Follow Your Conscience

Follow Your Conscience

The Catholic Church and the Spirit of the Sixties

PETER CAJKA

The University of Chicago Press
Chicago and London

The University of Chicago Press, Chicago 60637

The University of Chicago Press, Ltd., London

Published 2021

Printed in the United States of America

30 29 28 27 26 25 24 23 22 21   1 2 3 4 5

ISBN-13: 978-0-226-76205-0 (cloth)

ISBN-13: 978-0-226-76219-7 (e-book)

DOI: https://doi.org/10.7208/chicago/9780226762197.001.0001

Library of Congress Cataloging-in-Publication Data

Names: Cajka, Peter, author.

Title: Follow your conscience : the Catholic Church and the spirit of the Sixties /
    Peter Cajka.

Other titles: Catholic Church and the spirit of the Sixties

Description: Chicago ; London : The University of Chicago Press, 2021. |
    Includes bibliographical references and index.

Identifiers: LCCN 2020037871 | ISBN 9780226762050 (cloth) |
    ISBN 9780226762197 (e-book)

Subjects: LCSH: Catholic Church—United States—History—20th century. |
    Catholics—United States—History—20th century. | Conscience—Religious
    aspects—Catholic Church. | Conscience—Social aspects—United States. |
    Liberty of conscience—United States. | United States—Church history—
    20th century. | United States—Civilization—1945–

Classification: LCC BX1407.C75 C35 2021 | DDC 282/.7309046—dc23

LC record available at https://lccn.loc.gov/2020037871

♾ This paper meets the requirements of ANSI/NISO Z39.48-1992
(Permanence of Paper).

For Gráinne

CONTENTS

INTRODUCTION

In 1977, Father James T. McHugh accused Senator Augustus Hawkins, a California Democrat, of violating the conscience. Hawkins had attempted to broaden the beneficiaries of the Civil Rights Act of 1964 (which banned discrimination based on race, color, religion, and sex) to include female employees who became pregnant. The amendment he and the Senate Committee on Human Resources had written compelled employers to offer insurance that covered childbirth and immediate postnatal procedures. This coverage meant that female workers could start families and return to work without losing their position. McHugh, director of the Committee of Pro-Life Activities, an official Roman Catholic body tasked with scrutinizing federal legislation especially as it affected health care, found no language in the bill allowing employers to exempt themselves from financing abortions. In his letter to Hawkins, McHugh explained that such a clause would be necessary "to protect Church agencies from being faced by the amendment to support or provide abortion services in violation of our religious tenets and conscience convictions."[1] After not receiving a satisfactory response from Hawkins, Father McHugh wrote to the committee's chair, Senator Harrison Williams of New Jersey. His letter mentioned four times how the proposed legislation, as it stood without an explicit ban on insurance funding for abortion, threatened trespasses against conscience by making Catholic institutions and their managers pay for the procedure.[2]

In 1968, Jesuit priest James E. Straukamp had written a similar letter, charging both the US military and the US Supreme Court with a momentous transgression against an individual's conscience. Straukamp, a professor of history and acclaimed antiwar activist from the Sacramento area, addressed his words to the adjutant general of the US Army. He wrote on behalf of his spiritual mentee, Louis A. Negre, a college student seeking discharge from the army on account of his growing discomfort with the Vietnam War. In the spring of 1971, after twists and turns in the California legal system, Negre's case appeared before the Supreme Court, and the Jesuit's letter entered the official record of that court. Father Straukamp deployed conscience language in much the same manner as McHugh, a fellow priest. He contended that the State of California must remove its hold from the conscience of a reluctant soldier to allow that individual to disengage from an immoral war—much like McHugh's letter suggested that the state open a loophole for Catholic employers to opt out of funding problematic medical procedures. Straukamp told the state that Catholics had a long tradition of listening to subjective, internal authorities, and the army as well as the Supreme Court should recognize this religious prerogative. He defiantly wrote, "I counseled Private Negre that under the beliefs and teachings of the Catholic Church he is obliged to examine and form his own conscience in respect to participating or refusing to participate in war," explaining that "under Catholic doctrine [Negre] would be in religious duty bound to act in conformity to his conscience" if he became convinced in his sacred subjectivity that the war was unjust.[3]

Just a few months after Straukamp wrote his letter, Father Shane Mac-Carthy accused the powerful Cardinal Archbishop Patrick O'Boyle of trampling on conscience rights. O'Boyle, the archbishop of Washington, DC, applied a strict reading of *Humanae vitae* (*Of Human Life*), Pope Paul VI's 1968 encyclical, to Catholic life in the nation's capital. He prohibited priests from publicly critiquing the Catholic Church's condemnation of artificial birth control, and he demanded that the laity conform to the prohibition. Mac-Carthy, a young priest only three years out of the seminary, pointed out that conscience, not the law, had the final say on matters of reproduction. "For each individual man, his own conscience is the Norm of moral conduct. An ultimate subjective norm," he preached.[4] MacCarthy argued that if a Catholic properly attended to conscience and it reached a conclusion different from the law, he or she could follow the subjective authority, use contraceptives, and remain in good standing with the church. O'Boyle contended that the pope's infallibility meant conscience should obey authority. But the parish priest reminded the cardinal archbishop that *Humanae vitae*—or any law, for that matter—could not force a Catholic to act against conscience.

What is shared by all three of these episodes, which represent the stories told in this book? Four overlapping trends found in these conflicts, some apparent and others concealed just below the surface, are the main threads that bind the following pages together. First, in each case a breakdown of the law's moral authority, prompted by the unjust ends it promised to yield or by its limited applicability to an individual's situation, compelled these priests to call for official recognition of a Catholic's right to follow conscience, an immediate moral authority that grew in importance as the credibility of law (an external authority) faltered. Catholics turned to conscience because, as well known to students of the natural law tradition, unjust laws cease to be laws at all. Second, in each instance men who had undergone extensive seminary training and were ordained priests in the Roman Catholic Church stood up as the most outspoken defenders of subjectivity. That all three men wore clerical collars, offered Mass, heard confessions, and invoked conscience rights is hardly a coincidence, as explained below. Third, McHugh, Straukamp, and MacCarthy understood the right to follow conscience as a long-standing tradition championed by the Catholic Church for the past several hundred years. The priests strongly believed that authorities, whether church or state, should acknowledge the individual's right to refuse the law on account of the lofty place conscience-following held in Catholic moral and political teachings. Finally, these three stories feature a particularly Catholic notion of subjectivity and conscience as distinct from, but in conversation with, America's liberal secular tradition and its Protestant roots. The clergymen in the episodes invoked conscience, not to act secular, rational, and Protestant, but to uphold a church teaching to follow conscience in the face of unjust statutes. As Catholics, they joined an American discourse of conscience and individual rights stretching from the founding of the Massachusetts Bay Colony to the Cold War: individualism has long been an American value, and American Catholics contributed to its shape on their own terms in the twentieth century. By the end of that century, those Catholics invoking conscience had done so from the perspective of the pro-life religious right. But the Catholic case for conscience rights actually arose from draft protests during the Vietnam War. The long-standing problem with the teaching on conscience rights, from the perspective of members of the hierarchy like Cardinal O'Boyle, was its tendency to be invoked against church authority, which was done with stunning consequences in the debate over contraception in 1968.

Historians normally depict Protestants and secular rebels as having collectively blazed the trail of liberty in the modern world through their heroic efforts to safeguard conscience and individual rights.[5] The heroes and heroines in this pantheon—Anne Hutchinson, Roger Williams, Betty Friedan, William Ginsburg—deserve their places, but the group's membership is incomplete. This book tells the story of how Catholics became vocal champions of conscience rights and subjective freedoms during the 1960s and

1970s. In the halls of Congress, at the Supreme Court, in churches, at public rallies, and with countless articles in the religious and secular press, Catholics excoriated the law as unjust and advocated acting on one's subjective moral truths as a political and a moral solution.

This modern movement has medieval roots. Our story begins at the University of Paris in the late 1250s when Thomas Aquinas, recently appointed the master regent of theology, gave an address on conscience to his students. The Dominican priest made a provocative argument: an individual must always follow internal promptings rather than the directives of a superior. Then he took it a step further: the person who goes against subjective truths can expect to spend eternity in hell. Certainly, Thomas never encouraged Catholics to disobey church teaching (he advised Christians to study the law closely), but the more conservative elements of his writings can be easily pushed aside. Our narrative follows American Catholics as they internalize Thomas's uncompromising teaching on self-determination before it recounts how the faithful repeatedly injected this medieval church doctrine (learned in modern schools and seminaries) into public debates over sex and war.[6] Conscience discourse, it is important to note, entered the twentieth-century United States via other intellectual and discursive pipelines. One recalls the influential emphasis that William Penn and generations of American Baptists placed on freedom of religious practice; the genealogy of nonviolence stretching from Thoreau to Gandhi to Martin Luther King and the civil rights activists also comes to mind. Quakers, mainline Protestant pacifists like William Sloane Coffin, and other peace activists forged essential networks as they crafted a modern religious pacifism. An important transnational narrative about human rights features the rise of personal responsibility as a reaction to totalitarianism and the verdicts handed down at the Nuremberg trials. But historians have not yet isolated and analyzed the tremendous surge of Catholic conscience language in the 1960s and 1970s United States—a modern conscience discourse with medieval roots that held significant consequences for authority, ecumenism, and religious freedom. The claim made in this book is not that Catholics possessed a monopoly on conscience language but that the faithful made the push for conscience rights a salient social and political movement in the United States during and after the 1960s. *Follow Your Conscience* thus explores the proposition that modern autonomy is not only Protestant and secular but also Catholic and medieval.

The Catholic struggle for conscience rights brings into focus the intertwined nature of sex and war throughout the American Century. The rise of Catholic conscience claims is connected to a larger plotline of sexuality and state power. Scholarship tends to treat the deep reach of the military into twentieth-century American life and the sexual revolution as separate affairs, but in that century Catholics felt the tensions of each acutely, both pulls congealing into one broader antiauthoritarian logic that led men and women to reach for conscience as a primary moral guide.[7] The Catholic discourse of subjectivity reveals that if historians of the modern United States are to understand freedom and dissent in the American Century, sex and war must be intermixed in our analyses, not set on separate tracks. Conscience language swung between church and state in debates over the draft and the birth control pill, then traveled from antiwar groups to antiabortion circles. Catholics seized on Thomas Aquinas's ideas, increasingly circulated by Catholic peace activists after the draft for the Vietnam War began in 1965, to take control of their own reproductive destinies. Contradictions gave the conscience agenda an intellectual energy, sparking public debates in spiritual and secular spheres: a handful of Catholic leaders who stood opposed to autonomy in the area of sex claimed on other occasions that Catholic men could follow conscience in resisting the draft for the Vietnam War. Pro-life activists then borrowed conscience language from the antiwar movement. In the 1970s, Catholics rallied to protect doctors and nurses from the effacement of subjectivity that came with unwanted enlistment in abortion procedures. In these efforts, they were drawing from the same concepts deployed by early conscience rights advocates to help draftees avoid the termination of self-governance that ensued after induction into a military waging an unjust war. Catholics set conscience to different political ends, but recurrent overlaps of sex and war propelled its ascent.

Throughout the twentieth century, an unlikely group of advocates picketed on the front lines. Modern Catholic priests became exponents of conscience rights, taking up a role long reserved for Protestant dissidents. Members of the Catholic clergy, particularly Jesuits, significantly represent the major protagonists in various strands of this narrative. This book urges a sober confrontation with the reality that male Catholic clergy sought to promote the advancement of modern subjectivity and the liberation of the individual. Not all these men expressed admiration for the invocations of conscience—many priests became antagonists who decried the movement as an exultation of subjectivism—but enough priestly advocates for conscience rights stand out in the historical record to form a clear pattern. Priests stood against powerful bishops to uphold laypeople's rights to follow conscience on the matter of family planning, and they organized incessantly to protect the subjectivities of soldiers and medical professionals from the state. As confessors, clergymen accorded deep respect to the internal moral worlds of their penitents; as pastors, well read on modern psychological techniques, twentieth-century priests theorized at length about how to gently shepherd a layperson's conscience into a state of full maturity. As professors and theologians, Catholic clergymen mastered an intricate system of ideas about the objective and the subjective, then diffused their church's teaching on conscience and authority to a wide audience. Yet the main intellectual architects of American freedom, a tradition stretching from John Locke to John Dewey and beyond, have looked on priests as papal agents participating in a global conspiracy to throttle independent thought.[8] *Follow Your Conscience* flips on its head the pervasive story line about priest-ridden Catholics that had gained traction before the Civil War, helped define twentieth-century American liberalism, and notably endures into the twenty-first century. For the first three centuries of US history, priests served as the antithesis of democratic culture; but in the twentieth century, standing at a nexus of sex and war, Catholic clergymen became the nation's prime defenders of subjectivity.[9] The gauntlet of the modern, from the bombing of civilian targets during World War II to the draft for the Vietnam War, from the invention of the birth control pill to the legalization of abortion, awoke these clergymen to the tasks of defending self-sovereignty and drives of self-determination. In numerous public arenas during the twentieth century, they preached the gospel of conscience-following, warning the democratic state and their own Catholic Church to keep a safe distance from an individual's inner sanctuary.

A series of surprising alliances carried a Catholic take on conscience into the mainstream of American culture and around the world. If some conscience warriors tacked right, bringing religious prerogatives into conflict with secular notions of bodily autonomy, other defenders of subjectivity veered left, forging relationships with members of other faiths and secular humanists. Catholic priests turned to Jewish scholars like Sigmund Freud, Erich Fromm, and Lawrence Kohlberg to deepen their understanding of conscience development over the course of an individual's childhood and adolescence. Reflections on Nazism, the Holocaust, the Nuremberg verdicts, and the Eichmann trial convinced them that rearing robust subjectivities was a political imperative. Mainline Protestants and Catholics redefined conscience at a series of ecumenical conferences held in the 1960s and 1970s, with both groups recognizing the strengths and weaknesses of their respective traditions. In church basements throughout the 1970s, Catholics formed Amnesty International cells dedicated to freeing "prisoners of conscience," entering a partnership with a secular organization. Conscience language sprang from the friction between internality and law in the realms of sex and war, but the nomenclature of subjectivity also provided a common ground for Catholics to bond with Jews, Protestants, and human rights activists. *Follow Your Conscience* traces how the Catholic Church became a launching pad for conscience rights by way of some unlikely channels. In the early 1970s, the Catholic discourse of subjectivity became a common language in US politics as federal and state governments drew from the medieval and modern idea in formulating "conscience clauses," legal devices allowing doctors and nurses to refuse participation in abortion procedures.

The widespread impact of Catholic conscience language demonstrates that the American Catholic Church exerted major influence over key tenets of the nation's political and religious thought. Given the church and state dynamics along with the conscience advocates' liberal and conservative tendencies, a history of the Catholic campaign for self-rule helps explain the underpinnings of democracy and pluralism as practiced in the contemporary United States. Catholic conscience defenders deepened, and transformed, the nation's commitment to autonomy, a concept identified by historian James Kloppenberg as central to democracy. He defines it as an individual's exercising "control over his or her own life by developing a self that is sufficiently mature to make decisions according to rules or laws chosen for good reasons."[10] The Catholic faithful asserted self-control when the law asked individuals, as it frequently did during a brutal century, to contravene truths known to the internal self. They widened the scope of modern autonomy by repeatedly making law earn its authority over the individual. An ordinance that failed to produce just behavior (the legalization of abortion, conscription into an army fighting an unjust war) or neglected to consider specific individual circumstances (a church ban on contraception) could not be obeyed. Catholics strove to form a mature conscience for assistance in following rules and laws for reasons they deemed valid rather than out of rote obedience. This Catholic vision for the freedom of conscience also transformed prevailing notions of pluralism from group rights into individual rights: Catholics made clear that both state and church needed to make laws moral enough and simultaneously flexible enough to speak to the truths that citizens and church members alike held in their own souls. Father MacCarthy made the case for this type of flexibility in pointing out the limits of Cardinal Archbishop Patrick O'Boyle's call to obey the rules on artificial birth control, as did McHugh and Straukamp in their appeals to the state for recognition of individuality concerning abortion and conscription.

But this is not a story of progress. Freedoms for conscience came at a high price. Shaken loose from church and state authority, individuals with strong subjectivities enkindled a series of painful contests of wits and power in the church and in the nation, and ultimately Catholic defenders of self-sovereignty did as much to unsettle the US government and the Roman Catholic Church as they did to carve out tangible spheres of freedom for their constituents. Debates over the freedoms and limits of conscience, which reverberated in the US Supreme Court and special ecclesiastical courts in Rome, pitted laity against hierarchy, priests against bishops, citizens against the law, church against state, and religious rights against secular rights. A significant legacy of the conscience rights movement in the 1960s and 1970s is a constantly churning cycle of theological and political argumentation, in the United States and in the Vatican, with no end in sight.[11] A good Whig history features Protestants and progress; and this book, pushing back against that old but still appealing narrative, argues that Catholic priests are agents of liberation and that their efforts ended in intellectual and political gridlock.

This book grounds twentieth-century US history in Catholic sources of subjectivity and conscience. It tells a story about US history and the modern Catholic Church; it moves between religious and secular realms; and while primarily focusing on the history of an idea, it traverses the domains of social, cultural, political, women's, and legal history. This book answers historian Sarah Igo's call to "unfence" intellectual history and to study the "thinking that goes on out in the open fields."[12] If conscience, like privacy, Igo's object of study, has been an easily adaptable concept, one that encompasses confessionals, grade school lesson plans, radio talk shows, bedrooms, draft board hearings, parish pulpits, civil rights–inspired marches and sing-alongs, scholarly conferences, and preliminary arguments at the Supreme Court, its historians should be equally as venturesome. *Follow Your Conscience* necessarily includes what David Hollinger has labeled "the discourse of intellectuals," as many of its protagonists served as university or seminary professors. But it also shadows conscience language as it migrated from its home in Catholic theology into wider legal, political, and cultural discourses, where it was taken up by activists, college students, married suburbanites, concerned bishops, and US senators.[13] Only by charting the ironic twists and unexpected divergences of the idea will we be able to explain why it moved to the center of American political and intellectual life.

Chapter 1 examines the Catholic teaching on conscience in the centuries and years leading up to the Second Vatican Council. It lays the book's intellectual foundation by unpacking the doctrine's conservative and emancipatory tendencies along with the many procedures comprising this elaborate church teaching. It follows the careers of three priest-theologians, John

Ford, Francis Connell, and James Martin Gillis, to explore how these men understood and relayed the Catholic teaching on conscience to their contemporaries. Chapter 1 also captures the institutional structures and print cultures that conveyed the rights of conscience to millions of Catholics, who learned from catechisms, textbooks, and priest-confessors about the important role of subjective perception in moral decision-making.

Chapter 2 unearths the origins of the doctrine's rise in modern political life. As robust states in Europe and the United States conscripted men into massive armies in the 1930s and 1940s, a coterie of Catholics deemed civil law unjust and began recommending that Catholics exercise self-sovereignty. Catholic conscience discourse first entered the public sphere in response to totalitarianism and World War II, and the nature of the doctrine helped American Catholics keep the defense of autonomy consistent across nearly three decades of US history.

The Roman Catholic Church, with its elaborate just-war doctrine, will never be a "peace church" like the Jehovah's Witnesses, the Quakers, or the Mennonites; but members from various positions in the denomination—laypeople, priests, bishops, theologians, and activists—became outspoken defenders of conscience rights during the Vietnam War. Chapter 3 analyzes a stack of Form 150s, the paperwork Catholic laymen filled out to secure conscientious objector status from draft boards. Catholics bolstered their right to refuse the state with long-form essays explaining their duty to act on their own internal perceptions of the world. This chapter also shows how the Catholic Peace Fellowship "coached" Catholic laymen who faced conscription, often counseling them to explain in their conscientious objector applications their denomination's deep respect for acting on internal cues.

It was one thing for Catholics to object to a secular state's rights over their individual conscience, and another thing altogether for them to demand that the church itself recognize their right to exercise their conscience publicly and privately against church law. Chapter 4 homes in on Washington, DC, where the main event of what I call "the American Catholic 1968" took place. A wave of popular protests rocked the nation's capital after Cardinal Archbishop Patrick O'Boyle suspended more than thirty priests for publicly defending lay Catholics' rights to decide for themselves on the matter of artificial contraception. The dispute—captured by local and national media—catapulted conscience into the center of American debates about sex. The suspended priests coordinated marches, street rallies, sit-ins, public lectures, and a regionwide letter-writing campaign to prevent the cardinal archbishop from usurping traditional prerogatives of self-determination.

The events in Washington only served to reinforce the notion, already becoming accepted by theologians and confessors, that fierce obedience to law hindered personal development. That Catholic thinkers used the word *development* itself signaled a change. Chapter 5 considers how Catholics drew from the insights of modern psychology and Jewish thought to strengthen the medieval theology of conscience. They began to chart the developmental stages of "conscience growth" and commented frequently on the need for "mature consciences." Psychology is often construed as a means of breaking with religious tradition; but in the hands of American Catholic confessors and theologians, it bolstered the conscience's long-standing role as the person's immediate moral guide.

Chapter 6 traverses the many political realms (congressional committees, Senate hearings, presidential commissions, the Supreme Court) where Catholics presented the case for self-rule to the state during the Vietnam War. Their campaign achieved mixed results: while the bishops threw their weight behind the idea of conscience rights in 1972, the state remained unconvinced that a citizen could reject the particular wars offending individual sensibilities. The 1971 Supreme Court case *Gillette v. United States* laid bare the conflict between the Catholic Church and the state over conscription: several Catholic groups demanded that the court recognize Louis Negre's right to refuse military service in Vietnam after the formation of his conscience deemed the engagement unjust, but the justices voted down the idea 8–1.

Chapter 7 moves beyond the Catholic Church. The discourse of conscience rights generated in Catholic debates about sex and war spread across American society in the late twentieth century, shaping the nation in ways its advocates could never have anticipated. This chapter shows how Catholic concepts of subjectivity influenced ecumenism, the rise of global human rights, and, most significantly, the fate of reproductive rights and religious freedom.

Our story begins in the parochial school classrooms, confessionals, and print culture of the mid-twentieth-century American Catholic Church. The Roman Catholic Church of the earlier parts of the story was a profoundly institutional enterprise, fortifying its schools and seminaries against the transformative winds of modernity. Its adherents moved from fortress to fortress on an institutional archipelago that stretched from parochial classrooms to graduate philosophy seminars and, for those who heard the call of God, to convents and seminaries. The two decades before 1965 witnessed a rapid growth of the Catholic (and public) educational apparatus at all these levels.[14] It would have seemed counterintuitive to thinkers like John Adams or John Dewey, but the Catholics who came of age under this regime—whether layperson or priest, weekly Mass-goer or speculative theologian—knew about the inherent rights of conscience they possessed as members of the Catholic Church. Far from breeding the automatons that haunted the imaginations of Protestants from the colonial period to the first wave of Irish immigration up to the rise of fascist and communist powers, the institutional Catholic Church taught each of its journeyman pupils about the inviolability of their moral sense. With this faith in conscience, twentieth-century American Catholics changed the terms of American freedom and deepened the nation's commitment to democracy and pluralism.

ONE

The Conscience Problem
and Catholic Doctrine

Conscience is certainly the ultimate and deciding norm for personal action.

—John Ford and Gerald Kelly, *Contemporary Moral Theology* (1957)

In the mid-twentieth century, American Catholics found themselves living in a mental world where moral authority rested in two places: law and conscience. Whereas laws were external to the person and thought to be objective, the conscience was internal to the person and imagined as subjective. As two priests explained in their 1953 textbook for high school students, "Besides the external guide for morality known as the moral law, God has also supplied us with an internal guide known as conscience."[1] Catholics respected both the objective and the subjective sides of the equation, seeking to strike a balance between the two. The desired balance was explained in texts prepared for teenagers as well as in top-flight academic journals, spun in the latter in fancier language but with the same message. The leading Catholic intellectual of the day, John Courtney Murray, outlined the "two primary concerns that run through all Catholic moral thought" in his 1945 article for *Theological Studies*, the flagship journal of Roman Catholic theology managed by the Jesuits. First was "a profound concern for the sacredness of the laws of God," which must, he wrote, "be kept inviolate." Murray then hastened to add that Catholics had an "equally profound concern for the integrity of conscience," whose every need and circumstance "must be respected and whose inner freedom must be safeguarded."[2] Murray and the priestly authors of the 1953 high school text detailed a linguistic and theological structure for conscience that many Catholics, lay and clerical, had internalized by the middle decades of the twentieth century.

It requires a thick institutional apparatus to make doctrine a lens for defining reality. The Catholic Church possessed such gravitas. Over the course of the twentieth century, American Catholics built a nationwide chain of educational institutions in rural and urban communities. Many US cities in the Northeast and Midwest were dotted with Catholic parishes, grade schools, high schools, and universities. Enrollments rose at these institutions in the opening decades of the twentieth century, skyrocketing in the years just after 1945. These were the institutions where young Catholics learned the rituals and creeds of their faith; in these same spaces, they entered relationships with the saints and the real presence of Christ in the Eucharist. Here, too, they began to speak the language of conscience.

The public intellectuals of the institutional church—moral theologians such as John Ford and Francis Connell along with midcentury media savant James Martin Gillis—disseminated the church's teaching on conscience far and wide. These three men had much in common: all were born in Boston near the turn of the twentieth century; joined religious orders in their late teens or early twenties and became priests; and became notable figures in the twentieth-century institutional church. Ford and Connell were prolific writers, and they influenced Catholic life as professors of moral theology and as tireless advocates of the church's authority. Gillis left his mark as a public media personality. He served as editor in chief of the *Catholic World*, a prominent monthly, from 1922 to 1948, and for three decades he delivered hundreds of radio addresses and wrote a nationally syndicated newspaper column. All three men expounded lessons on conscience that were echoed in the high school and grade school texts used by thousands of nuns to drill their young pupils in Catholic doctrine.[3]

This chapter proceeds in two parts. The sections on law and confession in the first part explore the conservative side of the doctrine. To Catholics, the primary role of a conscience is to help them apply just and clear laws to a given moral situation. The sacrament of confession, a constant devotional practice for millions of Catholics at midcentury, brings law and conscience into the proper relationship between input (law) and output (correct action). But in order to see the importance of conscience in twentieth-century American Catholic life, we must shift our focus entirely to the emancipatory capabilities produced by the doctrine. Consequently, the second part of the chapter unpacks the many procedures that allowed Catholics to follow conscience, and it shows that midcentury Catholics defended rights of conscience *in the church*. The sections here detail the more radical half of the teaching and show how Father Francis Connell, an otherwise traditional theologian, embraced a truly revolutionary position on conscience rights.

Cosmic and eternal consequences would be exacted on those Catholics who acted against conscience.

Readers will note that Ford, Connell, and Gillis appear in both parts of the chapter. This is not to suggest that they were divided selves. Both the conservative and the radical sides of the doctrine were standard fare. Before we turn to Catholic doctrine, however, we must address Protestant and secular sources of the modern self and modern individuality.

Protestantism, the Enlightenment, and the Modern Individual

It is tempting to conclude that Catholics are "acting Protestant" in staking claims of conscience rights. After all, a long-standing tale of modernity attributes the initial percolations of self-governance to the Protestant Reformation. When in 1524 Martin Luther told Johann Eck at the Diet of Worms that he could not "go against conscience" because his internal sphere was "captive to the Word of God," the former Augustinian monk liberated himself from obedience to wicked priests, initiating the rise of modern individualism.[4] The modern individual, born in sixteenth-century Germany, bypassed worldly mediators for a direct connection to God's word and truth.

Then in the 1630s, Anne Hutchinson turned the transgressive conscience against the leaders of the Massachusetts Bay Colony, introducing the modern individual into the stream of US history. Her conscience, offering a clear line to God, told her that most clergymen in the colony were preaching a dangerous doctrine of works. Her message found favor among the women gathered to hear her preach each Sunday and even among some male ministers in the colony. As Hutchinson's critique called into question the authority of the clergy, it began to place the comity of the nascent New England community in jeopardy. Conscience claims left the private sphere. At her trial in the mid-1630s, John Winthrop and the Puritan court made Hutchinson a progenitor of conscience rights by arguing forcefully that her inner divinations would not be permitted to disrupt civic life. "Your conscience you must keep or it must be kept for you," Winthrop snapped at the outset of his interrogation.[5] Hutchinson persisted in making her case that the spiritual knowledge God set in her conscience placed her beyond the judgment of the magistrates. Even her longtime mentor, the sympathetic John Cotton, presented an argument that a subjectivity persisting in error ought to be disciplined. Resigning herself to the punishment, Hutchinson told her male judges, "If you condemn me for speaking what in my conscience I know to be truth, I must commit myself unto the Lord."[6] The court banished her and her family from the colony, setting in motion a chain of events that culminated in Siwanoy warriors scalping her and her children on the New York frontier in 1643. Thus, a legend of Protestant antinomian conscience was created.

Roger Williams's famous efforts to inoculate the gospel from state interference helped make the word *conscience* synonymous with Protestantism and religious freedom. His colony of Rhode Island, which historian Chris Beneke describes as having "developed some of the most generous provisions for conscience the world had ever seen," remains central to the origin story of American freedom.[7] Williams held to an expansive definition of religious freedom that included both assent to theological propositions and freedom of action. In his scathing denunciation of Massachusetts divine John Cotton for his denial of Hutchinson's rights, *The Bloudy Tenet of Persecution for Cause of Conscience*, Williams defined freedom of conscience as either "professing some point of doctrine in which you believe in conscience to be the truth, or . . . practicing some work which in conscience you believe to be a religious duty."[8] Without this freedom, he explained, one might as well live in Spain or Rome, where nobody read the Bible or had the freedom to hone their individual conscience.[9] He concluded that no civic authority could force a conscience to reach a certain end. His uncompromising stances on religious freedom, demonstrated in his leaving England for Massachusetts in 1630 and just five years later settling in Rhode Island after being expelled from the Bay Colony, lends credence to his campaign for subjective freedoms. Early reformers like Williams linked conscience language tightly with emerging concepts of religious freedom, inaugurating a pairing that held across centuries of US history.

Along with Hutchinson and Williams, William Penn helped develop an association between freedom of conscience and a stand against Catholic-like power. He described religious liberty in a 1681 book, *The Great Case for Liberty of Conscience*, as "the exercise of ourselves in a visible way of worship."[10] Agreeing with Williams, Penn thought religious freedom entailed not simply "mere liberty of the mind" but a considerable latitude to choose one's own denomination and rituals—a liberty, in other words, to make the freedom concrete.[11] To deny freedom of conscience was to "act Catholic." In the seventeenth century, Penn and other reformers believed that freedom of conscience was both central to a de-Romanized future and a mandate to offer liberation to other dissenting sects. Penn wrote, "I say, since the only just cause of the first revolution from Rome was a dissatisfaction in point of conscience, you cannot reasonably persecute others, who have right to the same plea."[12] Protestants must continue to expand religious freedom, a revolution they began in the sixteenth century.

In the minds of the Protestant reformers, religious freedom offered much more than access to diverse modes of worship; properly secured, religious liberty jump-started the process of modernization. Subjects who reached voluntarily chosen religious ends made good democratic citizens and productive capitalists. Men and women who chose their religion became active agents in the progress of society. According to political theorist Andrew Murphy, Penn believed that the destruction of conscience "undermine[d] civil rights, elevate[d] the church over the state, ruin[ed] the economy and reward[ed] hypocrisy."[13] As historian Tisa Wenger has shown in her history of religious freedom, these expansive hopes for religious freedom held their influence into the middle decades of the twentieth century, allowing Protestants and secular liberals to both portray the Catholic Church as the enemy of conscience rights and paint that church as a roadblock to modernity. Without freedom of conscience, understood as freedom to worship, a society could not become modern and the individual could not become autonomous. This argument justified US imperial expansion into Cuba and the Philippines, as only Protestant modernizers were thought capable of producing a truly prosperous and efficient society.[14]

A fear of Catholics grinding the United States down into a sluggish, stunted society, one bereft of religious freedom, held a grip on the liberal intellectual imagination for quite some time. Its spell lasted into the mid-twentieth century. Historian John McGreevy has shown how a wide range of prominent American intellectuals, including philosopher Charles Morris, religious historian William Warren Sweet, literary critic Howard Mumford Jones, and popular scholar Henry Steele Commager, subscribed wholeheartedly to the Protestant modernization theory as they expressed anxiety about collectivist tendencies in communism and Catholicism. Their influence reached its high tide in the 1950s.[15]

The belief that Catholics lacked conscience held an equally long tenure in the Anglo-American mind. From the seventeenth century to the middle years of the twentieth, Protestants mentioned consistently, and nonchalantly, that Catholic reliance on external authority prevented the development of their moral subjectivities. Popes, bishops, and priests made choices for their fold; what resided within Catholics, then, was not a conscience but a moral faculty controlled remotely by a member of the hierarchy that brought an individual to heel. In *A Letter concerning Toleration* (1689), John Locke commented that men and women of Rome "owe[d] blind allegiance to an infallible pope who hath the keys of their consciences tied to his girdle."[16] In his epic poem *Paradise Lost* (1667), John Milton expressed his belief that Catholics would eviscerate conscience if they took control of the state: "and from that pretense / Spiritual Lawes by carnal power force / over every conscience."[17] Protestants and their secular heirs rarely deviated from this assumption for the next three hundred years. In a 1945 article, theologian Paul Tillich commented that medieval Catholics made "conscience more and more dependent on the authority of the church."[18] He blamed the Jesuit order for placing "Jesuitic advisers" between God and man, blocking any connection between conscience and the divine. Tillich, in typical fashion, credited Luther with liberating the individual from the law. This Catholic lack of conscience had far-reaching implications, from making it an imperative to ground democracy and religion in Protestant sources, to an assumption about who could properly practice science and be considered a modern intellectual. A twentieth-century scientist thought that a lack of self-sovereignty explained why Catholics could not be objective: dispassionate analysis, he wrote, "depended on a moral preference for the dictates of the individual conscience rather than for those of an organized authority."[19] One needs a conscience to practice religion, democracy, and science; in short, a conscience is required to be modern.

The Enlightenment, captured in the thought of German philosopher Immanuel Kant, is the other famed source of individual autonomy. Kant defined *enlightenment* as having the courage to think for one's self without guidance from an authority figure, particularly a priest. To him, Catholics seemed to be the people least likely to take up his challenge "Dare to Know!" Kant also had much to say about conscience, an important constitutive node of his well-known "categorical imperative": the notion that one should perform acts that can be universal for all others. One should examine the self, discover universal moral truths, and then impose on the self the duty to obey those truths. For Kant, conscience was this very process of self-justification and self-appraisal. He pursued the classic definition of *autonomy* as applying universal rules to the self without some outside imposition or stamp of approval from a domineering power structure like a church. The modern self dared to know his or her own inner life and generated his or her own duty to obey higher norms. This was a process or an unfurling rather than the commanding or bestowing from a superior. Conscience is the process of looking inward and transcending to obey an outward universal norm.

In the American moral tradition, the Reformation and the Enlightenment converged to create what historian Amy Kittlestrom has identified as a new "practical approach for ascertaining truth and justice and for acting with moral virtue."[20] Protestants linked liberty of conscience with empirical discovery to provide democratic citizens with a special set of polity-sustaining virtues that encouraged seeking consensus and tolerating diverse viewpoints. By the opening of the nineteenth century, the Protestant Reformation and the Enlightenment had blended to form a potent argument for a religion-based self-culture, full of autonomous agents behaving in seemingly non-Catholic ways.

The above narrative, with Protestant reformers and Enlightenment savants as the primary architects of conscience and the modern self, overlooks Thomas Aquinas, a thirteenth-century master craftsman of religious subjectivity. Catholics are as defensive of conscience freedoms as are the Protestants, their separated brethren—a fact lost to most modern commentators. Indeed, the history of modern conscience claims did not begin at the Diet of Worms in 1524 or in Boston in 1637. Rather, it began at the University of Paris in the late 1250s when Thomas, recently appointed the regent master in theology, gave a series of lectures to his students under the title *Questiones disputatae de veritate* (*Disputed Questions on Truth*). Question 17 of his disputation dealt with conscience. Thomas made a provocative argument that echoed into the twentieth century when he claimed that "no one is bound by a precept except through his knowledge of that precept."[21] In other words, he argued that the law binds the individual to obedience only when the individual understands the law. Consequently, the teacher of the laws, be it the state or the church, was responsible for relaying each law with clarity and justness so that an ordinance connected to the individual's subjective authority, the conscience.

From this initial point of departure—and quite a radical one from its theological starting line—Thomas only grew bolder in his assertions. He claimed that individuals are bound to follow false conscience (a conscience that misunderstood the law) or suffer eternal consequences. "Conscience, no matter how false it is, obliges under pain of sin," the rising intellectual star wrote.[22] This is because, as he explained further, conscience conveys a directive; and even if the transmission is the wrong law, the sacred inner sanctum nonetheless swiftly hands the guideline to the individual. Catholics must follow the truth closest to the self. Thomas channeled the thought of his near contemporary Pope Innocent III, who once said that "whatever is done contrary to conscience leads to hell."[23] Thomas even suggested that following one's conscience overrode the commands of churchmen higher up the chain of ecclesiastical command. He stated this conclusion succinctly: "The bond of conscience is also greater than that of the command of the superior."[24] The *Summa Theologica*, his magnum opus completed in 1265, offered similar arguments. He explained that individuals who follow their conscience unexposed to truth cannot be held culpable for an illicit viewpoint or a deformed will.[25]

In the centuries that followed Thomas's medieval theorizing of conscience rights, a wide range of Catholic theologians, like Jean Gerson (1363–1429), Francisco de Vitoria (1486–1546), Francisco Suarez (1548–1617), and Francis Silvius (1581–1649), added more tricks and pivots to the doctrine of conscience. Italian theologian Alphonsus Liguori, writing five hundred years after Thomas, did more than any other to carry the Angelic Doctor's provocative suggestions about conscience into the era of the Enlightenment. In the 1750s, Liguori published *Moral Theology*, a text best described as a long reflection on what Thomas meant when he wrote, "Nobody is bound by any principle except through the knowledge of that principle."[26] The men and women trapped in vicious cycles of sin, coming and going from his confessional, troubled Liguori immensely and inspired him to write about conscience. He proved to be influential on generations of Catholic confessors, believing that the essence of the law rested squarely in its promulgation—to oblige a conscience to follow a law, the rule must be clear, just, and applicable to the penitent's situation. His aims were pastoral: the law must be relevant to a believer's life to save a soul. When a believer could not meet a code's stipulations, he simply accepted his fate, committing to a life of sin. Thomas provided a crucial piece in the puzzle by claiming that law only gains legitimacy by way of its capacity to be received into a believer's conscience.

In one of the most surprising twists of modern Catholic thought, Thomas and the fierce defense of subjectivity rose in stature in the opening decades of the twentieth century as the Catholic Church escalated its battle against secular knowledge. When Pope Pius X condemned psychoanalysis, psychology, evolutionary biology, and Marxist economics in 1907 with his antimodern encyclical *Pascendi*, he cemented the church's commitment to Thomism as the bedrock of all Catholic thought.[27] Catholics embraced what historian William Halsey has identified as a sense of innocence—an ability to float aloofly above secularity with an abiding faith in absolute truth as the surrounding culture plunged into relativism, probability, and the unconscious.[28] What scholars like Halsey missed in this argument for the anti-intellectualism of Catholicism is the rise of an intricate system of law and conscience that circulated widely and paradoxically, even in a church staunchly opposed to modernity and modern individualism. The early twentieth-century Catholic Church, in its catechisms, confessional manuals, and schoolbooks, handed down to millions of schoolchildren a sophisticated moral system designed to calibrate the proper relationship between law and conscience. The system's emancipatory sides came into full bloom and entered the public eye during the crises of artificial birth control and the

Vietnam War. While official texts from an increasingly antimodern church urged Catholics to obey the institution, they also spoke a subtle language of liberation from ecclesiastical and political authority.

The mid-twentieth-century inheritance of the Reformation and the elision of Thomas Aquinas created a subtle irony. Protestants and secular liberals of the 1950s well knew that Catholics talked about conscience frequently, but they concluded that Catholic subjectivities existed only to make laypeople obedient to the rules set by clergymen and popes. Paul Blanshard, author of a series of best-selling books on Catholic power, encountered the Catholic language of self-governance frequently during his research forays into Rome's global ambitions. Indicative that the concept had wide circulation, Blanshard placed conscience into a "glossary of double-talk" in his 1952 book, *Communism, Democracy, and Catholic Power*. He concluded that conscience "becomes in Catholic semantics the collective conscience of the Catholic clergy, which is directed by the Pope."[29] Conscience only ratified the rules of the priests; it did not disclose alternative paths of action. Pragmatism, a modern spin on American freedom, emphasized spontaneity, experimentation, inductive methods, and openness to new conclusions. Blanshard set out to prove that Catholic authority comes from outside the self and forecloses on each of these outcomes. But the relationship of conscience to authority, to which we now turn, is more complicated.

Conscience and Law

Conscience solved a practical dilemma in Catholic moral theology, making it alluring to midcentury confessors and moralists. The dilemma is best captured in a pair of questions: What connects individuals to divine or natural laws? How does the individual internalize objective rules and follow them in specific instances? Mid-twentieth-century Catholic theologians believed that God made objective laws that existed outside the person (and that Jesus Christ commissioned the Catholic Church to teach those laws), but the laws required a space within the person in which to nestle. Conscience played the crucial role of implanting externalized laws into a materialized personhood. Laws without conscience were like radio signals that never found a receiver to relay their message. As the Italian authors of *General Moral Theology*, a text translated into English in 1962, explained, "The law is the remote and objective norm of human operation and yet it cannot reach its efficacy if it does not touch the subject, if it does not enter into him."[30] Catholic moral theologians imagined conscience as the space within the person where the law could roost and become "proximate." The Italians wrote that law reached "its full efficacy in the moral order" upon entering a person via his or her conscience.[31]

When objective law and subjective conscience did meet, the synthesis created a true conscience, the optimal form of conscience. Catholic educators admitted that depending on an individual's cultivation and education, a subjectivity assumed one of several conditions. Textbooks introduced high school students to several specific conditions of conscience—true, false, erroneous, doubtful, and certain—each, it was explained, with a particular relationship to the law. A true conscience apprehended and applied the divine law to a given situation. The law entered this conscience, and out came the right action. *Living Our Faith*, a textbook written by two nuns and a priest in 1945, defined the true conscience as "one that correctly judges an action right or wrong according to the law."[32] As the word *true* obviously suggested, it would be far better for a Catholic to possess a true subjectivity than a false subjectivity. Anthony F. Alexander, a member of the Department of Religion at John Carroll University, wrote in a 1958 textbook for Catholic undergraduates, "With a true conscience a person appraises the moral value of the act correctly. With a false conscience he judges the act to be the exact opposite of what that act might actually be."[33]

Every penitent had the obligation to pursue a true conscience through education and a frequent confession of sins. Thus, every Catholic had an obligation to place moral laws into his or her internal sanctuary of selfhood. In turn, this metaphysical coupling of subjectivity to the law created an obligation within the Catholic person to apply the law to each situation. Finally, knowledge of the law begat an obligation to follow the true conscience. To accomplish these conservative ends, Catholic theologians routinely defined conscience as an "act of mind" that applied the divine laws to specific situations. Understood in this technical and cerebral manner, the word *conscience* itself implied knowledge about the laws and a capacity for moral reasoning to align action with decrees. For the listeners of his 1930 *Catholic Hour* radio program, James Martin Gillis (fig. 1) described conscience as the "mind itself uttering judgments upon matters that pertain not to speculations but to action"—action that must be considered, and executed, "here and now and not at some future time."[34] Conscience became a mental entity, in other words, when a Catholic pondered how to act in a specific situation.

Gillis was no stranger to the limelight. He entered the Paulists, an American religious order, and was ordained a priest in 1901. After a brief teaching career at St. Thomas College in St. Paul, Minnesota, that ended in 1910, he went on the road and preached at over 150 Catholic missions in the span of just a dozen years. This type of preaching involved visiting a Catholic

1. Father James Martin Gillis. Courtesy of the Office of Paulist
Archives for the Missionary Society of St. Paul the Apostle.

parish and usually raining fire and brimstone from the pulpit, entreating the
audience to seek forgiveness for sins and calling on the gathered faithful to
battle the forces of evil in a dark world. Gillis gained such acclaim as a missionary speaker (an exhausting exercise requiring hours of focused exhortation) that his Paulist superiors asked him to preach on the order's radio
station. After 1930, he also gave an annual address on *The Catholic Hour*, a
radio program carried by twenty-two affiliates of the National Broadcasting
Company. Moreover, Gillis wrote regularly for the *Catholic Mind*—a magazine with over ten thousand subscribers—and his regular column, "Sursum
Corda" (Latin for "Lift Up Your Hearts"), was syndicated and published in
diocesan newspapers nationwide.[35]

2. Father Francis Connell. Redemptorist Archives, Philadelphia. Used with permission.

Like many Catholic thinkers of the mid-twentieth century, Gillis insisted
that speculation would not be needed if a Catholic comprehended the law.
An individual required no existential reflections on Mass attendance or fast-
day regulations, only the internalization of the church's rules within the
conscience and the decision to perform or not perform the action, avoiding or committing sin by living by the book or not. Gillis's contemporary
Francis Connell (fig. 2), a member of the Redemptorist order, agreed. He
captured the conservative side of the doctrine of conscience perfectly in his
1953 book, *Outlines of Moral Theology*. Conscience, he wrote, "is an act of the
intellect, judging that an action must be performed as obligatory, or must
be omitted as sinful, or may be performed as lawful."[36] For thinkers like
Connell, the solution resided in the law. This definition of conscience as legalistic intellection surfaced frequently in midcentury literature.[37]

Ordained in 1913, Connell taught moral theology at St. Alphonsus Seminary in Esopus, New York, from 1915 to 1940. Then, identified as a major talent, he moved to Washington, DC, to accept an invitation to teach in the Sacred School of Theology at the Catholic University of America. When compared with Gillis and Ford, Connell was the most committed to the role of theologian as apologist. He earned a reputation as a theological crusader because of his campaign to persuade Vatican officials to condemn the work of John Courtney Murray, which it did in 1955. Connell deemed dangerous Murray's postwar intellectual campaign to bring Catholics to accept church-state separation, because it suggested that Catholic control of the state was undesirable. In an infamous pamphlet published just over a decade earlier, Connell seemed to deny the right of religious freedom to non-Catholics because, as he argued in so many words, only truth has rights.[38] He understood his task as a theologian to be bringing souls to Christ solely by way of the Catholic Church. Connell was both a formidable scholar (he declined admission to Harvard as a high school senior to attend Boston College) and a disciplined worker whose typewriter could be heard pounding paper late into the night. He was a frequent guest on Catholic radio, and he published regularly in the *Boston Pilot* and the *Brooklyn Eagle*. By the mid-1950s, Connell—following media evangelist Bishop (and later Archbishop) Fulton J. Sheen—began to appear on television. In addition to publishing several books and articles, he authored over six hundred pieces in the *American Ecclesiastical Review*, most of which were responses to readers' requests for moral guidance.[39] His advice, inside or outside the confessional, was of the follow-the-rules variety.

The conservative side of the Catholic doctrine of conscience had a wide circulation at midcentury. Catechisms, the basic teaching primers of the Catholic faith, taught that a well-formed subjectivity ought to serve as an applicator of natural law. For the first two-thirds of the twentieth century, Catholic youngsters learned the sacraments and doctrine of their faith from these didactic booklets. These came in many forms, but all the American texts derived from the famous Baltimore Catechism, issued by the Third Plenary Council in 1884.[40] Though formulaic and often tendentious, catechisms promised those who memorized their teachings a power to understand the workings of the universe.

Catholics learned at a young age that conscience held an important power: a proper understanding of one's internal moral faculty helped in comprehending God's law-filled world. They relied on a well-formed conscience to successfully navigate the divine legal order and the many quagmires of earthly existence. The order of law that exists outside persons implies that conscience, a process of reason, exists within persons to tether them to the moral order. The position of the church, one Dominican theologian wrote in 1931, was that "conscience would be futile and unwarranted unless there be some objective unchangeable standard of morality."[41] Conscience, a cerebral entity capable of reason, tuned Catholics in to the reality of this legal order. It would follow logically that if the moral universe were chaotic or opaque, persons would not need a process of reason to understand what did not exist. If natural laws or divine laws were fables, one would not need a conscience to apply those laws to a situation. These laws were real to Catholics, and so was the conscience.

Conscience and Confession

The moment of truth arrived in the confessional. The law-binding side of the doctrine of conscience had at its disposal a finely choreographed ritual. During the act of confession, lay Catholics off-load the sins weighing on their conscience; confessors, in turn, awake the conscience to the reality of moral laws. Most Catholics, urban and rural, blue collar or white, entered the order of objective and subjective by way of the dark booths installed in the sanctuary of their ethnic neighborhood church. As historian James O'Toole has shown, the sacrament occupied a central position in a Catholic devotional life from the early nineteenth century up to the early 1970s. Millions of Catholics—men, women, and children—found time on Saturday afternoons and evenings to tell their priest about their sins, large and small. The men of the church consecrated to God, whose lives were not always glamorous, could expect to spend four to six hours in the small confessional booth on a normal Saturday, besieged by long lines of fervent penitents.[42] The Catholic Church aimed to have all its members enter and exit the confessional booth, comporting conscience with the law, for their entire lives. Achieving the proper relationship between the external and internal authorities took a great deal of work.

Synchronizing the Catholic's conscience with moral laws began around the age of seven, the so-called age of reason, when members of the faith made their first confession. As preparation for the sacraments, particularly confession and First Communion, Catholics of elementary school age relentlessly "examined" their conscience—an exercise meant to produce an awareness of sins committed. The conscience slyly records exactly when and where a commandment was broken or a code shirked, so the examination made children aware of these transgressions. Awareness of a breach begot the obligation to confess. The dual tracks of external and internal authority existed apart from each another, but Catholics learned at a young age that the two guides shared a relationship.

Inexpensive pamphlets, almost always authored by priests, instructed Catholic boys and girls to examine their conscience with the Ten Commandments. A seemingly endless supply of conscience examination guides for elementary school students and adolescents based on the Decalogue came off Catholic presses at midcentury. Jesuit Aloysius J. Heeg's 1941 booklet, *A Little Child's Confession Book*, exemplified the genre. Heeg arranged his guide according to Moses's sacred injunctions: interrogating one's own conscience with the fourth commandment (respect your parents), for example, meant asking conscience, "Did I Sin by not minding my parents?" and "Was I mean to them?" or "Did I make fun of old people?"[43] A child's conscience, awaking to the reality of the objective order, would reply, "Yes, you failed to obey your father and mother, and you ignored them on six occasions." Heeg, in step with the era's practices, encouraged elementary students to identify sins and count them: "When I find a sin that I did, I see if I can tell it in just a few words, and say about how many times I did it."[44] The instructional pamphlets sat in a rack (usually located just inside the church entrance), cost a nickel or dime, and were to be read by Catholic children as they awaited their turn in the confessional. Making it to heaven depended on the crystallization of a conscience that knew instantly and unconsciously when a law had been broken.

Therefore, to be a proper Catholic internality, conscience thought in the language of laws. Confessors and catechists did not want a young Catholic's subjectivity to be like a ventriloquist's dummy, speaking the words of law enunciated by a master pulling strings; but teaching materials did seek to imprint the patterns of legalistic thinking onto the Catholic self's inner guide. *Catechism of Christian Doctrine*, one of many such volumes, maintained that perfecting a conscience requires "an adequate study of the laws of morality according to our condition in life."[45] Herder and Herder's *A Catholic Catechism* (1957), replete, as we see below, with strong defenses of the subjectivity of conscience, stressed the need to rear conscience under multiple sets of laws. "Conscience must be guided by the natural law, the Ten Commandments, the example of Christ, and the teachings and commandments of the Church," the guide held.[46] A highly functioning conscience evaluated each situation with the categories of external objective laws.

The priests who wrote catechisms had both theological and practical reasons for promoting the examination of a sacred personal vault in such a forensic manner: examinations shortened the queues outside confessionals by preparing each penitent to quickly rattle off a series of very specific sins to the confessor. It was relatively easy to state the offense and the number of times the offending act had been performed. But these inquiries also forced young Catholics to internalize the notion that the subjectivity must be weighed against the objectivity. In this way, confession opened up a back-and-forth between law and conscience, Catholicism's two most important metaphysical moral guides.

John Ford (fig. 3) coached Jesuit novices to seize opportunities for conscience appraisal presented to them by their penitents. Ford graduated in 1920 from Boston College High School, a Jesuit institution whose strong neo-medieval curriculum was anchored in Thomas Aquinas's *Summa Theologica*. A promising student, he was sent by his superiors to the Pontifical Gregorian University in Rome after his ordination in 1932. He completed a dissertation in 1937 and launched a career of research and teaching in the field of Catholic moral theology. Ford knew the power of good moral advice firsthand: experts helped him overcome alcoholism. A gregarious man and talented piano player who enjoyed a good time, he battled recurrent bouts with the disease in the early 1940s, ultimately turning to Alcoholics Anonymous to control it. In 1944, he burst onto the Catholic intellectual scene with a provocative article in *Theological Studies*, his field's top journal, denouncing Allied saturation bombing. Ford published a tremendous number of books and articles, and he began corresponding with Catholics from across the United States who sought his advice on matters ranging from Jesuit community life to conscientious objection to psychological testing. Over the course of his storied career, Ford accepted invitations to teach at Catholic University of America; seminaries like West Baden College in Indiana, St. Mary's College in Kansas, and the Gregorian University in Rome; and his alma mater, Boston College.

But perhaps Ford's most important contribution as an educator to the twentieth-century Catholic Church is the generation of confessors he mentored at Weston College, the Jesuit house of formation in Weston, Massachusetts.[47] Ford taught the novices that questioning penitents about their conscience was a matter of timing and proper technique. Questioning the conscience harmonized the believer's inner sanctum with the divine order and revealed a precisely defined path to eternal life. Ford believed that fates were decided in confessionals. Confessors had to know how to nudge a conscience toward the law. "When a penitent asks: is it a sin to kiss, or pet, or go to the movies, or go out with a married man," Ford lectured, "do not answer the question directly. Instead find out what is on their conscience."[48] The confessor might ask why the penitent inquired about these particular sins. The act itself could be set aside in the name of reaching a deeper

3, Father John C. Ford. Fr. John C. Ford, RG 12 Personnel photos. New England Province Archive. Jesuit Archives and Research Center, St. Louis. February 4, 2020.

understanding of sin, of one's place in the cosmos of external and internal. After all, Ford concluded, when overcoming ignorance of the law and properly tuning a conscience, "so much depended upon education."[49]

Without its duty to sync the law with conscience, the entire operation of the church would be moot. The system flowed from top to bottom, from law to conscience. God's existence was obvious, one priest wrote, because of the "moral order in the universe, mirrored in the stern commands of conscience to do what is right and avoid what is wrong."[50] God created an objective order and gave individuals a conscience to approve or condemn actions that conformed or deviated from the moral law. Catholics had the obligation to equip themselves with the type of conscience that correctly applied the law to a given situation. The confessional fused transcendent rules with immanent subjectivities.

The Radical Side of the Doctrine

The emancipatory dimension of the church's teaching on conscience begins with the significant checks that Catholic moralists placed on the law. It was axiomatic that a subjective guide could not be programmed by an external authority to internalize divine laws. The Catholic Church set the context for the conscience to catch sight of the divine law; the individual Catholic then had to take self-guided steps to connect his or her or sacred selfhood to transcendent norms. Catholics referred to the process of interlacing subjective conscience and objective law as "formation of conscience." John Ford described the necessity of this operation in a 1958 manual, *Contemporary Moral Theology*, coauthored with Gerald Kelly, a fellow Jesuit and moral theologian stationed at St. Mary's College. Both priests recognized the limits of law: Catholic educators had to admit the reality of conscience, explain the divine laws, and hope the penitent would bring the two to coalesce. Church authorities could never produce an educated conscience with the wave of a wand or pound a true conscience into existence by having their laity goose-step through proofs or statements meant for memorization. The role of these authorities in educating the child's conscience, Ford and Kelly admitted, was "to inform him of the meaning of these divine laws, as interpreted by the Church, and to inspire and encourage the child, in as much as possible, to observe the laws."[51] The educator, like the confessor, could not simply wrench conscience into the grooves of the law.

Authorities had a role to play in conscience formation, but any approach would have to strike a delicate balance between pushing for obedience to laws and respecting the reality that only the subject could join law and conscience. To reach a true understanding of the moral universe, conscience could be neither left to its own devices nor brought to heel with force. Too much autonomy or too much coercion, Catholics worried, might corrupt or destroy a person's capacity for accurate internal perceptions. A 1940 editorial in *Commonweal* warned that subjectivity was "not self-operative," but it hastened to point out that too much force entailed a "perversion of conscience." A process of some subtlety was therefore required. "There is an art—a cultivation—of the conscience, as there is an art of seeing or hearing or knowing," the editors explained rhapsodically.[52] Catholics had an innate moral authority that required a laborious process of self-formation to be synced with the natural law. A balanced process of education and refinement—neither autonomy nor forced obedience—put the conscience in harmony with the divine order.

Conscience formation shares attributes with a higher aspiration in the Catholic faith to balance, and properly utilize, the separate but overlapping operations of faith and reason. The formation process calls for the individual to proceed with a faith in the teaching authority of the church. The dialogue between objective and subjective encourages the Catholic to trust that ecclesiastical authority has promulgated laws with the goal of helping individuals become virtuous and happy agents. Faith makes it safe to err on the side of obeying a rule. For Catholics, faith also entails a willingness to allow the church and its rules to hold influence over the self. A solid baseline in the molding of a conscience, then, is a simple faith that following the laws accords with the interests of the individual for this world and the next. But this faith cannot be blind. The Catholic Church encourages its members to exercise their powers of reason to verify the claims made by authority figures. Conscience formation obliges Catholics to make sure that a law meets high standards of justness, clarity, applicability, and legitimacy. Catholics exercise their reason to analyze evidence that obedience to a law, issued by the church or the state, does in fact produce proper behavior in the world. Lawmakers must meet a high standard, appealing to intellect as well as trust, to command a conscience. But reason has its limits. Therefore, if such a quest for empirical knowledge fails or produces more confusion than clarity, one can safely place the conscience into the church's keeping. And yet it remains a sound teaching that reason must be utilized in appraising a law. Conscience formation moves a Catholic between the realms of faith and reason, allowing both approaches to enter a fruitful relationship in the broader mission of seeking and discovering a moral truth.

Confessors asked conscience to testify, but they never peered into that sacred space. Priests were like any other human authority in that they could neither read a conscience nor simply declare the conclusions it held. Only God and the individual really know what rests in an individual's inner sanctum. As Jesuit Daniel Lord explained in his 1941 pamphlet *When We Go to Confession*, Christ possesses a supernatural power to read an internal regulator, whereas the priest does not. "For Christ, standing back of His priest, follows the course of the confession and sees deep down into the human conscience," Lord wrote. "He knows whether or not the sinner is sorry. He knows why he came to confession."[53] The priest might not get access to that information, and he could never discern the penitent's true motivations or even contriteness of heart. Pope Pius XII reminded all Catholic priests of the absolute sanctity of conscience in an important address given in 1952. Only a priest may crack open a conscience as a "master of the Sacrament of penance," Pius announced. But the pope was quick to point out that the penitent still retained his or her rights of conscience. Even when in the confessional, behind a heavy cloth or a door and speaking to a priest through a screen, he explained, the person's "conscience does not cease to be a jealously guarded sanctuary whose secrecy God wishes to be safeguarded with the seal of a most sacred silence."[54] The pope used this particular address to denounce situation ethics (the notion that each situation had its own moral rules) but predictably could not bring himself to completely disregard subjectivity. The potent subjectivity of conscience—and the rights accorded to it by church teachings—endured both the confessional and priestly interrogation.

If a Catholic could not make a conscience true, the goal that midcentury Catholic pedagogues had for their pupils, then he or she ought to make it certain. For Catholics of high school age, teachers and textbooks began to differentiate between several conditions of conscience, some of which had the powers to rebuff, ignore, or trump the laws. In Catholic thought, certain conscience held an important liberating power in its ability to disregard official codes. As moral theologian Henry Davis explained, "One must obey the conscience when it is certain . . . the certain conscience is the conscience of one who is subjectively certain that the dictates of his conscience are correct."[55] Davis was articulating the belief held by midcentury moralists that God respected Catholics who acted with a cocksure, even misguided conscience. The certain conscience may very well have been objectively incorrect (misapplying God's law to the situation at hand) but certainty made an action acceptable nonetheless. Confidence covered up any errors. A text for high school sophomores, *Through Christ Our Lord*, put it frankly: "Follow your conscience if you are sure it is right."[56] A Catholic needed only certitude to make a particular action "legal" in the world of external and internal. If subjectivity could not be readied to become true, it should be made certain. As Edwin J. Healy, a Jesuit seminary professor from Indiana, wrote in his textbook *Moral Guidance*, "One must follow the commands of the certain conscience. Even if this certain conscience is false, it is to be obeyed."[57]

By-the-book confessors valued certitude so highly because, as they explained to Catholic penitents, the actions most offensive to God are those performed with a doubtful conscience. The doubtful conscience comprised a supremely undesirable condition wherein the penitent did not know where God stands on a particular issue but took a concrete action nonetheless. Doubt was not the same as ignorance: a penitent with a doubtful conscience possessed the means (manuals, confessors, and teachers) to alleviate the doubt; but the penitent with that diffident internality did not take the time to study church laws and undertook an action under the cloud of incertitude. The manualists hoped that the undecided subjectivity motivated a penitent to properly educate (i.e., "form") his or her conscience: the doubtful conscience, aware of its undesirable state, would be replaced with truth—or be transformed into a certain conscience (shielding the penitent from sin) and proceed to action from there. Actions performed with a hesitant subjectivity were strictly prohibited by confessors. A 1963 guide prepared by two Dominicans instructed penitents that "in practical doubt about the lawfulness of an action one may never act."[58] Acting with an equivocal conscience suggested to manualists that a penitent wavered on the existence of God's transcendent legal order.

But doubt also had a liberating potential: Catholics did not have to obey a law if they lacked confidence in that law's authority. At several junctures, Catholic respect for conscience overrode enforcing regulations, and doubting consciences could also find a loophole. If a Catholic doubted the authority of specific guidelines or instructions but had to act immediately, the church's theologians urged him or her to form a confident conscience and act decisively. Francis B. Cassily's 1931 textbook, *Religion: Doctrine and Practice*, explained the emancipatory possibility of doubt by using the example of fasting on days set aside for abstinence from meat during the liturgical year. If served meat on such a day but unsure of the specifics or the rules, a Catholic could resolve in conscience to eat the meat, and no law would be broken.[59] No sin was committed with an assured conscience and doubt of the law. *Through Christ Our Lord*, another textbook for high school students, elucidated this teaching in easy-to-understand terms: "there are occasions when it is impossible to find out what the Church says," and if a Catholic were pressed to act immediately and had no recourse to a priest, a confessor, or a catechism, such a member of the faithful "must follow the dictates of conscience . . . even if one makes the wrong decisions through ignorance, one will commit no sin in this case."[60] This held only if a Catholic remained doubtful about the exact advice of the law.

Theologians called these actions reflex principles or reflex acts. If a Catholic was hazy about the exact nature of the law's advice or authority, a reflex act, a rapid turn toward conscience, became the preferred approach. According to Dominican priest Bede Jarrett, because someone could not act in a state of doubt, that person needed to take a leap of faith behind a certain conscience. If that person was unsure of a code, and it didn't appear completely wrong to ignore the rule, he or she had to act. Conscience moved to the driver's seat and law went to the backseat. "In this way by a reflex act, by getting as it were behind my conscience, I have in reality made my conscience sure and I can proceed to act on it," Jarrett wrote.[61] Francis Connell noted in his 1953 textbook that the reflexivity of doubting the law and forming conscience transformed the doubting conscience into a certain one.[62] This gave the Catholic a green light to perform the action. While theologians debated how much liberty one could take with the law, all acknowledged the conscience-affirming powers of this reflex principle. Catholics should never follow a dubious law but rather a confident internal drive.

The erroneous conscience also occupied a special place in the universe of objective law and subjective conscience. Catholics with this defective type of internality sincerely believed they knew the objective truth but in fact did not. They earnestly took an action to be good when such a move was a sin. As Father D. F. Miller defined it, erroneous conscience would judge that "a certain action about to be performed [was] good, when actually it [was] contrary to the objective law of God."[63] An erroneous subjectivity, to paraphrase Miller, would be convinced it was correct when it was in fact objectively incorrect.

The redeeming quality of a mistaken conscience was that on many occasions, the subject was unaware of the erroneous application of the law: such a person operated in ignorance. One could theoretically possess a conscience that completely ignored the objective laws because such an internality had never contemplated the existence of such laws in the first place. Father Miller explained that one followed an erroneous conscience without sin unless a priest or a manual somehow induced doubt. If the penitent picked up a scent, however faint, that the action might not be in line with the objective law of God, following such an error-ridden internal sanctuary invited sin (it became doubtful). One then had a duty to consult the rulebook. "The man must obey his erroneous conscience, but in so doing he sins if he could have corrected it," as one priest warned.[64]

Persons with an erroneous conscience failed to apply the laws of God to a given situation. Yet their erroneous conscience, if it persisted, would maintain its moral immediacy and internality. Thus, such a subjective core still commanded considerable moral power to define reality, and it also retained its rights in church and society. Historian Ulrich Lehner identified the late eighteenth century as the time when Catholic thinkers turned to the erroneous conscience, known also as the invincibly ignorant conscience, to explain why Protestants deserved rights. Protestants believed Protestantism to be true because it was the only faith they knew. Participants in what Lehner calls "the Catholic Enlightenment" excused them for failing to see the truth of Catholicism. "If one grew up Protestant," Lehner explains, "one's conscience was formed from the earliest days accordingly, and one could not expect to overcome it."[65] In the twentieth century, Catholic moralists accepted the erroneous conscience of their fellow Catholics in much the same manner. If ignorance endured education (an unlikely but possible outcome), the Catholic who acted with an unsound inner light was not to be blamed for the error. "Some persons have a wrong or erroneous conscience," a high school text explained, but "as long as they do not know better," they are not culpable for the blunder.[66] Catholics retained the sacred obligation to follow conscience no matter how enlightened or ignorant a conscience remained about the moral law.

Acting against an erroneous conscience came with grave consequences. Failing to follow even this malformed subjective stance displayed a willingness to ignore God, thus inviting the same potentially soul-damning sin committed after breaking a confident conscience or acting with doubt. The erroneous entity gave the individual the wrong advice—but it was guidance from a sacred internalized chamber nonetheless. "The reason for man's obligation to follow an invincibly erroneous conscience is that failure to do so would mean that he was acting contrary to the subjective norm of morality and was therefore committing a sin," theologian Dominicus Prümmer explained in a 1955 moral theology manual.[67] One could not act against conscience, no matter how invincible its ignorance of the law.

Erroneous consciences troubled John Ford, but even he admitted they had rights to exist, and, per the objective-subjective worldview and its rules, they had the power to keep coercion at bay. On one hand, as Ford lectured a class of future Jesuit confessors in 1959, over the course of the twentieth century Catholics had come begrudgingly, but admirably, to respect the erroneous conscience. He told his students, "Nowadays we just say absolutely that in a case of invincible ignorance it is a sin not to follow one's conscience when it commands an objectively sinful act." If, even in the light of contact with the law, a subjectivity remained impervious to the truth, Catholics had come to respect conscience enough to let it walk away uncorrected. An internal conviction had achieved an "invincible ignorance" if teaching and confessing could not convince the penitent to replace false ideas with true ones. Ford wrote in his lecture notes, perhaps ambiguously, that Catholics of his day were "very lenient . . . but logical."[68]

Connell joined Ford in acknowledging the inoculation of the erroneous conscience from law. In lectures delivered at midcentury, he reminded Catholics of their obligation to properly knead their internality to lift the cloud of error and connect that inner sphere to the divine law. The church tasked the individual to discover the truth, the reality of right and wrong that existed outside the self. But it remained possible for the individual to have an erroneous conscience even after heavy doses of Catholic education, just as it remained possible for someone to conclude that an action is right when in fact it is wrong. Connell reassured his audiences that God doesn't punish individuals for following their faulty conscience—quite the opposite. God actually rewards individuals who follow their conscience untouched by or tragically shielded from the divine law: "In these circumstances God will reward one who follows his [erroneous] conscience," Connell commented, "for each one's conscience is for him the immediate norm of right and wrong."[69] One had to use all the means at his or her disposal to destroy ignorance. But if ignorance repelled all of an individual's repeated assaults or the educator's lessons, Connell explained in another lecture delivered in the 1950s, the conscience still retained its rightful place as the person's chief guide. A flawed sphere of morality buried deep in the individual cannot be rightly called invincible until "one has first used all of the ordinary means to form a conscience that is objectively correct." Yet it remains, Connell conceded, that a conscience stubbornly sealed from the law or treated with inadequate moral training "is the proper conscience for the individual."[70] A sacred interiority plagued by error still reigned as the individual's immediate norm and proper guide.

The important role of conscience in a Catholic's moral life seemed quite obvious to the church's theological experts at midcentury: it served as the closest guide at hand for moral actions. The power of the conscience came from the simple fact that it dwells closer to the individual than do divine laws. As Father Prümmer put it in his moral theology manual, "Conscience is the proximate norm of morality which must act as the guide for the whole of man's moral life."[71] This type of subjectivity served as the individual's nearest guide for morality and could step up as the primary moral guide if law failed to provide clarity. While the law was distant and external to the Catholic, the conscience was within reach and already present within that individual. In the words of various midcentury Catholic moral thinkers, conscience comprised "the immediate norm of all morality," "the proximate norm of all our actions," and the "proximate and subjective norm."[72] Ford told a class of future confessors in 1959 that a denial of its immediacy smacked of heresy: that conscience is the "norm of proximate perception" is "de fide [of the faith]."[73] To earn the rank of de fide is high status for a Catholic concept—it means that such a teaching has been promulgated by a pope or a plenary council as an official tenet of the faith. Its importance was beyond reproach in the Catholic moral tradition.

The very same catechisms that prepared Catholic students for confession carried lessons about the potency of the individual's subjectivity. Catechisms served up the instruction on conscience's powerful internal authority in a very raw form intended for the pupil's memorization. *Catechism of Christian Doctrine No. 4* explained to readers that "we are never permitted to act against our conscience" whatever it commands or forbids.[74] A catechism from 1930, prepared for parochial schools, urged students to "always obey the voice of conscience" and "never do anything your conscience forbids."[75] It was axiomatic that a Catholic could never go against conscience. Reverend Felix Kirsch and Sister M. Brendan's 1939 catechism, *Catholic Faith Explained,* put the theology succinctly: "It is never right to act against conscience."[76]

Herder and Herder, a longtime publisher of religious books considered friendly to the Catholic Church, took the lesson on conscience to its seemingly logical conclusion in a 1957 catechism: if authority commands one thing and conscience says another, it is conscience that a Catholic must follow. "Not even orders or threats from other people should ever force us to do anything against our conscience," the catechism coached.[77] If it appeared to a Catholic that internal resources possessed more moral authority than a law, the conscience must take the lead. There was nothing controversial in mid-twentieth-century America about having young Catholics memorize this proposition.

Catholics also gleaned from catechisms that acting against conscience constituted a grave sin. To dismiss the internal voice once it arrived at a conclusion indicated a willingness to disobey a direct order from God. A catechism prepared by a Redemptorist priest warned, "If we disobey our conscience, we disobey God's voice in us, and thus commit sin."[78] The catechism produced by Herder and Herder put it tersely: "Anyone who goes against the clear judgment of his conscience commits a sin against God."[79] Catholic commentators would take the idea found in the catechism to a more serious conclusion in editorials and speeches given at midcentury: members of the church who contravened their own conscience were in jeopardy of losing their soul or plummeting to hell upon death. James Martin Gillis reminded Catholics in 1930 that church teaching had linked acting against conscience to a dispossession of the soul since the thirteenth century. The high medieval church made clear that "a man cannot go to hell except by violating his conscience."[80] Lay Catholics were warned by their priests that an individual who violated conscience hollowed out his or her own internal moral world, entering a type of living hell. Conscience comprised the individual's ultimate authority, a final court of appeal for reason, so to break that ultimate internal authority meant emptying the soul itself.[81] Acting against the conclusions contained in one's subjective sanctuary carried grave consequences, temporal and eternal.

The lesson on the subjective power of conscience also appeared in mid-century American Catholicism's most "legalistic" texts—the moral theology manuals. These "how-to" theological works containing extremely detailed instructions taught aspiring confessors to pinpoint how and when a penitent committed a sin. As such, the texts naturally placed a heavy emphasis on the laws. But in the sections on conscience, without which no manual would be complete, moralists carefully outlined the sacred nature of Catholic subjectivity. How conscience was addressed in Henry Davis's 1952 manual, *Moral and Pastoral Theology*, was standard for its time. After defining conscience as "the herald of God," Davis declared that "a man must obey the conscience when it is certain." He then took the theology one step further, drawing another tenet from the orthodoxy: "God judges man on the dictates of obeying his conscience."[82] God checks to see whether individuals follow conscience, not on how carefully they attend to the law. Statements like Davis's were common fare in the Catholic manual tradition and a lesson encountered by every seminarian who aspired to hear confessions, administer penance, and forgive sins.

Radical Priests

The doctrine further held that every Catholic possessed rights of conscience *in the church*. If the church promulgated a rule that went against a Catholic's conscience, the rule became illegitimate and did not have to be followed. Priests were fond of pointing out the fact that these rights could be found in actual church doctrine. Though dead for over half a millennium, even Thomas Aquinas, the Catholic master teacher and modern theologian in chief, had made clear that the church places its bets with conscience. A Dominican reminded fellow Catholics in a 1953 article that Thomas sided with self-determination in power struggles within the church. "It might be thought that the order of the superior, whose authority is from God, is absolutely binding," he wrote, "yet this is not the opinion of St. Thomas who considers that the law of God supports the subject's conscience, in relation to which the order of the superior is only that of another man."[83] As a religious superior or a confessor, these mere men had no special power over the Catholic conscience. The laws they promulgated had to be just, reasonable, legitimate, and applicable to hold court over a selfdom.

Father Gillis took conscience rights to their natural end point: the doctrine not only created a buffer from the rules of superiors, it also allowed conscience to distance itself from and judge the rules of the Catholic Church itself, including ordinances seemingly issued by God. A Catholic conscience might find God and the church's guiding precepts inadequate, forcing it to make its own decisions. These laws, like all others, had to be considered at length for their clarity and reasonability before being granted authority over a sacred subjective sphere. "In a sense," Gillis explained, "the human conscience does and must sit in judgment upon the commands that come even from the mouth of God."[84] The Ten Commandments and the rules of the church "make their appeal to conscience, and if conscience does not recognize them or understand them, the Ten Commandments are not commandments to their conscience."[85] Gillis's biographer Richard Gribble found a tendency in his subject to swing rapidly from one end of a Catholic doctrine to the other, a trend reflected in Gillis's commentary on conscience.[86] A Gillis radio program or lecture moved from one iteration of the teaching, law over conscience, to the other dimension, conscience over law, in a matter of seconds.

On occasion, Catholics went so far as to assert that the subjective understanding of an act in conscience determines the objective nature of the act. At the heart of the Catholic doctrine of conscience rested a set of epistemological questions: What determines reality: individual perception or the law? What reality did subjective knowledge of the moral good create, if any at all? Catholics took extreme positions on these questions. The individual might not know much about the truths that govern the universe, but it didn't quite matter: they created a reality through the truths known in conscience. The doctrine of conscience had Kantian qualities of philosophical idealism; the mind imposed categories on the world and created the realities in the world. Conscience, in other words, constructed the reality of the moral order outside the person. The doctrine also recalled early modern philosopher Rene Descartes's assertion that a mind is ontologically distinct from matter. What you think, the doctrine of conscience said, *therefore is*.

Gillis reveled in detailing the subjective powers of conscience in his lectures and radio shows. "A bad action done in good conscience becomes good, and a good action with a bad conscience becomes bad," he told his *Catholic Hour* listeners.[87] If conscience told its host not to undertake an action and if he or she did anyway, this action became a sin regardless of the end of the act. The reverse also held true. If conscience countenanced an action, the action became good despite the outcome. Gillis took the argument to an outlandish conclusion in his radio address: if Oliver Cromwell had been convinced in conscience that he had to butcher the Irish, the subjective power of conscience is so formidable that it means that his actions were not murder. Even when he dropped the outrageous Cromwell example, Gillis explained the subjective power of Catholic internality with consistency.

"What is done in good conscience is virtuous, even if bad," he lectured in 1940. "Whatever is done with a bad conscience is sin even though the solution itself may be materially good."[88]

At midcentury, however, it was Francis Connell who had the greatest knack for taking the doctrine of conscience to its most extreme orthodox forms. Anyone tempted to call him a conservative has not looked closely at his early speeches or the lecture notes for his graduate seminars. In a 1949 address given at the Knights of Columbus Forum in Brooklyn, the revered Catholic University of America theologian admitted that proponents of contraception, divorce, and euthanasia were all following their conscience. The natural law seemed obvious to Catholics, but Connell thought the remnant had to admit that not everyone in American society recognized these divine ordinances. "Hence, we do not say that those who hold the lawfulness of contraception and divorce and euthanasia are all going against their conscience," he lectured. As held in the doctrine, materialists and secularists committed no sins when following conscience and advocating for sex, divorce, and mercy killing. Connell insisted that the real tragedy rested in the failure of these moderns to have their subjective lifeworlds reared under the auspices of the church. Catholics, he noted, "claim that such persons are unfortunate in that they have not the guidance of the Catholic Church to help them in forming their consciences."[89] Natural law was available to all through reason, but modern progressives could not connect their internal orb to the law because they had no assistance from the institutional church. For Catholics, the doctrine of conscience could explain many things, even the sins of non-Catholics.

Connell found himself paying homage to both sides of the law-conscience equation on a televised episode of *Moral Decisions: The Individual and His Freedom*, aired by the National Broadcasting Company in 1955. That episode opened with two characters, "Paul" and "Mary," debating whether to give a lethal overdose of medicine to their very sick mother to end her life. The camera then panned to Father Connell, who offered a short lecture on the relationship between conscience and the natural law. His first oration of the show detailed how conscience ought to import the laws. An objective standard promulgated by God existed outside human beings, and "conscience is intended to find out what is right and what is wrong, and what is good and what is bad, not to make actions good or bad."[90] The show then featured questions from figures representing other sides of the euthanasia debate. Question 4 came from a "farmer leaning on a fence," who told the audience, "I figger that the good Lord's gonna judge me on what I think is right and wrong. I'll let my conscience be my guide." The camera then shot back to

Connell, the moral expert invited to the show to provide the viewers at home with moral clarity. The audience might have expected a high-powered theologian employed at a notable university to slam the yokel's careless theology, but even the conscience of a hardened rural laborer possessed a capacity to create truths deserving of respect. Connell could not deny the other, equally orthodox aspect of the Catholic teaching on conscience. God would in fact judge this farmer on whether he followed his conscience regarding an action as serious as euthanasia. "It is true, God judges each individual according to his conscience honestly formed," Connell explained. "If a person sincerely believes that a certain action is good, even though it is wrong, God will not punish him, but on the contrary will reward him for his . . . good will and sincerity."[91] The gateway to heaven is narrow, and those who pass enter only with a confident conscience.

Connell saved the most extreme examples of the rights of conscience for lectures to his graduate classes at the Catholic University of America. The individual who acted on impulse with a conscience temporarily unhinged from reason might not have committed a sin. Connell used the example of the husband who kills his wife's murderer to illustrate his point. Having come home to find his wife dead and the murderer standing over her body, "the husband might be so overwhelmed by grief that he would kill the murderer, yet not be guilty in conscience of any sin, because his emotions deprive him temporarily of the use of intellect and of free will."[92] Connell also used the doctrine of conscience to exculpate the teenage driver who slammed his car into another person's property. "If a boy drives a car recklessly and inflicts damage on one's property, he is not obliged to make restitution if he sincerely believes that he was not guilty in conscience," Connell said.[93] However, should the civil law judge him guilty, he must pay his debt to society. But he remained guiltless before God, because the powerful subjectivity of conscience determined the moral reality.

Conclusion

One basic rule governed Catholic moral life at midcentury: right or wrong, the individual must follow conscience. The nature of the act, as understood in the depths of the self, determined the goodness or badness of an action. The standing of the action proceeded only from what conscience concluded. Conscience always had to be followed, right or wrong; it was morally dangerous to the simply follow the law.

Yet this description is not meant to imply that the doctrine of conscience is as straightforward as its medieval Catholic creators intended it to be—bound to law here, freed from law there, as if the required motion were easily apparent. The twentieth-century church had a conscience problem, and it passed the dilemma on to the modern state. In the 1960s, even the most educated priest had to double back and offer numerous caveats in a basic summary of the doctrine. Consider, by way of conclusion, a 1964 article by a priest that was published in the magazine *Emmanuel*. First, he warned against any disregard for the law. Those in the church who taught "others to break the laws," he explained, would be ranked on the Day of Judgment as "the least in the kingdom of God."[94] Then came the requisite mention of the individuality required to fuse law and conscience: the self-directed bridging of subjective and objective must occur if law were to gain authority over the individual. The priest made clear that an individual should consider each formal instruction at length "by the purpose for which it was enacted" and by "its preference over conscience," testing it for applicability, clarity, legitimacy, and justness.[95] Laws did not have power over conscience upon delivery. Like other moralists of his generation, this cleric recognized the limits of the law. Finally, and all in the same article, the classic disclaimer of conscience rights and conscience's truth-generating capacity: every layperson and priest, he wrote, "affirm[ed] the subjective supremacy of the individual conscience." Then he drove home the point that "right or wrong, conscience must be obeyed."[96] Each articulation of the doctrine included points and counterpoints. The conservative and radical sides of the teaching set the terms for debates in church and state in a century beset by demanding questions about war and sex.

American Catholics of the 1960s and 1970s inherited this medieval and modern program. The conscience problem made its way into Second Vatican Council documents. In these writings, its twinned nature of restraint and liberation was less a symbiosis and more a fault line. The council's *Pastoral Constitution on the Church in the Modern World* shrouded conscience from external surveillance and domination by calling it the "most secret core and sanctuary of man," and it reinforced the power of Catholic subjectivity by declaring that conscience did not lose its dignity even if it "err[ed] from invincible ignorance."[97] Yet the council fathers made clear that conscience should be made ready to become a home for the law, especially the natural laws that governed sex and condemned birth control. Spouses should enter bedrooms with a "conscience dutifully conformed to the divine law" and ought to be "submissive to the Church's teaching office."[98] The bishops wrote that conscience became good conscience the more the divine law "[held] sway." According to *The Declaration on Religious Freedom*, "man [was] not to act contrary to his conscience," but all formation of conscience must consider "the sacred and certain doctrine of the church."[99] Conscience was free, and yet everywhere it was in chains. Herein lay the problem for American Catholics and the modern America they inhabited.

The doctrine could only be truly grasped by those who accepted its tensions and its split personality. Midcentury Protestants and secular progressives like Paul Blanshard and Paul Tillich lopped off the liberating side of the doctrine, interpreting confessionals and clergymen as crushers of conscience. Catholics of the 1960s and 1970s, for their part, sometimes made the opposite mistake: they left behind the conservative elements of the doctrine and the importance Thomas Aquinas placed on proper attention to the law to argue for an unadulterated right to follow conscience. Conservative Catholic commentators, among them Cardinal Archbishop Patrick O'Boyle and William F. Buckley Jr., were not completely wrong when they accused Catholics of radicalizing Thomas's teaching on conscience and neglecting the emphasis he placed on obedience to authority. But, as we are about to explore, the most conservative Catholics were willing to invoke conscience rights to disobey the state on matters of conscription and military service, but then they tended to deny the rights of conscience in the church. They wanted to shut down claims of conscience in the religious sphere while invoking them against the modern state. Conscience should be obedient to the church but also prepared to reject deference to secular laws that undermine God's power in the world. Conscience has a legacy as a double agent, shoring up the hold of authority over the individual in some instances or liberating the individual from authority in others. Where and when the conscience bound the individual to obey authority or uncoupled the individual from authority became a matter of serious debate in the modern United States.

Conscience shared a relationship with civil laws in addition to its calibrations with divine and ecclesiastical laws. Connell's example of the teenage joyrider with a confident conscience seems trivial, but the fraught relationship between civil law and conscience was anything but in the twentieth-century United States. A confident subjectivity might deign to shape moral reality outside the individual, but civil law did not have to recognize the actuality created by a Catholic conscience. Catholics found themselves caught in the crosshairs of conscience and civil law as governments in the United States and Europe developed robust systems of mass conscription to fight world wars and cold wars. It is to the clash between the powers of conscience and the civil laws of the twentieth-century state that we now turn.

TWO

Political Origins:
Totalitarianism, World War II,
and Mass Conscription

It is the teaching of the Church that I must always follow conscience. . . . I can never try to shelter myself behind authority, and say that though my conscience objects, I have a right to put it aside and follow authority blindly. . . . I am certainly wrong, for that I case I should be using authority to break up my conscience.

—Father Bede Jarrett, *Catholic Worker* (1941)

Since the Pope has not pronounced the Allied Powers to be waging a just war, the decision as to its justice (and accordingly to one's participation in the war) is the responsibility of the individual conscience.

—Dwight Larrowe to Bishop Edward D. Howard (1942)

Father John K. Ryan, professor of philosophy at the Catholic University of America in Washington, DC, brushed aside the suggestion that individuals were capable of judging large-scale political programs. "It is certainly not within the moral and mental competence of each citizen to decide upon the wisdom and morality of the most momentous questions of national policy," he wrote in a 1941 article on conscientious objection.[1] Published in the *Catholic Educational Review* in June of that year, Ryan's article appeared as Hitler's Panzer divisions rushed toward Moscow. Over a year earlier, in October 1940, Congress approved the first peacetime draft in US history. The nation had not formally entered the war then raging in the Pacific Ocean and continental Europe, but the United States, led by the quiet efforts of president Franklin Roosevelt, had been busy organizing manpower and machines for more than two years. But Father Ryan (not to be confused with influential Catholic economist John A. Ryan) would not publish an article on individual and society, war or no war, without mentioning the Catholic doctrine of conscience. For Catholic moralists, discussion of the state's laws, the external guides for citizenship, proceeded with recognition of its partner, the conscience, the internal and subjective guide for morality. Despite the complexity of national policy, Ryan wrote, "the supremacy of conscience . . . still remains."[2]

Ryan could have been drawing from ideas found in Henry David Thoreau's canonical 1849 treatise, *Resistance to Civil Government*, but Catholic priests like him hardly needed help from Thoreau—or any other American individualist—when it came to articulating the rights of conscience. The notion that Catholics had to refine their subjective perceptions and judge civil law was stated in the church's doctrine for all, even Catholic teenagers, to see. Thoreau, too, wanted US citizens to stand in judgment of unjust state policies and rebel against them, subtly and overtly. "Must the citizen ever for a moment, in the least degree, resign his conscience to the legislator?" he wondered. "Why has every man a conscience, then?"[3] Thoreau watched in the 1840s as men set aside conscience to join a "file of soldiers, colonel, captain, corporal, privates, and powder-monkeys," which marched proudly but mindlessly into battle against the Mexicans. He was convinced that thoughtful individuals scrutinized a public behavior before handing a precious selfdom over to the man in charge. Catholic priests, whom many nineteenth-century Protestants would have looked on as conformers par excellence, also considered it anathema to displace subjective moral responsibility onto the state or any other authority figure, whether in times of peace or of war. Modern men of the cloth learned this lesson, not from the canonical writings of nineteenth-century American radicals, but from a church doctrine formulated in the thirteenth century and repeated in Catholic schools and seminaries in the twentieth.

This chapter traces a nearly three-decade period in which the US security state reached unprecedented size and power, and the American public witnessed severe wars. Though the history of the security state during these years is one of aggressive intensification, this chapter shows that the Catholic teaching on conscience remained remarkably consistent. Defenses of self-sovereignty surfaced in mainstream publications like the *Catholic Educational Review* and *America* as the Selective Service System pulled thousands of Catholic men out of the urban neighborhoods and the small farming towns, dispatching them to America's many military bases, the killing fields in the Pacific Islands or northern Africa, or the beaches that edged France. Not only did the teaching remain steady, but a small yet dedicated cross section of Catholic priests began to apply the rights of conscience to civil law in a series of new arenas where modern warfare raised fresh moral problems: totalitarianism, mass conscription, obliteration bombing runs, state contraceptive programs, and the rise of the Cold War garrison state. Indeed, conscience rights became a real option for Catholics to invoke during World War II as the faithful confronted the unjustness of conscription laws and military orders that asked men to contravene deeply held truths.

Conscience Formation and Catholic Citizenship

Thomas Hobbes's definition of law in his 1651 classic, *Leviathan*, is a useful point of departure to begin assessing conscience formation and its political ramifications. Hobbes, stricken with a fear of anarchy induced by the first and second English Civil Wars (1642–49), famously advanced the argument that a sovereign's primary duty is to provide security, material and territorial, for his or her people. The quest for security left no room for a religious doctrine that divided moral authority between external (law) and internal (conscience). Whereas Catholics distributed moral authority equally between law and conscience, Hobbes's thought rendered moral authority and civil law indivisible. The English political philosopher put it bluntly: "The measure of good and evil actions, is the civil law."[4] The Catholic process of conscience formation, wherein the individual was presumed to judge the justness or unjustness of the civil law, would, to use Hobbesian phrasing, "distract" or "weaken" the body politic. Consciences, according to Hobbes, presented an unacceptable risk to national security.

The doctrine of conscience required that Catholics submit all civil laws to evaluation. As the *Catholic Worker* explained to readers in 1941—with a line Hobbes would have found horrifying—"Conscience must sit in judgment of the claim of authority before investing it with the sanction of moral law."[5] In terms of war, should a Catholic find the war just—forming his or her interiority by bringing the universal law to bear on his or her subjective circumstances—that person could take up arms. But the doctrine of conscience allowed the individual Catholic to reach the exact opposite conclusion. The radical tradition allowed subjectivity to project its own image of reality. The law might be judged unjust after a period of deliberation, shifting moral authority decisively to the conscience. If a Catholic found an entire war or a specific command unjust, the church bound that individual to follow conscience and not a civil law. Here we do well to examine the words of Jesuit Paul Blakeley, written in March 1942, nearly three months after the United States declared war on Japan: "If my conscience, seriously consulted tells me that a war is unjust, then I can take no part in that war."[6] For Hobbes, there was no need for moral cogitation; the law arrived with moral authority qua its status as law. For Catholics like Father Blakeley, the law was to be tested to ensure its justness.[7]

In the fine print of twentieth-century catechisms and religion textbooks published in the 1920s and 1930s could be found a contract between the Catholic Church and the modern state. The terms of the deal appeared to be quite simple. The first part of the compact stipulates that unjust laws issued by the state did not have any power over the individual's internal life. But, on the other hand, if legislatures and executives passed legitimate and reasonable rules, the injunctions earned authority over Catholic interiority. Catholics would have to obey the state's laws if the government upheld its end of the bargain. In response to the question, "Do civil laws bind in conscience?" the *Catechism of Christian Doctrine No. 4* (1926) answered, "Yes; laws properly so called passed and promulgated by any State bind in conscience no matter what may be the form of government."[8] The qualifying words "properly so called" are important to note: civil laws became laws only by channeling the divine law into worldly affairs. If the laws were improper and ran askew of the divine law, the ordinances could not bind a Catholic conscience to obedience. As regards an "unreasonable" civil law, a 1932 textbook, *Religion: A Secondary School Course*, explained, it "cannot be said to enjoy the approval of God and does not oblige us in conscience."[9]

Catholics found civil laws reasonable when the laws, issued by a legitimate body, pursued the "common good." The common good was a notoriously vague notion, but civil laws contributed to its realization by providing stability and security for all a society's many members. Catholic social thought upholds the state's rights to protect the common good with military action. But it devolves to each Catholic individual to assess for himself or herself, through a process of conscience formation, whether laws or wars were oriented toward the common good. The law lost power over conscience if an individual Catholic decided that the law did not seek the proper end. "If a law is contrary to the common good it does not oblige in conscience," explained *Religion: A Secondary School Course*.[10] God does not expect Catholics to indiscriminately obey laws made by civil authorities but rather to form and follow conscience.

The considerable circulation of the rights of conscience during World War II far outstripped the number of Catholics recognized by the state as conscientious objectors (COs). Catholics numbered only 135 out of the total pool of officially recognized 11,887 COs.[11] The bishops opposed conscientious objection during World War II, as did the majority of American Catholics. A special camp created for Catholic COs in Stoddard, New Hampshire, folded in 1943 after the bishops withheld financial support. The Selective Service System, in a remarkable feat of mobilization, pulled a total of 10 million men into the military over the course of that war. Catholics comprised over a quarter of the armed forces in the global conflict. Following a conscience did not separate a Catholic from the civil law, as foretold in doctrine. But a new discomfort with obedience to political authority was spreading among American Catholics.

Totalitarianism and the End of Isolation

The first American Catholic to apply the doctrine of conscience to politics was James Martin Gillis, a critic of America's burgeoning New Deal state and a conservative in politics and theology. As historian Peter D'Agostino notes, Father Gillis was American Catholicism's foremost critic of Benito Mussolini in the 1930s. Gillis's deep suspicion of state power, stemming from his conservative social and political positions, led him to fetishize independent moral rigor and thoroughly denounce any dependence on the government.[12] He initiated the push for conscience rights in the political sphere in his nationally syndicated newspaper column. Initially, his targets were the US high-level courts that refused Douglas Clyde Macintosh, a Canadian Baptist, his prerogative to follow his conscience on the matter of war. A district court in New England had denied US citizenship to Macintosh in 1929 after the prolific Yale professor indicated in his immigration paperwork that he would only fight in wars he personally deemed just. A World War I veteran, Macintosh personified the Catholic theology of conscience formation: he assigned to himself the right to judge the civil law before granting it authority over his inner selfdom. Gillis's first editorial on the case explained that the church's defense of the erroneous and confident conscience—"If upon mature deliberation, I am convinced that certain action is immoral, I must not take part in it. I may be wrong, but I must follow my conscience"—applied to Macintosh's claim to judge the justness or unjustness of any future wars.[13]

Gillis, a passionate and hard-headed thinker who fulminated against the perceived relativism of modernity (he regularly criticized materialism, contraception, capitalism, and Freemasonry), forcefully denounced the Supreme Court's denial of Macintosh's subjective truth-creating capacities after the justices upheld the lower court's refusal to grant him citizenship in 1931. Father Gillis thought the modern US state put forth a new philosophy of governance with its decision in the Macintosh case. "Allegiance to God is expressed immediately, as everyone knows, by obedience to conscience," he concluded, "but according to the theory now insinuated [by the Supreme Court] one must serve the State even at the expense of conscience."[14] The justices demonstrated a callous disregard for conscience, an individual's immediate moral guide—a faculty Macintosh was obliged to form and follow.

The withholding of Macintosh's citizenship was not the judicial system's only denial of conscience rights as fascists took power abroad and US politicians clamped down on conscientious objection at home. In 1934, just three years after the Macintosh case, the Supreme Court ruled against two college students from the University of California–Berkeley, both Methodists, who sought exemption from mandatory enrollment in military science classes. The Jesuit editors of *America* magazine sardonically observed that the court's conclusions rested "on the theory of the supremacy of the State over the rights of conscience."[15] They knew that Catholic social teaching upheld the state's rights, extending from its duty to provide security, to fund and manage military academies. Berkeley, a land-grant college awarded property in the Morrill Act of 1862, agreed to ready men for military service in exchange for the financial boost provided by the land. But the Supreme Court's philosophy, as expressed by justice Pierce Butler, its only Catholic member, troubled the priests. In 1925, Butler ruled favorably to the Catholic Church in *Pierce v. Society of Sisters*, striking down an Oregon law making it illegal for parents to send children to Catholic schools. With his opinion in the Berkeley case, however, he ignored a universal truth that held for the Jesuits and for their fellow citizens. The courts mistakenly understood morality as purely external and objective, failing to recognize conscience, the internal and subjective receiver of the law. The Supreme Court made no attempt to "effect a reconciliation of conflicting rights, but simply set aside the rights of conscience alleged by the individual."[16] For the Jesuits and for Gillis, court decisions of the early 1930s augured a reign of political domination.

Rome played an important role in applying conscience rights to mass politics. Totalitarianism inspired Pope Pius XI to seek out exemplars who lived the doctrine for special acknowledgment as saints. In 1935 the pontiff, whom historian Samuel Moyn credits with making the initial gestures toward human rights at the end of that decade, canonized Thomas More and John Fisher.[17] These Englishmen were said to have followed conscience in refusing to sign the Oath of Supremacy in 1534, a heroic stand that made them saints for a contested political moment. The path to canonization was four hundred years in the making: King Henry VIII executed More and Fisher in the summer of 1535; Pope Leo XIII beatified them, along with fifty-two other English martyrs, in 1886; and both men were finally taken off the waiting list and made saints in 1935, shortly after Hitler and Mussolini grabbed the reins of political power in continental Europe. In the twentieth-century Catholic rendition of the classic tale, Henry executed

Thomas More, a renowned scholar and Chancellor of England, and John Fisher, an accomplished theologian and Bishop of Rochester, for refusing to recognize the king as head of the church. In his address marking the announcement of canonization, Pius XI claimed to have made saints of More and Fisher to inspire contemporary heroes and heroines under totalitarian rule who would "rather die than offend their conscience, the purity of their faith, and the purity of their soul."[18] The canonization of the two men marked the genesis of a conscience-following legend that culminated in plays performed in New York and London theaters as well as the 1966 film *A Man for All Seasons*, winner of the Academy Award for Best Picture.[19]

The profound threat that political power presented individuals in the 1930s can be seen in how British and American Catholic writers suddenly invoked More and Fisher to contrast the rights of conscience with the concepts of totalitarianism and the national will. Catholics met burgeoning state power structures with praise for preserving subjectivity. More and Fisher, Jesuit Francis Talbot wrote, "were opposed to the totalitarian state" and went to early graves "in defense of their inalienable right to serve God as their consciences demanded."[20] The Anglo-American Catholic press celebrated the English saints for living out the doctrine of conscience rights in a politically coercive environment. For a British priest writing in 1935 in the *Downside Review*, a quarterly published by monks from Stratton-on-the-Fosse, More and Fisher would not have allowed inner sanctuaries to be crushed and controlled by big government powers like modern National Socialism and communism. The English saints "consistently formed conscience according to the will of Christendom," the priest wrote. "Their conscience thus formed (not their private opinions), they opposed to the national will."[21] When More and Fisher molded their conscience according to the teachings of the church, the process revealed the state's law as unjust, and the law lost authority over a Catholic's intimate stronghold of personhood. These were saints for a totalitarian moment. As one American Catholic magazine rejoiced, "Catholics throughout the world will seek their intercession with equal fervor."[22]

The *Catholic Worker* became a hub of conscience language in the late 1930s.[23] The political problems of the era increased the frequency with which journalist and social activist Dorothy Day's reporters delved into the annals of church history for crisp articulations of the doctrine. Writers for the newspaper recognized the late medieval and early modern period as a creative moment in Catholic theorizing of conscience rights. In September of 1938, the newspaper profiled Francisco de Vitoria (1483–1546), an influential Spanish Dominican; he earned a reputation as a thorn in the side of princes for subjecting the wars waged by the royals of his time to the just-war theory. The *Catholic Worker* quoted Vitoria as arguing that truths known in conscience define the moral realities of the princes' wars, an idea that became useful in Europe's and America's new totalitarian moment: "If in their conscience the subjects are convinced of the injustice of the war . . . it is not [just]."[24] That same issue of the paper also quoted theologian Juan Lopez de Vivero (1450–1524), whose fifteenth-century writings urged medieval subjects to preserve their conscience, if nothing else. "If it seems to a subject that the true prince . . . wages an unjust war and calls together his subjects for such a war," Lopez once wrote, "the subjects, whose conscience would thus be harmed, must not comply with the orders given them."[25] The *Catholic Worker* was reinforcing modern conscience rights with medieval sources in September 1938, the same month that Germany annexed Czechoslovakia.

Around that time, Dorothy Day set in motion one of the most passionate cases for conscience rights outlined by a Catholic thinker when she asked Monsignor George B. O'Toole, a philosophy professor at Catholic University of America, to write a series of articles on conscription. In these writings, published in the paper in 1939 and 1940, O'Toole defended conscience rights from the claims of the Selective Service System. The *Catholic Worker* received so many requests for copies that it published O'Toole's articles in a ninety-page pamphlet, *War and Conscription at the Bar of Christian Morals*.[26] War seemed unavoidable as Father O'Toole's corpus went to print: German armies occupied the capitals of Denmark, Holland, Norway, and France. The US government had begun conscripting men into the army: as of the autumn of 1941, all male citizens between the ages of twenty-one and thirty-five had to register with local draft boards, their names to be sent into a lottery system. But O'Toole's popular pamphlet, which he dedicated to the church's "conscript boys," argued that total war had thoroughly corrupted civil laws, obliging all Catholics to follow conscience and refuse induction into the military. The military, with its use of indiscriminate killing machines, severed any connection to the divine laws, forfeiting authority over a Catholic's inner chamber. "Contrary immoral practices such as the bombing of civilian centers, the hate-propaganda, and the bloodthirsty bayonet drill" are all part of an official war program, O'Toole observed, concluding that "where such immoral methods are the order of the day, no Christian can in conscience participate."[27] Conscience, not civil law, perforce became a Catholic's guide, even before formal declarations drew America into the global conflict. "The fact of the matter is that all modern nations are secularized and that they have legislated religion and morals out of all public life whether civil or military," Father O'Toole explained, "relegating Christian ideas to the privacy of the individual conscience."[28]

World War II

Defenses of conscience in political life were becoming more common among Catholics in the 1930s, but the discourse remained somewhat marginal. James Martin Gillis stood outspoken on the matter, and while Pope Pius XI made saints of Thomas More and John Fisher, the push for Catholic self-determination was largely a preserve of Day's radical followers at the *Catholic Worker*. The sheer brutality of World War II, and the proliferating instances of coercion it required, gave the political iteration of conscience rights the opening it needed to become more relevant in modern America. The argument for Catholic self-governance gained a legitimacy among American Catholics, including Jesuit theologian John Ford, in the early 1940s. Its origins as a political project can be traced to the latter years of the war when bombing civilian innocents and the mass distribution of prophylactics became common practices of the US military. Many priests kept the doctrine on an even keel, discussing the medieval teaching and its finer points of error and truth in periodicals like the *Catholic Mind* and the *American Ecclesiastical Review*. But a significant development in the history that this book is tracing is also apparent. An increasing number of Catholics began to argue during World War II that subjectivity needs defending from the coercive powers of the militaristic liberal democratic state. So many reputable theological and cultural authorities suggested that the doctrine could be applied to the question of conscription that raising it against the state became a more readily available option.

Jesuit Daniel A. Lord, a popular Catholic media icon like James Martin Gillis, defended self-sovereignty in a remarkably stark manner as wartime patriotism blossomed in the United States after Hitler's blitzkrieg attack on Poland. Lord, a man of many artistic and musical talents, earned a reputation as being a martinet of a censor in the early 1930s after he helped craft the Motion Picture Code, an official set of regulations that sanitized movies and aimed to make them morally wholesome. In the Protestant and secular imagination, Lord qualified as a Catholic reactionary; but like other Catholic thinkers trained in the Thomistic mode, he was a fierce defender of conscience rights. His invitingly titled 1939 pamphlet, *So You Won't Fight, Eh?*, available for only a nickel, explained in plain terms that Catholics were, as stated in Church doctrine, bound by the rules surrounding sacred

subjectivity not to fight in an unjust war. Lord detected a shift from isola-
tionism to militarism in American culture after Hitler flouted international
diplomacy and invaded his neighbors. "It took just about a month of blitzkrieg," Lord observed, "to change the whole temper of America from one of
restful pacifism to one of strenuous militarism."[29] He saw the writing on the
wall: the United States was gearing up for war. The Jesuit feared that conscience formation would be left behind when the nation charged headlong
into global conflict. He recapitulated the doctrine for a mass audience of
young men: "If a country is engaged in a clearly unjust war, then conscience
has to enter in."[30] Then Lord took the argument a step further: "The man
who fails to examine his conscience and fights an unjust war is guilty in the
sight of God."[31] Willing conscripts never took the time to form conscience
properly. They neglected to appraise the law for its justness before submit-
ting to obedience. They simply served their selfhood to the authorities on a
platter, neglecting to refine their own subjective moral resources and consequently committing a grave sin. Lord urged Catholics to form conscience
before turning up for military service.

Catholic priests rolled out defenses of the erroneous conscience as the
United States prepared for war. The most impassioned defense came from
Father Cyprian Emmanuel in an article for the *Catholic Mind*. It was published in October 1940, the same month that Congress approved a peacetime draft, but, like Lord's pamphlet, before the United States entered the
global conflict. Despite an individual's detailed study of the draft law and
his or her literacy in basic Catholic theology, he wrote, "it can happen that
one remains in complete or partial ignorance of the law or misunderstands
its true meaning," thus creating "an invincible erroneous conscience" within.
Emmanuel took his case to its logical conclusion, as outlined by doctrine:
"The individual is obliged to obey the dictates of such a conscience just as
rigidly as though it were in perfect accord with the law, not because it is erroneous, but because his conscience is convinced in good faith that it is true."[32]
In Catholic thought, in peace and in war, in a confessional or at a draft board,
the erroneous conscience comprised a sacred space beyond the state's coercive reach because it generated an objectively true reality for the individual.

The Imperial Japanese Navy's surprise attack on Pearl Harbor—an air
strike that left over two thousand Americans dead and another eleven hundred wounded—did not compel Jesuit priests to suppress the Catholic
Church's classic teachings on self-rule. The urgency and sovereignty of
the conscience remained lively even as the United States became the formal enemy of Germany and Japan. On December 13, 1941, two days after Hitler declared war on the United States, an editorial on conscientious

objection appeared in *America*. The magazine's Jesuit editors noted the long-established tenet of Catholic political theory that the state possessed the right to raise an army. But the editors pointed out that if a Catholic individual's self-directed process of conscience formation turned up evidence of an unjust war, that person had no choice but to ignore law and inaugurate the requisite regime of self-determination. As the editors explained, "Ordinarily, presumption favors the government . . . [but] presumption must yield to evidence, and should the individual citizen conclude that he must in conscience accept what he deems to be evidence overthrowing the presumption, his conscience must be his guide."[33] *America* published another editorial on Catholic conscientious objectors just two weeks later. When the editorial appeared on December 27, 1941, Japan had defeated US forces at Wake Island and marched victoriously into Hong Kong.[34] Its editors realized what was at stake. The Japanese attack on Pearl Harbor and the empire's rapid expansion made shoring up security an imperative for the US state. Still, in light of these facts, if the Catholic CO found the war unjust, *America* admitted, "he has to follow his conscience, it is true."[35] He must also accept the state's punishments.

Priests, particularly the Jesuits, refused to bury the rights of conscience during the war, even when the opportunity presented itself. Layman Dwight Larrowe, director of a camp of Catholic COs in New Hampshire and a member of the Catholic Worker movement, wrote to the editors of *America* magazine in March of 1942, accusing these Jesuits of gainsaying the rights of conscience in the months following Japan's attack on Pearl Harbor. Larrowe felt that the magazine had not done enough to clarify the church's teaching on subjectivity for its readers (despite two editorials). Editor and Jesuit Paul Blakeley was taken aback. He immediately endeavored to clear his magazine's name of having committed any such apostasy. "Let me say I have never heard of a Catholic moralist who holds that a man may disregard, or act against his conscience," Blakeley huffed in a published response. "I did not write that a man might follow his conscience. I said that he must."[36] Indeed he had. Priests believed that the Catholic tradition of self-sovereignty held in the face of any authority—political or ecclesiastical—despite a threat to national security that made raising an army imperative. Jesuit Stephen Brown suggested that priests discuss conscience rights in a normal home-front homily, as he explained in 1942 for the *Homiletic and Pastoral Review*, a trade journal for the busy parish priest. Parents, religious superiors, legislators, judges, and the president of the United States could never force Catholics under their command to violate self-generated truths: "If they command one thing and conscience commands another, it is conscience that must be obeyed, because the authority which commands through the voice of conscience is higher than they, higher than kings and emperors, for it is the authority of God himself."[37]

At the time of Brown's orthodox if intense retelling of the doctrine, German field marshal Erwin Rommel still held his ground in North Africa and the Japanese had taken the island of Guadalcanal, a landmass not far from the coast of Australia. The United States had entered the war, but the outcome was far from determined. Brown's fellow Jesuit John Ford, reviewing the homily for *Theological Studies*, Catholic moral theology's premier journal, deemed it "an excellent popular explanation of what conscience is and how it works," recommending that it "would serve as a good basis for Sunday sermons."[38]

Clergymen contended that quick moral deliberation on the battlefield could yield a true conscience, making obedience to an unjust command impossible. A Catholic might identify a military order as objectively contravening the laws of God, refuse to obey, and be completely correct in the eyes of God. Father Cyprian Emmanuel defined objective COs in a 1941 report as "those whose conscience is in conformity with the objective existing law."[39] The soldier who refuses to execute a prisoner of war in cold blood, for example, possesses "a conscience as true and valid in every sense of the word, since his conscience is based on the objective natural law."[40] Like the person with a certain or erroneous conscience, these individuals became obliged to follow conscience; the only difference was that the objective conscience-follower spliced a real objective norm with his subjective frame of reference. A seminarian at the Catholic University of America argued in a 1942 dissertation that these brave objectivists "must follow their conscience and in so doing they are acting in a manner both formally and materially correct."[41]

Catholics pushed the lingo of conscience into new arenas as a global war and its proliferating death machines raised unforeseen questions about the justness of law and its authority over the individual. The slight but noticeable circulation of conscience language in the 1930s and 1940s occurred because civil laws, in addition to conscripting men into the military, also pressed claims on sacred selfdoms in the areas of sexuality and the specific action of saturation bombing. A posting along the state's wartime supply chains, for example, could gently coax a Catholic into off-loading his moral responsibility onto someone higher in the chain of command. The state required Catholic quartermaster sergeants (the soldiers placed in charge of supplies) to maintain an inventory of prophylactics. The Catholic Church stood strongly opposed to any state-sponsored program to regulate sexual behavior, no matter how benign its intent. During the war, the state commanded military officers, Catholics among them, to hand out condoms to fellow soldiers. As historian Leslie Tentler notes in her pathbreaking study of Catholics and contraception, the US bishops protested the violations of conscience that occurred as Catholics were forced to distribute "prophey packs," but the prelates achieved precious few results.[42] The US government dispensed more than 50 million condoms a month in the early years of the war to prevent the spread of venereal diseases among the troops.[43]

Catholics met these new threats posed by the democratic state with assertions of self-rule. A priest from Ohio voiced his concern about contraceptives in a 1942 letter to Father John LaRue, an editor at the *Ecclesiastical Review*. "There is a standing Army order that contraceptive devices must be kept in stock and issued to soldiers on demand," the priest noted, explaining that a Catholic quartermaster "must either violate his conscience by keeping and issuing these devices" or face a military trial for insubordination.[44] LaRue forwarded the letter to John F. O'Hara, Apostolic Delegate for the Military Forces and former president of the University of Notre Dame, who would be appointed Bishop of Buffalo just after the war. The chain of correspondence brought O'Hara to disclose his willingness to defend Catholics' rights of self-sovereignty in military courts. He had already been due to appear before the Judge Advocate General's Corps (JAG Corps) on the question of Catholics and the involuntary supplying of contraception when he received the letter forwarded by LaRue. O'Hara disclosed his legal strategy to his brother priest: "My defense before the Judge Advocate General will be that the Army cannot force a man to act against his conscience."[45] He was unwilling to make his position public for fear of the "hair-splitting correspondence that would result."[46]

The drive to prevent the spread of venereal disease also motivated the US Army to build red-light districts, where soldiers visited prostitutes who had passed a medical exam. The military, going beyond its condom policy, encouraged doctors, Catholic physicians included, to send troops to these officially designated prostitution zones in order that soldiers' sexual appetites might be appeased without inducing a public health crisis. John Ford, writing in *Theological Studies*, urged Catholic authorities to defend Catholic doctors. These educated and moral men likely would find ways to avoid participation and clashes with authority, Ford hoped, but the doctors' "rights of conscience [were] paramount, and at times they [must] assert them boldly at whatever cost." The doctors would be all the more likely to keep their moral composition intact if exercising prerogatives of a sacred selfhood "were approved and defended by ecclesiastical military authorities."[47] In this way, the hierarchy would get to keep the Catholic remnant away from participation in sin on a grand scale.

Ford also used the influential pages of *Theological Studies* to defend the conscience of US Army Air Forces officers ordered to drop explosives on civilian populations. In Ford's mind, even if doctrine enabled a consistent defense of conscience and provided Catholics with a shared idiom of subjectivity, the doctrine needed to be refined in light of threats posed by modern states. The tremendous violence of World War II exposed a new frontier the doctrine had yet to conquer—namely, the conscription of bombardiers into dropping explosives on noncombatants. Eric Genilo, a theologian and Ford's intellectual biographer, found that Ford moved between two modes of thinking and writing: a "standard mode" and a "crisis mode." In his classroom at Weston College among young Jesuits, Ford discussed the radical side of conscience rights in the standard mode, casually explaining the teaching and its implications. But in the public sphere, with the state producing a barrage of violence the world over, he snapped into crisis mode.[48] He vigorously defended inner sanctums from being seized by military authorities bent on dropping bombs on civilian targets. In a 1944 article on "obliteration bombing"—the piece of writing that launched his writing career—Ford argued that men who refuse to bomb city centers have crystallized a true conscience, the highest form of conscience. Catholics who refused to drop explosives on populated areas had synthesized the subjective element of moral life (the conscience) with the objective benchmark of moral life (the divine law not to murder innocents). Ford conceded at the outset of his article that the Catholic Church had no specific law on modern war, and so it remained difficult to bind a conscience to a particular path.[49] But he constructed a case that the church could promulgate a clear law obligating Catholics to refuse orders to bomb nonmilitary targets.

The official church needed to drain the civil law of its moral authority on this matter, and quickly. Ford's article reported ninety total bombings by 1944 from the Royal Air Force and the US Army Air Forces on "industrial centers" in Germany that had large civilian populations. Ford's main body of evidence for a violation of the natural law came from the bombing of Hamburg in late July 1943. US and British planes bombed a city that was unusually dry that summer. The bombs dropped on the city center produced a tornado of fire—a towering pillar of flame—that engulfed Hamburg. When the smoke cleared, the Allied forces had killed over forty thousand German civilians in a matter of days.[50] Given the erasure of innocent lives, Ford reasoned that a "burden of conscience" could be established in moral teaching so that Catholics were not to pull the levers that loosed bombs on civilian centers. He built his case on repeated statements made by Pope Pius XII in which the pontiff condemned the murdering of innocent civilians. Catholics could be bound in internalities to refuse the military's orders to bomb civilian targets, liberating the Catholic bombardier from orders that, if carried out, threatened the eternal destiny of his soul.

The state's erasure of the distinction between civilian and combatant meant that it abandoned its connection to the divine law, freeing Catholics to follow conscience. In other words, it broke the contract with Catholics that it had entered in the 1920s and 1930s: laws had to be "reasonable" and aimed toward creating a "common good" to have a say over a Catholic conscience. Conscience was on its own when law failed to meet this threshold. In a 1943 article for the *American Ecclesiastical Review* published after the Allied bombing of civilians was well under way, Jesuit Joseph Connor, a colleague of John Ford's at Weston College, surrendered to the thinkers applying conscience to political questions, granting them an intellectual victory. By the middle phases of the war, with the Germans defeating continental Europe, Catholic theologians, likely concerned about the questions fellow citizens would raise about Catholic patriotism, conceded only reluctantly that the unjustness of 1940s civil laws activated the obligation to follow strong inner convictions. Most Catholic moralists, Connor among them, believed that the defensive nature of World War II made it a just war. But Connor conceded that the methods of total war opened the door for the cases made by O'Toole, Daniel A. Lord, John Martin Gillis, and Cyprian Emmanuel. "Besides the Church's deep respect for individual conscience," he noted, the American Catholics who supported the war, himself included, were "up against the fact that the objector was aided in forming his conscience . . . before the war, by some very reputable Catholic authors and periodicals."[51] The Catholic conscientious objector "may say that the Catholic religion teaches the obligation of following the dictates of conscience," he admitted, raising a white flag, and "he may quote Catholic writers in defense of this position."[52] The Catholic CO who invoked conscience had a very real backing in the literature, even as Catholic authorities argued that World War II was a just war. The global conflagration offered space for moralists and priests to legitimate conscience-following in political life.

The Cold War

After World War II, the United States bulked up its military strength considerably and built itself an even more powerful national security apparatus.[53]

Congress passed the National Security Act of 1947, outfitting the state with the Central Intelligence Agency, a new Air Force, and a new cabinet position, the Secretary of Defense. The security apparatus would be put to the test as president Harry S. Truman and his advisers imagined countries all over the world as dominoes ready to fall to communism.

Congress renewed the draft in 1948 as relations with the Soviet Union deteriorated. The need for a garrison army created new problems for stands of conscience. In the fall of 1949, state authorities detained Bluffton College history professor and Quaker activist Larry Gara in a jail cell just outside Toledo, Ohio. The Sixth Circuit Court of Appeals found Gara guilty of violating the 1948 Selective Service Act for counseling his student, Charles Ray Rickert, to refuse registration with his local draft board. The court granted that Gara could criticize the draft, but the justices would not allow the professor to encourage young men to forgo registration. A split decision in the US Supreme Court upheld the lower court's conviction.

American Catholic thinkers deployed their own doctrine of conscience, a product of medieval Thomism, to protect this Quaker. It was an old song and dance, but Catholics performed it in new venues throughout Cold War America. Father Gillis dedicated three incendiary *Boston Pilot* editorials to the Gara situation. The courts seemed to prefer domination over recognition of a citizen's duty in cases dealing with subjectively held truths, prompting Gillis to ask, "Is the conscience free when it dictates what the state approves and not free when it dictates what the state disapproves?" If so, he wondered aloud, "wherein do our laws and our customs differ from those of totalitarian states?"[54] Only the Catholic Church, the historic defender of conscience rights against the Leviathan, could protect subjectivity from aggressive state power.[55] Gillis ended the 1950s the same way he had begun the 1930s: defending the Protestants' rights of conscience from the overreach of US courts with a neo-medieval Catholic teaching.

Jesuit Robert Drinan—a young priest with a freshly minted District of Columbia law license and later a Democratic congressman from Massachusetts—thought the judges misunderstood Gara's advice. Gara had not, as found by the court, simply advised a student to refuse to register for the draft. He had related to his student an orthodox teaching to follow the dictates of well-formed and confident subjectivity.[56] Drinan conceded that COs may have possessed consciences of the erroneous variety, but certainty always covers up the flaws of erroneousness. "The most casual acquaintance with the CO position," he wrote, "convinces one that many pacifists have the moral obligation to follow their subjectively certain consciences whatever may be thought by others of its objective validity."[57] When Drinan's defense of conscience appeared in the *Catholic World* in March of 1951, US forces were engaged in heavy fighting with Korean troops along the 38th parallel; and General Douglas MacArthur, a military leader who fantasized about dropping atomic bombs on his enemies, was a month away from being removed from command by President Truman. The Catholic commitment to the doctrine of conscience—despite its radical potential to drain the civil law of moral authority and jeopardize national security—remained steady during the Cold War.

Unsurprisingly, Catholics sided with conscience in their own conflicts with government agents at the US Department of Justice. In a confidential memo sent to T. Oscar Smith, chief of the department's conscientious objector section, Patrick Aloysius O'Boyle, the archbishop of Washington, DC, reminded him that the church stood against the violations of conscience that came with forced bombing runs or involuntary participation in the distribution of prophylactics.[58] As O'Boyle told Smith, "A Catholic, even in a just defensive war, consistently could refuse to act against his conscience and take part in certain military tactics which we hold to be a violation of Divine Law, for instance, bombing non-military objectives." O'Boyle further clarified for Agent Smith that a "Catholic in the Armed Forces of our country must refuse in conscience" to distribute contraceptives or, as a Catholic doctor or nurse, participate in an abortion or a sterilization procedure.[59]

O'Boyle's letter was a significant moment in the history of Catholic conscience rights, because it took the doctrine forcibly into the overlapping domains of sex and military obedience. The convergence of sex and war in World War II augured a much larger one that came during the 1960s as Catholics fought fiercely over artificial birth control and the state drafted thousands of men into an army fighting communism in Southeast Asia. John Ford and a few others made the pitch for conscience rights in the pages of academic journals, but O'Boyle set the doctrine and its implications right in front of an influential agent of the state with an official letter. Catholics could join an American army fighting against godless communism, but no unjust law would force them to violate conscience to bomb innocents, perform illicit medical procedures, or hand out contraceptives. A war could be just, but specific orders could be unjust, and conscience then would take over.

The story of how O'Boyle came to explain the church's teachings to the Department of Justice is the more astonishing aspect of the 1957 exchange. Agent Smith asked O'Boyle to clarify the church's position on conscientious objection after reading a copy of Pope Pius XII's 1956 Christmas Address. Pius seemed to hand the Justice Department just what it needed to prosecute Catholic COs: an outright denial that Catholics could object to conscription and remain in line with church teaching. The pontiff stated explicitly in his talk that "a Catholic citizen cannot invoke his own conscience in order to refuse to serve and fulfill those duties which the law imposes."[60] He likely directed his words toward Catholics in Eastern Europe who objected to military service after the Soviet invasion of Hungary. But because the he did not specify, the pope's words could be taken as universal. The director of the Justice Department's conscientious objector unit, Agent Smith, who spent his days and nights in hot pursuit of men who dodged the garrison state, would have been more than happy to take Pius's sentence as a stand-alone synopsis of the church's position. A Christmas Address is hardly ex cathedra, but the festive oration carried some weight with Catholics around the world. Perhaps Justice Department agents would find it useful against Catholics in appeal board hearings.

But the dualistic nature of conscience confounded even Pius XII. His fellow Catholics disagreed with his interpretation, which was in fact quite lopsided. O'Boyle, an archbishop and later a cardinal, placed clear limits on the use of papal authority to end the debate on conscience rights by fiat. Involuntary bombing runs on civilian targets, compulsory distribution of prophylactics, and forced participation in medical procedures like abortion and sterilization were exceptions to the pope's rule that "a Catholic citizen cannot invoke his own conscience in order to refuse to serve and fulfill those duties which the law imposes." Political life as a citizen of a modern nation-state simply did not merit total obedience to civil laws or military orders. The church required Catholics to refuse to perform duties imposed by a law when those duties included immoral, unjust, or illicit actions.

What makes the 1957 letter to Smith all the more remarkable is not only the stack of memos that had accrued in the days before it was sent off to the Department of Justice but also the authors of those memos. O'Boyle often asked top theologians for advice. Quite naturally, the archbishop turned to John Ford and Francis Connell for their input on how to respond to Agent Smith's request. The archbishop then relayed the theologians' interpretations to Smith. Both men took the pope to task for his lack of nuance. In his analysis of the pope's address, Ford observed several times that Pius simply forgot about the erroneous conscience. The pontiff's statement, he wrote, "[did] not settle the question whether a Catholic in this or other areas might have an erroneous conscience and still be in good faith."[61] Here, Ford, a theologian unafraid to invoke papal authority to support his points in many other areas, critiqued the pontiff for his limited field of vision. The pope failed to deal with the complexities of the doctrine. Connell, in contrast, allowed the pope to save face by claiming Pius only meant that self-rule could not be invoked by a Catholic to avoid serving a state that met the requisites for a just war. But he was quick to point out that the pope had not completed the theology of conscience in a satisfying manner. The Catholic, Connell wrote, "could and should object on grounds of conscience" to participation in any military activity that targeted civilians.[62] The papal pronouncement had to be qualified. Catholics can, and must, invoke conscience to "refuse to fulfill the duties of law" if the law demanded immoral actions, no matter what a pope says at a Christmas party.

Conclusion

This chapter has explored the political origins of conscience rights. The idea rose at two distinct paces. The first tempo was a steady recitation. From the early 1930s to the late 1950s, Catholics responded to the growth of the modern security state with consistent invocations of conscience rights. At the dawn of the totalitarian moment and with the escalation of the Cold War, they met state power with calm but powerful assertions of subjectivity and subjective truth-creation capacities. The writers at the *Catholic Worker*, Pope Pius XI's canonization of Thomas More and John Fisher, clerics like James Martin Gillis and Robert Drinan defending Protestant COs, and the priests who wrote about erroneous conscience turned to the Catholic idea of conscience in the face of increasingly coercive civil laws. These Catholics, most of them clergy, kept the doctrine of conscience consistent in the face of robust state power.

The second tempo, a rupture, occurred during the latter stages of World War II. Catholics pushed the doctrine of conscience rights into several new areas of inquiry in response to total war. The writings of clergymen like Cyprian Emmanuel, Daniel Lord, George O'Toole, and James Martin Gillis argued that the faithful could claim conscience rights against the liberal democratic state. These were incremental gains. But during the second half of World War II, invoking conscience against the state gained a real intellectual legitimacy among theologians like John Ford and Joseph Connor. Otherwise reluctant and patriotic Catholic thinkers like these two Jesuits were forced by saturation bombing and the indiscriminate killing of citizens (not to mention the involuntary distribution of condoms) to concede that the state's immoral laws no longer deserved authority over a Catholic conscience. The individualizing and traditional logics of Catholic conscience rights, long a moral teaching, became a nascent political program in the mid-1940s. From these humble origins—steady incantations, incremental applications, a wartime breakthrough—the rights of conscience would spread widely in US political life.

THREE

The State's Paperwork and the Catholic Peace Fellowship

The Church, in teaching the primacy of the human conscience, believes that a person must take all of the beliefs, teachings, and morals that have assimilated [*sic*] into his conscience and add to that the laws of the Church and then make a just decision.

—Layman Patrick O'Sullivan to Chairman of Draft Board No. 77, Asheboro, North Carolina (1972)

Conscientious objection can be claimed and based on the Catholic faith's teaching on conscience alone, without recourse to any other precept.

—Layman Allen Westmore to Chairman, Appeal Board, Middle District of Pennsylvania (September 30, 1967)

Andrew Vincenzo handed the Selective Service System his past, present, and future in the conscientious objector application he filed in the New York City borough of the Bronx on October 4, 1965. Vincenzo learned catechism at the city's St. Martin of Tours Grammar School and the basics of moral theology from Jesuits at Regis High School. He spent two years in the Reserve Officer Training Corps on his way to finishing a bachelor's degree at Fordham University. Like other men of his generation who enrolled in Catholic colleges and universities, he earned the equivalent of a minor in theology and trained for war as part of his academic career. Then he endured a year at Brooklyn Law School before heading off to St. John's Abbey, a Benedictine monastery in Collegeville, Minnesota, to test out a vocation in the priesthood. It turned out not to be his calling. In the fall of 1965, US combat troops began arriving in Vietnam and Vincenzo found himself back in his native Bronx, ordered to report for duty. He was among the first round of young men called up by president Lyndon Baines Johnson to fly off to Vietnam to halt the spread of communism.

The stakes of a seminary departure were unusually high at that time. Vincenzo's decision to forgo training for the priesthood made him draft eligible. Yet his extensive Catholic training also left him well versed in theology. After the state called him up for military service, he tracked down a Form 150 (Special Form for Conscientious Objector). On it, he wrote down his street address, date of birth, and Social Security number. He then attached a series of essays explaining his decision to refuse induction. Vincenzo, a Catholic, should have been prepared to defend his nation and suffer on faraway battlefields for God and country. And to be an American Catholic in 1965 meant guarding the nation against its communist enemies abroad and reaping the rewards of hard work at home. The United States had welcomed Catholic John F. Kennedy into the White House in 1961, and it beckoned college-educated men like Andrew Vincenzo into the middle class. As a college-educated Catholic working as a claims representative for the Social Security Administration, Vincenzo embodied the nation's change in attitude toward its Catholic citizens.

Catholics became enthusiastic patriots during the 1950s, forging a synthesis between devotion to God and devotion to country. Catholic influence could be felt in many quarters. The 1950s witnessed Bishop Fulton J. Sheen take home several Emmy Awards for his television series, *Life Is Worth Living*. Moreover, the Catholic population of the United States rose sharply at this time, accounting for one-fourth of the nation's population. Catholics joined the Federal Bureau of Investigation at unusually high numbers, giving rise to the quip that Fordham and Notre Dame boys checked the American credentials of their peers from Harvard and Yale rather than the other way around. And Catholic colleges and universities helped their alumni faithful climb ladders of power in a range of careers. These institutions of higher learning underwent a particularly explosive increase in enrollment, from a total of 92,425 students in 1945 to 384,526 by 1965.[1]

More important, Catholics were uniquely responsible for starting the war from which Andrew Vincenzo, a son of the institutional church, sought exemption. Tom Dooley, a Catholic physician in the US Navy who helped refugees from communist North Vietnam escape to South Vietnam in 1954, introduced Americans to the plight of the Vietnamese. His 1956 best seller, *Deliver Us from Evil*, portrayed malevolent communists torturing and massacring faithful Catholics. His account, steeped in the paternalism of modernization theory, made millions of Americans sympathetic toward the Vietnamese—whom he portrayed as a benighted people in need of US aid to "develop." Francis Cardinal Spellman, a prominent Cold Warrior and Vincenzo's own archbishop, demonstrated his support for the war with annual visits to the South Vietnamese capital of Saigon to spend time with Ngo Dihn Diem, the Catholic dictator installed by the United States to lead the new republic. Diem convinced secretary of state John Foster Dulles that he was worthy of the appointment by making it appear as if his devotion to the church made him a strong anticommunist. In reality, Diem was a vicious autocrat obsessed with tiny administrative details who ruthlessly murdered his political opponents or interned them in labor camps. But the United States stuck with Diem, partly because of his Catholicism.

Despite the nationalism and anticommunism of his denomination, Vincenzo, like hundreds of Catholic men nationwide, inscribed the theology of conscience—an idea subversive to civil law—onto his copy of Form 150 (fig. 4). His theological treatise on the Catholic's duty to follow conscience ran for several pages. He began, "We apprehend God in the particular case through the dictates of conscience, and here disobedience to conscience is an act of rebellion against God." Catholics encounter God's will in the confines of an inner sanctuary and commit a grievous sin if they contravene God's will as known in conscience. Hence the Catholic Church, Vincenzo's spiritual home, made it incumbent on him to follow "the voice of my own conscience which is trying to act in this matter as Christ would have acted in the same position."[2] His inner voice told him that Christ would object to any participation in the Vietnam War whatsoever.

Draft boards across the United States—from Palo Alto to Charlottesville, from Milwaukee to Atlanta—received exegeses on Catholic subjectivity similar to the one Vincenzo sent to the Bronx office. Men who moved from island to island on the archipelago of Catholic education during the 1940s and 1950s, from entering grade school to completing theology coursework at a university, wrote up long-form explanations of why doctrine required Catholics to act on a well-formed subjective frame of reference rather than the draft law. These essayists often directed the Selective Service System to an appended typewritten essay in which the sources of their belief and their story of institutional upbringing in the church awaited the state agents.[3] It must have come as a shock to the men who sat on local draft boards that the institutional church taught its people to be so profoundly individualistic and antinationalist.

Vincenzo may have appeared as a total pacifist, but the logical sequence outlined in the essay section of his draft dossier revealed him to be a selective conscientious objector. This category of objection meant that the individual would participate in just wars but must refuse to take up arms

PANEL A QUESTIONS CONTINUED   (SSS-N.Y. City Form No. 54)

QUESTION 10 CONTINUED
    Besides believing in a Supreme Being, I am a practicing Catholic. From the time
Jesus ordered Peter to put asie his sword, there has been a tradition of conscientious
objection-the refusal to take part in war-among His followers. In the earliest days of
the Church, this was a tradition embraced by virtually all Christians. One of the
Greek Church Fathers, Clement of Alexandria, spoke of the Christian community as "an
army that sheds no blood."
    As the Christian community grew, the refusal to bear arms continued, but, when
Constantine lifted the yoke of secular persecution, the nonviolent witness gradually
became considered a counsel of perfection rather than a binding precept. By the middle
of the 4th Century, laymen were permitted to remain in the army after Baptism, By the
middle of the 5th Century, the turnabout was so complete that the Emperor excluded all
but Christians from military service.
    Still, throughout the Church's history, even in the midst of such "holy wars"
as the Crusades, there remained those, such as St. Francis of Assisi and his followers,
who remained unarmed.Other Catholics who have refused to bear arms include St. Martin
of Tours, St. Maximilian, the Cure of Ars and such more recent individuals, as yet
un-canonized, as Franz Jagerstatter, an Austrian peasant beheaded by the Nazi
government for his refusal to serve in the army, even as a noncombatant.
    My personal religious belief is that participation in any war today cannot
be justified in conscience not only because of the arguments presented in the answer
to Question 8 but also because of the Fifth Commandment which states "Thou shalt
not kill" and because of the requirements of the natural law in traditional
Catholic doctrine. God is love and in war every means is used except love.
    As a Christian as well as a Catholic, I believe that Jesus Christ by His
Life and His Example showed unmistakably to each of His Followers the power of Love
and the futility of War and Human hate directed against other human beings.
    Moreover, Catholic theologians lay down certain principles concerning
conscience. A man is always bound to follow his conscience, We apprehend the law
of God in the particular case through the dictates of conscience, and here a disobedience to conscience is an act of rebellion against God. Nor can the injunction of
any authority, ecclesiastical or civil, make it lawful for a man to do that which his
conscience unhesitatingly condemns as certainly wicked.
    As the Redemptorist theologian and Vatican Council peritus, Father Bernard
haring, has written(in THE LAW OF CHRIST, Vol. 1:
    "Conscience has a voice of itself, but not a word of its own; it is the
    word of Christ(spoken in creation, in the Incarnation of the Word,
    through the influence of grace) which speaks through this voice. Of itself
    conscience is a candle without a flame, but Christ, the Light, shines
    forth with His brightness and warmth from it."(pp.135-136.)

    In summation, I base my convictions on a new appreciation of Christian
tradition, the witness of the early Church and of later Church figures, particularly
St. Francis of Assisi and Pope John XXIII, the witness of the New Testament, the
application of the just war theory, and the voice of my own conscience which is
trying to act in this matter as Christ would have acted in the same position.

4. A page from an essay written by Andrew Vincenzo in 1965 to secure his exemption from
the draft for the Vietnam War. Vincenzo elaborated on several tenets of the Catholic Church's
traditional teaching on conscience. University of Notre Dame Archives, Notre Dame, Indiana.

in unjust wars. As discussed in the previous chapter, Catholic doctrine held
that the individual discerns just war from unjust war, which is where selec-
tivity entered the picture. The principle of selective conscientious objection,
the just-war framework, and the rights of conscience were overlapping logics in a particularly Catholic approach to resisting the draft for the Vietnam War. Vincenzo made the case that because the war was unjust, his conscience bound him not to participate in any form; if the war was just (and
stopping the spread of communism still qualified as good cause), his inner

core would have urged participation. As historian Helen Ciernick observes in her analysis of James McFadden, a Catholic selective conscientious objector who challenged the court system in California, Catholics confronted the draft law in a straightforward manner because they thought that "the individual citizen must be allowed to make thoughtful moral judgements about orders his/her government has issued."[4] Catholics challenged "the system" directly to carve out legal recognition for conscience rights.

Catholics were particularly vocal in this arena, but they did not seek selective conscientious objection alone. By the late 1960s, as Catholics, Jews, Protestants, and secular activists pursued this approach, historian Ronit Stahl notes, "the viability of 'selective conscientious objection' wracked the nation."[5] In 1971, US Supreme Court justice Thurgood Marshall would offer a majority opinion dismissing the idea as out of step with the nation's tradition of recognizing total pacifists, religious or secular. For the first several years of the draft for Vietnam, however, selective conscientious objection had tremendous traction at the grassroots level. Advocates across the religious and secular landscape of American life thought that the logic of this intellectual operation was consistent and reasonable. As Stahl shows, that operation was strenuous, "deriving its legitimacy from parsing, distinguishing, and evaluating war's causes, means and ends."[6] The state, beginning at the draft board and rising all the way to the House of Representatives and the Supreme Court, viewed the idea of selective conscientious objection with horror: if a citizen could select which wars to fight in, the draft would be completely ineffective and the nation could not be secured or defended. The fight over conscience rights, and the nature of citizenship itself, began with paperwork and the initial hearings at a young man's local draft board, which in a few specific cases inaugurated a long march to the very heights of US judicial power.

Catholic prospective draftees sourced the Form 150s exquisitely. These essay writers explained to hundreds of draft board officials and the Selective Service System that their church had been defending the rights of conscience for nearly two millennia. From their reading of history and their desire to live out the church's teachings, they drew the lesson that the liberal state ought to permit Catholic men to walk in the footsteps of this tradition during the Vietnam War. This chapter provides an analysis of the official paperwork American Catholics filed with the state to earn conscientious objector (CO) status, offering glimpses into the real-world, life-and-death implications of conscience debates between the two parties during the 1960s and 1970s. Many lay Catholic men created friction with draft board officials on their own; but the Catholic Peace Fellowship, a new advocacy organization for Catholic conscience rights, was happy to lend a hand.

The Catholic Peace Fellowship

Draft dossiers—each an assemblage of essays, cover sheets, information forms, and letters of character reference—often had a common destination: Catholic men mailed their papers to the Manhattan office of the Catholic Peace Fellowship (hereafter CPF). Men like Andrew Vincenzo sent essays to be edited and fine-tuned there before the documents were to be scrutinized by a draft board officer. Vincenzo's application did not have to travel far when compared with the paperwork of his peers. Applications arrived at the CPF's Manhattan office from Minnesota, Ohio, North Carolina, Michigan, Massachusetts, Maryland, Connecticut, Upstate New York, and, in one case, Belgium. That office—like other draft counseling centers in the United States—redacted, tweaked, and reorganized the essays. CPF officers did not hesitate to put words into Catholics' applications, including invocations of conscience. But many laypeople like Vincenzo mailed their draft application to the CPF already demonstrably fluent in Catholic procedures of self-actualization.

The CPF was the child of a historic pan-Protestant peace coalition and Dorothy Day's storied Catholic Worker movement. The leaders of the Fellowship of Reconciliation (FOR), the nation's premier Protestant pacifist organization, sought to bring Catholics into the peace movement just as the state was preparing to ship tens of thousands of men off to Vietnam. Jesuit Daniel Berrigan and Presbyterian activist John Heidbrink convinced James Forest, a convert to Catholicism and a Catholic Worker stalwart, to start a Catholic subsidiary of FOR. Forest, who left his post as a US Navy meteorologist during World War II because of a conscientious objection to war, recruited fellow Catholic Worker Tom Cornell to serve as his co-secretary, and the CPF was born in 1964.[7] As Forest and Cornell would later explain to journalist John Deedy, the organization aimed to alter the "whole social situation" with a program of revolutionary nonviolence.[8] Deedy concluded that the CPF had achieved a visibility in the Catholic Church and the war resistance movement that far outstripped its meager number of managers and staffers, which never rose above a dozen.[9] The group's expansive program included publishing educational materials, conducting relief work, counseling COs, and planning antiwar rallies. Certainly, the CPF had many irons in the fire; but as the paper trail shows, the activists placed a campaign to protect the rights of conscience at the center of their social revolution.

Co-secretaries Forest and Cornell spread the concept of Catholic self-rule across America, one counselee at a time. When a Catholic officer stationed at Kelly Air Force Base in San Antonio, Texas, wrote the CPF seeking justification for his conscientious objection to the war, a position that crystallized in the months after the launch of the Tet Offensive in January 1968, Forest wrote him a paean on the inviolability of his conscience. The church's rock-solid commitment to self-sovereignty meant that Jesus and the church approved of the young officer's quest for an honorable discharge from the Air Force. "The teachings regarding formation of and obedience to conscience are ironclad and central to the practice of the faith," Forest told the officer. "To disobey conscience is, by definition, to die to grace."[10] Forest may have added rhetorical flourishes to Thomas Aquinas's core definition of conscience, but the theology was sound. According to tradition, a Catholic invited a spiritual death and psychological obliteration by acting against conscience. The young man had no choice but to leave the Air Force. His commanding officers—if Catholic doctrine had any bearing on reality—had to watch him walk out the door, or they would be terminating his opportunity to receive God's gifts.

The CPF received nearly twenty letters weekly from young Catholic laymen seeking advice; some wanted to know how to avoid conscription and how to articulate persuasively the church's teaching on war.[11] Other young Catholics already in the military expressed discomfort with the morality of the Vietnam War and required guidance on how to secure an honorable discharge. Also each week, twenty-five men visited the CPF's Manhattan office, located just off Wall Street at 5 Beekman Street.[12] Forest theorized conscience rights from that office, but occasionally he switched into activist mode. In 1969, he joined the Milwaukee Fourteen in breaking into a Selective Service office, removing four thousand draft cards, and setting the papers on fire in a nearby park.

For his part, Cornell actively coached Catholics on how to make an appealing case for conscience rights. He suggested to a CO, "You might write something like this: One's highest obligation in life is to fulfill God's will for one, and the way we know God's will for each one of us is through our own consciences."[13] He noted that it should be explained to the draft board that the guiding rule of moral and political life for Catholics is to act in accordance with their subjectivity. A sentence like this, then, ought to appear on Form 150: "This is one's highest duty—to live according to one's best insights and conscience, for this is the way the will of God is transmitted to us."[14] Cornell relayed a long-standing component of the teaching when he explained how a sacred internalized orb imported God's will into the person. The recently completed Second Vatican Council called conscience a medium in which God speaks to man. Even the old manuals and proofs of the institutional church called it "proximate authority," or the person's "immediate moral guide." Cornell had gained firsthand experience of the draft in 1956 when, freshly graduated from Fairfield University, a Jesuit college in Fairfield, Connecticut, he objected to conscription into the peacetime army raised during the Cold War. The FBI and the US Attorney General spent four years investigating his case and assigned him to alternative service. Cornell continued to butt heads with the Selective Service System as it conscripted troops for the Vietnam War. He was thirty-four years of age and a father of two when he publicly burned his draft card in 1965, an act that landed him in jail for six months.

The CPF's services would be in high demand in the years immediately following its founding in 1964. The state called up three hundred thousand men each year from 1966 to 1969 with the hopes that a huge ground force would eliminate the Viet Cong and push back North Vietnamese troops. President Lyndon Johnson may have dragged his heels in response to General William Westmoreland's demands for more troops in the middle years of the war, but the four-star commander— who coined the name of the military strategy of search and destroy—got his army's boots on the ground. By 1967, half a million US soldiers were in Vietnam, with Catholics and their many chaplains among them. As the ground force increased, so did CPF membership in the United States. A year after troop numbers in Vietnam crested, the CPF had an official membership of three thousand, vindicating the Fellowship of Reconciliation's decision to create a Catholic subsidiary and lining that organization's coffers with much-needed revenue.[15]

Forest established the CPF as a principal source of conscience language with *Catholics and Conscientious Objection*, a booklet he published in 1965 with formal approval from Terence Cooke, Apostolic Vicar of the United States Armed Forces. He unflinchingly answered the question, Can a Catholic be a conscientious objector? in the affirmative. Solving his own riddle, he wrote, "The constant teaching of the Church regarding the primacy of conscience, the Church's consistent application of this teaching in defense of Catholic conscientious objectors, and, not least, the continued presence of such objectors throughout Church history, would indicate that the answer is unqualifiedly yes."[16] Forest's pamphlet offered a selective though not untenable genealogy of the church's military history. He backed up his claim for the primacy of conscience by citing the examples of St. Maximillian and St. Martin of Tours, two early Christians who objected to fighting for the Roman Empire. He mentioned a suggestion made by St. Basil the Great that soldiers who killed men in battle be forced to abstain from receiving the Eucharist for three years. Moreover, Forest told the classic tale of St. Francis of Assisi, a legendary peacemaker, and he mentioned that St. John Vianney deserted Napoleon's army in 1809 and hid in a nearby forest. All the examples that made it into Forest's pamphlet—though not the fabrications that sometimes occurred when Catholics picked up a pen to write about their saints—were clearly a departure from the many Catholic heroines and theorists who accepted the tragedy of war and the possibility of a just war, a storied lineage that included Augustine and Thomas Aquinas. Still, Forest provided an excellent synopsis of the doctrine for young Catholics facing the draft. The pamphlet's main points could be easily paraphrased by a lay Catholic CO preparing his paperwork and even directly quoted in the essay section of a Form 150.

Father Lyle Young, an Australian priest who served as the lead draft counselor on site in the Manhattan office, lent a clerical gravitas to CPF's gospel of conscience rights. Along with Tom Connell and Jim Forest, Young did not regard the CPF as a rogue band of activists operating on the fringes of the Catholic Church. In these men's own minds, they were doing the Lord's work in an important vineyard that had sprung up almost overnight with the state's decision to raise a citizen army to fight an unjust war abroad. As Young advised a Catholic enrolled at Berea College in Berea, Kentucky, who had been convinced that Catholics could not be good COs, maintaining a sturdy internality guaranteed that he followed the laws of the church as set down by Christ. Regarding peace and war, he assured the student, "whatever you say about these matters acting on the drive of your own conscience will surely be in conformity with the mind of Christ."[17] Another young correspondent, a recent graduate of a Minnesota high school, doubted the justness of Vietnam but hesitated to render any sweeping judgment. Young suggested that the nineteen-year-old place his faith completely in the ability of his conscience to both align his desires with the church and disclose realities to himself. He counseled, "Your own personal feelings on war, peace and resistance to war fit in perfectly woth [sic] what the church has said about Conscientious Objectors, and men who respond to conscience in this way."[18] A response to conscience placed the individual well within the behavioral parameters approved by the church.

CPF counselors specialized in helping each draftee acquire the perfect letters of recommendation. Forest encouraged all Catholic COs to gather four to six character-reference letters to be filed with their final draft dossier. Letters were to come from "respected persons in your community" who can testify to "good character" and the "reasons for taking your position."[19] Forest knew how to work the Selective Service System. He told a lay Catholic from Pennsylvania that sincerity mattered more than any theological quibbles a CO had with his mentors or priests: "It is not necessary that these persons agree with your analysis or themselves sympathize with conscientious objection, all that is required is that they believe that you are sincere and that they state their opinion forcefully."[20] For this reason, doctors, lawyers, and teachers ("professionals") would serve as excellent letter writers, but the most valuable recommendation came from a local priest. A compelling letter from a clergyman testified to the authenticity of the objection but "also provide[d] some background information on the Catholic conscientious objector position." If a parish priest refused to write a character reference, the CPF would track down a proconscience priest and have him write a letter. "If you have any difficulty in locating a priest who is sympathetic to your position and recognizes the validity of the conscientious objector position, please let us know and we will be very happy to put you in touch with several priests in the Boston Archdiocese who have indicated in the past their willingness to provide such letters," Forest wrote.[21] The CPF had priests on call, including Father Young, who were willing to separate faith from citizenship with the wedge of doctrinally legitimate self-rule.

Forest regularly provided a letter-collection service for his CPF clients. When his close friend Stephen "Shorty" Spiro found himself scheduled to appear before a New Jersey Selective Service appeal board in 1965, Forest asked some of American Catholicism's most famous spokesmen, many of them priests, for official application letters explaining the church's support for conscience rights. Shorty fit the profile of the classic Catholic just-war objector, Forest assured potential advocates, so the letter should almost write itself. He was a regular at the Friday meetings for the "Clarification of Thought," a weekly gathering at the New York City Catholic Worker during which Catholics discussed just-war teachings and many other matters. Shorty, demonstrating his knowledge of doctrine and his commitment to following the church, lectured a New Jersey appeal board on how the war forced him to "rely on his own conscience," which the Catholic Church "teaches must be our ultimate and final guide."[22]

Forest wrote Thomas Merton, John Ford, Philip Berrigan, Daniel Berrigan, and John Wright, the Bishop of Pittsburgh, asking the luminaries to place Shorty into the genealogy of Catholic conscience-followers for the judges to see. The records do not make clear whether Wright or Merton responded to Forest's request, but both Berrigan brothers and Ford were happy to oblige. Ford penned a letter on behalf of Shorty in which he defended the rights of an erroneous conscience to a fair hearing from the state. He could have been more direct, but his letter made clear that the state could not lay its hands on a flawed subjectivity, a sacred space with a divinely granted immunity from the coercion of civil law.[23] Jesuit Daniel Berrigan, in the initial stages of a long career of Catholic peace activism, sent a letter directly to General Lewis B. Hershey, the director of the Selective Service System. In it, Berrigan insisted that Spiro's actions accorded with church teaching. "From the point of view of religious conscience and the doctrine of Mr. Spiro's Church it is clear that reasons alleged by Mr. Spiro are orthodox and worthy of praise," the priest wrote.[24] Forest even coached the potential letter writers—all of them clergy and CPF members—on how to articulate the church's teaching on self-sovereignty. He ended a letter to Bishop Wright, a rising star in the hierarchy (who gave a sophisticated lecture on conscience in 1964 to the Thomas More Society), with a friendly suggestion: "If you could give us a statement which points out that [Shorty's] position is orthodox and objectively sound, and that, in any case, he is required to follow conscience and seems sincere in doing so, this would be fine."[25] Despite the effort, and the gravitas of the letter writers, Shorty received five years of probation and a permanent record as felon—a sentence foreshadowing the difficulty selective COs would have convincing the state. He was one of over 3,305 men prosecuted for refusing induction in 1965, a sharp increase from only 380 the previous year.[26]

The creation of the CPF marked a turning point in the Catholic Church's campaign for conscience rights in the political sphere. Forest, Cornell, and Young institutionalized the defense of these rights, giving the framework built up during the era of totalitarianism and World War II a structure and a base of operations. Full-time activists stationed in the New York City area helped Catholic conscripts articulate their claims of theological self-direction to local draft board officials, the first line of the military's induction machine. The men who visited the Manhattan office or exchanged letters with its staff were never told to feign a malady or express longings for anarchy. They were never instructed to desert the military or flee to Canada. Instead, Forest and Cornell told their young clients to lay out the medieval doctrine and its modern emancipatory potential in no uncertain terms for their draft board officials and appeal court judges to consider. But the laity, products of Catholic grade schools and high schools, knew their theology too. An important interplay of counseling from CPF staffers and a surge of conscience language spoken at the grassroots of American Catholicism was at work in each Form 150 that this chapter analyzes. Both the CPF and the American Catholic laity spoke the language of subjectivity, sharpening each other's theologies.

Theology in Form 150

Lay Catholic men in their twenties assured their local draft board that deeply held truths would not be contravened for any authority figure, ecclesiastical or political. Andrew Vincenzo, with a line that appeared in catechisms and moral theology manuals, put it confidently in his essay: "The injunction of any authority, ecclesiastical or civil, [cannot] make it lawful for a man to do that which his conscience condemns unhesitatingly as certainly wicked."[27] Law could not decide what was moral or immoral; only a well-formed subjectivity could. When a conscience reached a state of certainty about the morality of an action, conscience must be followed, no matter what an authority figure promised as a form of retribution. The lessons learned in the parochial school classroom about the undisputed hegemony of interiority came in handy when young Catholic men wrote about why their religious beliefs required opposition to unjust wars. They were invoking conscience as their contemporaries attended teach-ins at New York University, the University of Wisconsin, and the University of California–Berkeley.

Lay Catholic COs vowed to never displace individual moral responsibility onto any military authority. Whether filling out papers at home or doing so in a dorm room, they projected that obeying commands delivered in the heat of battle would force them to violate their church's long-standing rules on following conscience. Military orders made it impossible to discern the justness or unjustness of a given law before giving a commander authority over conscience. A Catholic soldier might be asked to massacre women and children; he might be dragooned into a helicopter crew sent out on a sortie to gun down farmers. As Norris Davidson, a University of Virginia student, explained in his essay, "The code of military obedience—follow the leader, be he right or wrong—negates the obligation of each man to follow his conscience."[28] Anthony Francis, a Catholic who grew up in a patriotic household and followed his father's footsteps into the Air Force, found unblinking obedience to officers ethically impossible: "One is surrendering his free will to an extent which I feel to be incompatible with my belief that a man is obliged to maintain his freedom to decide on the basis of his own conscience and moral principles the morality of all situations he faces."[29] After the My Lai Massacre, which received US press coverage in November 1969, a Catholic could not be blamed for thinking that the military might force him to contravene his obligations of self-rule.

Catholic COs graced their essays with the Second Vatican Council's definition of conscience, a hybrid of old teachings and existential language. The typical draft board officer, often an accomplished white man from the local community, might be forgiven for not being up to speed on medieval theology, but certainly he had heard of Vatican II, whether he was Catholic or not. The council bishops phrased the classic teaching on the impenetrability of a believer's sacred nucleus in a mystical parlance: "Conscience is the most secret core and sanctuary of man. There he is alone with God, Whose voice echoes in his depths."[30] The teaching was not new, but the language itself, which appeared in several draft applications, conveyed the church's heightened sensitivity about the power of subjectivity.[31] But pushing aside the nuances and juxtapositions in the actual conciliar texts, Catholics facing the specter of the draft celebrated what they took to be the Second Vatican Council's enthusiastic endorsement of conscience rights. According to papers filed by CO Charles Bronson, a student at Aquinas College in Grand Rapids, Michigan, Vatican II trumpeted "the frequent and consistent teaching of the Catholic Church regarding the primacy of conscience."[32] The council, praised Edmund Thompson, a former seminarian from the diocese of Natchez-Jackson in Mississippi, "recognized the supremacy of conscience as our final guide and strongly supported those who conscientiously oppose war in any form."[33] Bronson and Thompson were not wrong, of course, but they were highly selective in their remarks. Council texts affirmed both the emancipatory and the conservative nature of the doctrine, but potential Catholic conscripts focused much more on liberation from law than obedience to it.

A particular descriptor became increasingly important in the antiwar context: the notion that the church granted conscience a primacy. Catholics first linked conscience to primacy in 1963 and 1964 during the early years of the contraception debate.[34] The modifier appeared in writings on conscription shortly after its debut in those on sexuality. Jim Forest cited the "constant teaching of the Church regarding the primacy of conscience" as a reason for why Catholics could become conscientious objectors to war. Father Lyle Young mentioned primacy to make the case to one CO that Catholics must be conscientious objectors to civil laws that failed to mimic natural laws.[35] A number of Catholic COs followed the CPF's lead and transcribed the primacy of conscience into their paperwork. But what did it mean for conscience to acquire primacy? The term *primacy* has a vague association with St. Peter, whose prelacy among the apostles singled him out as the first pope. Essays, of course, require a writer to define his or her terms, and Catholic COs rose to the challenge of outlining the rather capacious phrase for their draft board. Primacy suggested three things to lay Catholics: first, the path to following law began by satisfying conscience that adhering to the law resulted in moral behavior; second, primacy required moral decisions to be made through conscience and never around or without it; and finally, conscience could not be bypassed or short-circuited. James Upton, filing his papers in Burlington, Iowa, framed the issue concisely: a designation of primacy "teaches that the individual is responsible to his own conscience

for his actions."[36] To give conscience something less than supremacy suggested that an individual followed orders uncritically. The essay by Patrick
O'Sullivan, a CO who linked arms with Quakers for a protest vigil at a post
office in Virginia, claimed that the primacy of conscience "calls criminal"
those who "in the name of obedience" simply follow commands.[37]

The mandate to follow conscience as handed down to lay Catholics by
confessors and religious teachers extended to life as a citizen. Catholics reasoned that conscience reigned in other realms of life, and so its sovereignty
held absolutely and unquestionably in the political arena. Form 150 essayists pursued a lofty goal: convince the draft board that a church doctrine
from the Middle Ages defined the realities of conscription in the modern
United States. The paperwork filed by John Riesman, raised Catholic and attending a public university in Milwaukee, gave conscience a broad mandate:
"I have been taught that it is each person's conscience that dictates right and
wrong. I have been taught, for example, that we are commanded by God to
be obedient to our parents, but when in our consciences we know they are
commanding us to do wrong it is our moral obligation to disobey them.
So too is it with matters of the State."[38] Riesman narrated a life of following
through on his theological commitments: he claimed to have picketed the
Milwaukee induction center in 1965, and he mentioned playing the guitar
and singing folk ballads at antiwar rallies. Limits were not to be placed on
conscience by the Selective Service System or by one's parents. Doctrine applied to all situations, both moral and civil; it did not exist in one realm and
suspend its application in another. The teaching on conscience appeared so
frequently in Catholic paperwork because conscience organized the Catholic citizen's response to the complex conscription policies of his modern
host state.

Thus, Catholics did not produce their own response to the draft: conscience, a supernatural phenomenon, took the wheel. Catholic historians locate the supernatural—what Robert Orsi calls "the presence of the
Gods"—in external visible manifestations (Marian apparitions, miracles, visions) or physical objects (rosary beads, baptismal waters, transubstantiated
bread).[39] Conscience, nestled within the Catholic self and reified with a language learned from Catholic educators, constituted a subjective space inside
each person where the divine entered. The supernatural, in other words,
occurred not only in manifestations outside the person in objects, visions,
and transubstantiated bread, but within the body and mind of the Catholic subject. Catholics wrote about a supernatural protagonist, conscience,
which guided their lives. A college senior who faced the draft in the spring
framed it frankly in his essay for his Albany, New York, draft board: "My

conscience must be the guide for my life for God makes known his wishes through my conscience."[40] Drake Wiesman, a former Franciscan seminarian who filed his essays in Bloomington, Indiana, reflected on how "it is conscience which, ultimately, indicated for me how to live, tells me what I must do, and what I cannot do."[41] These sentiments that conscience possessed a spirit of its own featured strongly in the state's paperwork.

Even lapsed Catholics described a preternatural process of looking for God's ultimate directives on the grounds of conscience. Certainly, the routine praying of the Our Father, the Hail Mary, a Latin Mass, or a decade of the rosary were ingrained in Catholic minds with a daily or near-daily repetition; but the language of conscience, though less frequent, trailed only slightly behind these other refrains of sacred language. These men could not forget their moral training even if they tried. A narrative written by Brody Jacobson in 1965 recounted his having undergone thirteen years of Catholic education before leaving the church and subsequently entering the US Navy. "At the present time I do not consider myself to be a practicing Roman Catholic although I do realize that the morality I express is in accord with Roman Catholic Teaching," he related candidly to the navy chief of personnel in his application for a discharge. "I believe that human life has been created through or by some force which, although I don't understand it, I can sense, and I am aware of its direction through my conscience."[42] That unknown force filling his internal sphere was beckoning him to leave the military. Quentin Clarkson, baptized in the Catholic Church, was working as a postal clerk when he wrote his essays in 1967. He, too, had fallen away from regular Mass attendance, but his application highlighted his time in catechism class as a grade-schooler and a middle-schooler. He could still relate the orthodox teaching on conscience several years after putting down his catechism and departing from the gaze of the institutional church. "I believe my conscience is the medium by which the supreme laws of nature, which are my religious beliefs, are relayed to me," his essay read.[43]

The cosmic stakes of a transgression against conscience served as a central reason why no authority—including the modern US state—could force a Catholic to violate a confident subjectivity. Catholics informed their draft board of their refusal to face God's judgment with the sin of disobedience to conscience marked on their soul. Their paperwork warned the guardians of the Selective Service System that betraying one's inner confident self jeopardized the chance to taste the sweet reward of heaven. The bureaucratic tracts contained the lesson, long an axiom of Catholic tradition, that God does not judge humans on their close adherence to the laws, civil or ecclesiastical, but rather on their willingness to follow the moral truths that dwelled comfortably in the deepest confines of the self. Yani Turkic's essay read, "My church, Roman Catholic, teaches that one should follow conscience at all times and that he will be judged by God, not on what others say is right or wrong, but on how he acts in accordance with the dictates of his conscience."[44] The liberal state can punish men and women for breaking the law, but the pain that God seemed ready to impose on those who violated conscience would be far worse and last far longer. Catholics were obliged to dwell deeply on the justness or unjustness of the US involvement in the war in Vietnam and follow the conclusions that bubbled up in conscience, an internal sphere with a direct line to God that used the believer's body as a protective membrane. "If, after examining a moral question . . . a Catholic's conscience tells him to act in a certain way, he is bound upon pain of moral sin and eternal damnation to follow his conscience," George Schultz explained to his New Jersey draft board. Imagine a Catholic man forming his conscience after learning about the absurd mission to take Hamburger Hill near the Laotian border: a loss of three hundred men to capture a small mountain, plant an American flag at the top, and subsequently fall back from the hard-fought position at the behest of one's commanders. Schultz's papers further detailed for his draft officers how the Council of Trent made clear that the man who acts against conscience is immediately dispossessed of his soul.[45] To force a violation of the principle of self-governance stripped him of his inner vitality and condemned him to hell. Catholics felt that draft board officers and Selective Service agents had no choice but to let them follow conscience.

To force Catholics to break conscience was like asking a member of the faithful to renounce the church itself. Draft essays flattened out the history of the doctrine, making the teaching appear perennial, having never been subject to development or transformation in almost two millennia. These accounts suggested that the faithful, always and everywhere, obeyed their subjectivities. Stanley O'Leary told his draft board that "historically the Catholic Church has held its members must be guided by the law of God and of the Church as understood through their own consciences."[46] He took his elaboration even further: his draft essay claimed that the teaching on conscience was *ex cathedra* ("from the chair of St. Peter") and among "the oldest traditions in Catholic doctrine."[47] The latter statement had some plausibility, but the former was completely false. Modern popes have pronounced only two doctrines ex cathedra: Mary's Immaculate Conception and her bodily Assumption into heaven. But O'Leary expressed a desire found in many draft dossiers, no matter how outlandish his claim: in following directives generated by an agentive internality, Catholics imagined themselves as living out a long-standing tenet of the faith.

Catholic men stretched the teaching in their draft dossiers considerably, but not beyond the tradition. They did not invent tradition so much as accentuate, rather selectively, a teaching that had rested on the books for hundreds of years. The interpretative move made sense in light of the fact that thousands of young men would die on the battlefields of Vietnam, never to return home. War had calcified the doctrine into a stable, univocal process. Dennis Ackerman, who left seminary and took up studying psychology at the University of Michigan, insisted in his paperwork that "this freedom of the individual to follow his own conscience is deeply inscribed in Catholic theology."[48] Conscience-following qualified not only as an academic theology but more usefully as a simply stated matter of Catholic conviction. "Basically," as one CO put it, "the official statement of the Roman Catholic Church places the decision of participation in war on individual conscience."[49]

Essayists explained for draft board officers that Thomas Aquinas discovered the power of a Catholic conscience in the thirteenth century. His original formulation had tremendous staying power, for it could be adapted to multiple ends and put to widely divergent uses in the modern world, especially and perhaps most important in the refusal to go to war. Darren Scaft, an Americorps volunteer, explained to his draft board that "each individual Catholic must follow the dictates of conscience, for as St. Thomas Aquinas states, 'conscience is the proximate norm of morality.'"[50] Lay Catholics brought up Thomas because his writings condensed a complex theological genealogy into a single, provocative kernel. Just-war theory was important, as Catholic CO George Schultz noted, but "a more central consideration, emphasized by St. Thomas Aquinas, is that of conscience. A Catholic must obey his conscience above all else."[51] Thomas would be pleased if a Catholic, following conscience, resisted an unjust war or even became a Protestant. Catholics, acting on the Angelic Doctor's advice, swore they would follow conscience to any end, even set it against the church itself if necessary.

Lay Catholics drew from the same idea Martin Luther King, Jr. had discussed in his 1963 *Letter from a Birmingham Jail*. In writing some of the most consequential paragraphs of his classic epistle, King turned to Thomas to clarify the nature of an unjust law: a "law that is not rooted in eternal law and natural law."[52] Segregation did not constitute real law, because it was rooted in a desire for power rather than an eternal or natural truth. King also channeled St. Thomas when he referenced how the conscience "tells" the individual the law is unjust, inspiring that person to break the law and challenge its authority. As the theology long held, this sacred subjectivity assumed the important role of alerting the individual to the law's real nature, whether just or unjust. King and the Catholic laity agreed that conscience assisted in clarifying for the individual that an unjust law had no foundation in truth, and therefore that such a statute held sway only by way of the perverted police or judicial powers behind it. Illegitimate ordinances had no special standing in God's eyes and welcomed a transgression against them in the name of a higher truth. But King and these lay Catholics diverged in other ways, which illuminate their unique positions as rooted in the Social Gospel and medieval Thomism, respectively. King posited the existence of corporate conscience at the local and national levels, a collective entity that could be goaded into producing justice in the world. He explained how civil rights activists "present our very bodies as a means of laying our case before the conscience of the local and national community."[53] In contrast, Lay Catholics concerned themselves much more with following conscience as an end in itself, preserving the individual's moral integrity (and a chance at salvation), rather than as a means, as King put it, to "arouse" the conscience of the community. Catholics embraced an individualism King would have found unhelpful in the quest for civil rights. Nonetheless, lay Catholics and civil rights activists like King both granted a thirteenth-century Dominican theologian an important moment in the 1960s United States.

The priests who wrote character-reference letters assured the Selective Service that the Catholic men who invoked conscience were creatures of tradition. These young men appearing before local draft boards were good Catholic boys. They were products of the institutional church and its highly structured processes of moral formation. They had memorized catechisms, served countless Masses as altar boys, and enrolled in seminaries to find out whether God was calling them to become his priests. The reality they created in these institutions—that conscience properly formed is the believer's premier moral guide—ought to have some bearing on life as a citizen in a modern nation-state. Father Terence O'Shaughnessy, a Dominican who chaired the theology department at a Catholic liberal arts college, declared his student Charles Bronson, who objected to the war, a man of tradition. O'Shaughnessy told the draft board that Bronson did not have to wait for the hierarchy to grant him approval. In following his conscience, he acted on his religious training as a Catholic, which urged self-sovereignty in the face of unjust laws. O'Shaughnessy wrote, "If the conscience of a man should see a particular war as unjust, even though no special or official condemnation of this war has ever been made by his church, it would be in keeping with Catholic theology that this man follow the dictates of his own conscience."[54] Francis Connolly, a parish priest from Lenoir, North Carolina, told the local draft board that the state had to keep a distance from the sacred nucleus of his former parishioner, Patrick O'Sullivan: "The Roman Catholic Church, of which O'Sullivan is a member, teaches that war may be necessary in some cases, but that the conscience of the individual citizen must be respected by the government when it comes to bearing arms or aiding the war effort."[55] Many priests, whether from a religious order or a diocese, the Catholic academy or the parish, had learned these traditions in seminary. It required no protracted theological exegesis to spell out the tradition for the state. A defense of conscience rights could fly off a priest's typewriter in his parish study or professorial office in a matter of minutes.

Conclusion

When cancer took Stephen "Shorty" Spiro's life in 2007, his fellow Catholic Worker and close friend Thomas Cornell, a deacon, delivered the eulogy. A graduate of Farleigh Dickinson University in Teaneck, New Jersey, Shorty, like many Catholics of his generation, lived in the paradox created by his rising stature in American society and rejection of the state's unjust war. American society spurred the rise of Catholic education, yet those same institutions equipped their students with theological resources to undermine state power. Cornell noted how Shorty decided to brand himself as a selective conscientious objector despite the uphill battle such a designation meant he would have with the judicial system. Cornell claimed that the judge in Shorty's case "recognized his sincerity and his larger purpose" and gave him five years of probation.[56] The sentence came with a permanent record as a felon that would only be expunged by president Gerald Ford several years later. The records do not make clear whether men like Andrew Vincenzo and Patrick O'Sullivan received exemption from the state or faced additional proceedings after their initial draft board examinations. As historian Michael S. Foley notes in his influential study of the draft, the system itself was intensely localized, making generalizations difficult, and local draft boards destroyed their records in the 1970s when the Selective Service System went into "deep standby" status.[57] It was likely that many of the young Catholic men performed alternative service in their community—an appointment easier to obtain as the war pushed into its later years and rising numbers of CO cases strained the courts. The historical record does make clear, as explored in chapter 6 of this book, that the state rejected the conscience-rights-driven case for selective conscientious objection—whether put forth by Catholics, Jews, or Protestants—for the entire run of the war. While Shorty's case was stopped short of the US Supreme Court, another Catholic selective CO, Louis Negre of California, managed to push his case all the way to the nation's top court in 1971. The just-war framework and the theology of conscience gave the Catholic Church a profound stake in how the state treated selective COs.

The more immediate impact men like O'Sullivan, Vincenzo, and Shorty had on the church and American society was to push the conscience question into the front of many minds. In the summer of 1969, four years after Vincenzo filed his papers, nearly three dozen scholars descended on the Bronx to attend the scholarly conference "Conscience: Its Freedoms and Limitations." Many of the participants were Jesuit priests who taught at Fordham—perhaps some of Vincenzo's professors, the very men who inspired the young New Yorker to explore a calling as a Benedictine monk. The conference planners selected conscience as their theme because, as Father William Bier later explained, "it seemed that this concept had moved recently into a central position in the Church and the world."[58] Selective COs made conscience rights a chief concern in the nation's civic life. Yet the conference participants knew that selective conscientious objection could not be considered in isolation to other conscience rights movements in the areas of sexuality and psychological development. The debate about artificial birth control made it quite evident that "a consideration of conscience had become unquestionably central in the life of the Church."[59] Bier noted that theologians placed emphasis on "the maturity of conscience" out of a new awareness that each individual must be committed to personal growth.[60] The task set for the conference was to explain just how free or how limited a Catholic conscience should be in matters of war, sexuality, and personal development. Conscience rights promised a bright ethical and moral future yet simultaneously threatened to create a generation of individuals bent on asserting their own wills and subjectivities.

Scholars organized the conference to deal with the dual nature of the phenomenon as occurring inside the church and between the church and the state. The papers, unsurprisingly, did not reach a consensus about how free or how limited a Catholic conscience should be. Some presenters made the case that the turn to conscience was natural and necessary given the ambiguity of the cultural moment. Others argued that the future of the Catholic Church hinged on its ability to form mature consciences in each of its many members. Political scientists Richard Regan and John Rohr, both Jesuit priests, suggested that both the church and the state place considerable limits on conscience-following in civic matters like military service.

The conference was not a lighthearted theological debate: a deep anxiety pervaded the papers presented there. It was nerve-wracking enough to dwell on how Catholic COs and the Catholic Peace Fellowship threatened to divide the categories of Catholic and American, permanently damaging a relationship between faith and citizenship that a generation of older Catholics worked hard to create despite opposition and stereotypes from Protestants and liberal intellectuals. But American Catholics from around the nation also watched and listened from 1968 to 1971 as three dozen priests sparred with powerful Cardinal Archbishop Patrick O'Boyle over conscience rights on the matter of artificial birth control. These two streams of conscience rights were blending, demonstrating that an overlapping debate about sex and war generated a profound antilegalism among a group of white middle-class Catholics. Sex and war. The battlefield and the bedroom. The revolution for conscience rights had opened up on two fronts.

FOUR

Sex, Conscience, and the American Catholic 1968

We also feel that the position of the Washington Priests on the importance of conscience is integral to the best traditions of Catholic theology.

—Priests from Dayton, Kentucky, to Lawrence Cardinal Shehan (1968)

It has never occurred to me that personal decisions intelligently arrived at and made as a matter of conscience are anything but precious to and the very foundation of the Catholic faith.

—Layman Vincent Brown to Father Louis Quinn (1968)

On August 4, 1968, Father I. Joseph O'Donoghue publicly read a pastoral letter from Cardinal Patrick O'Boyle, archbishop of Washington, to the congregants of St. Francis De Sales Church, Washington, DC. The letter critiqued the stand for conscience rights taken by O'Donoghue and his fellow clerics in the aftermath of Pope Paul VI's condemnation of artificial birth control. O'Donoghue read the cardinal's words, and without sharing his own views on the matter, he then recited statements issued by bishops from Italy, the Netherlands, France, Britain, and Germany, who encouraged following conscience on matters of family life.[1]

Word traveled fast. Cardinal O'Boyle received an anonymous phone call from a parishioner of O'Donoghue's upset by his mixed messages. A chauffeur drove O'Boyle to Francis de Sales, off Highway 1 and well east of Washington's city center, where O'Donoghue served as assistant pastor. There O'Boyle sought out the priest and suspended him on the spot, revoking his teaching functions and barring him from hearing confessions. He informed O'Donoghue that he had five days to pack up his things and move out of the parish rectory. O'Donoghue dragged his feet for a month. On the day he was set to leave in September 1968, 250 parishioners descended on St. Francis to protest his removal. O'Donoghue took the opportunity to do some street preaching on conscience. "The issue," he told the crowd of supporters, "is the competence of your conscience and mine to arrive at truly Christian decisions after hearing all sides."[2] *Time* magazine covered the story for a national audience.

O'Donoghue's impromptu speech heralded a social movement for conscience rights, with roots both medieval and modern, that was about to rock the nation's capital in 1968. On December 23 that year, Father John Corrigan arrived at the First Congregational United Church of Christ, a sanctuary six blocks from the White House, ready to deliver an invited lecture. Corrigan, a popular assistant pastor from St. Gabriel's, a parish north of the city, had become the primary spokesman for the rebel priests. Corrigan was a man on the run. Two months earlier, O'Boyle had suspended him from the priesthood and, like O'Donoghue, ordered him removed from archdiocesan property. Just two days before the anniversary of Christ's birth, he spoke to the Protestant gathering about the struggle with Cardinal O'Boyle for recognition of conscience rights in the Catholic Church. Before the Second Vatican Council of 1962–65, it had been virtually unknown for a Catholic to set foot in a Protestant church; but times had changed, and Corrigan entered a once forbidden house of worship to preach about his own archbishop's shortcomings. He insisted that he and his fellow priests were being punished by O'Boyle for openly approving a deep tradition of the Catholic Church: when law became unclear, this teaching held, a Catholic formed and followed conscience, making a self-generated moral truth to guide personal behavior with confidence. The church's laws on birth control became fuzzy in 1968, so Corrigan promoted the natural shift to conscience. "The ultimate norm of morality is the will of God," he explained to his listeners. "However, since this cannot absolutely be known, then the proximate norm of morality must be one's well-formed conscience."[3] Controversially, Corrigan and his fellow dissidents applied the doctrine of conscience to the explosive issues of church law and contraception.

Cardinal O'Boyle's public debate with his priests marked an event that rippled out into the archdiocese throughout the fall of 1968, inspiring a wave of street demonstrations, passionate preaching, protest marches, letter-writing campaigns, and direct action in the name of conscience rights. The priests were inspired by the various social protest movements of the late 1960s as well as the Civil Rights movement. Men of the cloth who defended conscience rights in the District of Columbia in the fall of 1968 operated on the same global wavelength as that year's Prague Spring dissidents, French university students who barricaded Paris streets in May, African American sanitation workers who went on strike in Memphis from mid-February through mid-April, feminists who picketed the Miss America Pageant, and youth movements from Berlin to Mexico City. The clergymen coordinated direct action exercises. They joined a movement to challenge authoritarianism and break the institutional constraints that hindered their destinies, both individual and collective.[4] But clergymen like O'Donoghue and Corrigan joined this global insurgency from a unique angle: they were inspired by Thomas Aquinas and doctrine to liberate the laity to truly possess and live out conscience formation and following.[5] They put their priesthoods on the line to uphold this medieval right in a newfangled realm: artificial contraception. O'Boyle spoke for the clarity of the law. O'Donoghue, Corrigan, and their fellow priests pulled for conscience, a concept that they thought heralded a bright ethical and moral future for Catholics worldwide. The priests opened a second front in the struggle for conscience rights. Catholics had long agitated for recognition of conscience by the state, an effort that began in the 1930s and escalated after the US invasion of Vietnam; but in the fall of 1968, they demanded acceptance of conscience rights *in and from the church* on matters of sex.

This chapter tells the story of the clash between a band of Washington, DC, priests and Cardinal Archbishop O'Boyle over conscience rights in the arena of sexual morality. It explores the origins of the priests' campaign before charting their sixties-style social movement for conscience rights. The Washington, DC, priests made the rights of conscience a significant intellectual battle cry of global 1968. But this chapter is also about O'Boyle and his interpretation of the doctrine. The middle portions of the narrative demonstrate how the rebel priests took up the emancipatory aspects of the tradition, while O'Boyle favored restraint of conscience under the law. The Catholic Church's debate about artificial birth control in the immediate aftermath of *Humanae vitae* can be understood as a dispute over how much power to accord law over the individual believer's conscience or to what extent a conscience can trump the law. This center section of the chapter investigates the warnings offered by the cardinal in homilies, lectures, articles, and pamphlets about the dangers of refusing to form conscience under a clear teaching. Ultimately, as the latter sections "The Revenge of Doctrine" and "The Ambiguity of Victory and Defeat" recount, neither the priests nor the cardinal could declare victory in the immediate aftermath of the conflict. But, as evidence recounted below suggests, the stand made by priests like O'Donoghue, Corrigan, and MacCarthy—along with the draconian punishments handed down by Cardinal O'Boyle—revealed the limits of the law to many American Catholics, thus shifting more authority to the conscience after 1968. The operation itself, as noted above, derived legitimacy from the theological framework developed by Thomas Aquinas in the 1250s.

Controversy Origins

The controversy over conscience rights began innocently enough. On June 27, 1968, O'Boyle and four other bishops issued a routine document, *Guidelines for the Teaching of Religion in the Province of Baltimore and the Archdiocese of Washington*, reaffirming the church's stance on the immorality of artificial contraceptives. The statement did not develop or evolve doctrine in any significant manner. The Vatican had maintained a public stance against birth control since 1930, when Pope Pius XI issued the encyclical *Casti connubii (On Christian Marriage)*, a response to the liberal position taken by the Anglicans at the Lambeth Conference. Anglicans countenanced the use of birth control in the confines of marriage, whereas Pius XI proclaimed that married couples should receive children as if "from the hand of God."[6] Throughout the 1920s, birth control advocate Margaret Sanger found her most vociferous opponents in the Catholic hierarchy. Joseph Hayes, archbishop of New York, successfully executed a plot to have Sanger arrested in 1921 after she delivered a public lecture on birth control.

The church's stance on artificial contraceptives had not changed, but the Second Vatican Council—and the student and worker rebellions of 1968 from Columbia University to the Parisian suburbs—meant that O'Boyle's pronouncements would be received in a different light. O'Boyle had promulgated *Guidelines* in an archdiocese where for some time his priests had been reconsidering their role in the church, transitioning from dutiful shepherds to public interlocutors. Priests of the Archdiocese of Washington had recently "come of age," to use the language of the times. After Vatican II, they organized a public lobby to represent the laity and lower-ranking clergy. The organization came together initially as a series of informal meetings to read the Bible and share fellowship, known affectionately by its early members as the "Scotch and Scripture Crowd."[7] Under O'Donoghue's direction, the group rebranded itself in 1966 as the Association of Washington Priests (hereafter AWP) and invited all priests in the archdiocese to join its ranks. Nearly a third of the district's shepherds answered the call.

The AWP was among the first group of its kind in the nation: a conspicuously organized junta of priests publicly acknowledging their prerogative to pass judgments on relevant issues in the Catholic Church. O'Boyle, well aware of the AWP, never discouraged its formation or even its mission. In fact, he unknowingly subsidized the insurgency by sending many AWP members to the Catholic University of America for master's degrees, a decision he would later regret.[8]

In a surprising move in 1959, Pope John XXIII called the Second Vatican Council. The council, which opened in 1962, had bishops and theologians meeting in Rome to discuss a wide range of issues facing the Catholic Church, including religious freedom, the legacy of democracy, the liturgy, relations with Jews, and even modern telecommunications. The bishops gathered at St. Peter's Basilica and filled two long wooden stands, usually speaking Latin while debating these heavy issues. O'Boyle himself gave two speeches at the council, both in the church's mother tongue. A chief outcome of Vatican II was that the Catholic Church would no longer identify as a "Perfect Society," designed by God and built as a hierarchy. Instead, it was a "people," arranged into a set of horizontal rather than vertical relationships. The bishops dealt a deathblow to the *Syllabus of Errors*–style Catholicism that condemned modernity as sinful and anathema (in 1864, Pope Pius IX issued the infamous document, listing religious toleration, the separation of church and state, and salvation outside the Catholic Church as grievous errors).[9] Vatican II used no such denunciations. Instead, it envisioned the church traveling as a pilgrim in the world, taking up the "joys and hopes" of the world's people, Catholic and non-Catholic alike.

The Second Vatican Council made several short-term impacts on American Catholics, but two were particularly important to the Washington, DC, priests. First, the council's definition of the church as "the People of God" inspired AWP members to think of themselves as representatives of the laity. The priests took it upon themselves to make the people's interests known to the archbishop. The people, as depicted in secular democratic political theories, now had representation. The AWP was not quite a House of Representatives, as none of the men had been elected; but it spoke for the laity in meetings restricted to clergy. Second, Vatican II seemed to emphasize collegiality, a notion the AWP took very seriously. Directives would not be issued by a bishop or pope as fiats from the top down. Instead, priests banded with fellow priests and bishops with bishops in subsidiary units, often forming organizations like the AWP to "dialogue" on the problems facing the church. After dialogue, these silos made recommendations to superiors on how the church should be improved. Collegiality set in motion an institutional devolution that permitted lower church units to address local problems. The principle allowed priests to close ranks around their own interests, reaching conclusions without relying on episcopal interventions. The AWP deemed such a tactic necessary, because as pastors and confessors, it knew the true needs of the people.

Just over three weeks after receiving copies of Patrick O'Boyle's *Guidelines*, the executive committee of the AWP wrote a letter to the cardinal archbishop. It pointed out how the statement provided "no room for either probable opinion regarding the practice of contraception or the right of conscience so clearly enunciated in the documents of Vatican II."[10] A pronouncement of law at the expense of conscience on so important a matter as procreation could only be corrected through public dialogue and representation of the marginalized position, the very reasons for the AWP's existence. When ten days had passed with no official response from the archdiocese, the association released its letter to the local media, taking what would normally be a debate among priests in archdiocesan buildings out into the public spaces of the nation's capital. The *Washington Sunday Star* ran the letter on its front page.[11]

It so happened that Pope Paul VI issued his encyclical *Humanae vitae* (*Of Human Life*) the very next day, July 29, recommitting the Catholic Church to its stance against artificial contraception. The pontiff had been pondering his decision whether to approve or disapprove of the Pill since the Pontifical Commission for the Study of Population and Births (known as the birth control commission) delivered its official report to him in 1966. The committee urged official approval of the Pill, but Jesuit theologian John Ford, visiting the pope three or four times in the mid-1960s, persuaded the pontiff and his allies to hold the line. Following Ford's advice, the pope rejected the committee's recommendation, and artificial birth control remained gravely immoral in the eyes of the church as of the summer of 1968. Hence O'Boyle's defense of church law in *Guidelines* received strong reinforcements from Rome.

But Rome did not intimidate the Washington priests. They mounted the barricades the day after Pope Paul issued *Humanae vitae* to defend the rights of conscience. On July 30, they joined a small cadre of Catholic University of America professors in releasing "Statement of Conscience." Over six hundred theologians signed the statement, including Charles Curran, a rising star in the discipline and a professor at Catholic University. The theologians' statement and the tumult at Catholic University have garnered the attention of historians, but the AWP carried on the struggle begun by the "Statement of Conscience," making its words far more consequential than they otherwise would have been. The association's executive committee issued its own

"Statement of Conscience" the evening of July 30, setting the AWP on a collision course with Cardinal O'Boyle.

It had become common practice in the protest culture of the 1960s for groups to issue statements condemning an institutional practice or a societal abuse. But a "Statement of Conscience" as the AWP meant it entailed a public affirmation of the conscience's important and traditional role in moral decision-making. The AWP held that the teaching to form and follow conscience applied to a Catholic couple's decision to use artificial birth control. Its statement declared, "Spouses may responsibly decide according to conscience that artificial contraception in some circumstances is permissible, and indeed necessary to preserve and foster the values and sacredness of marriage."[12] The association's members, as parish priests and confessors, then pledged a "pastoral response" to Catholic families struggling with the question of artificial birth control. The rebel priests vowed to "respect the intelligently and responsibly formed conscience," even if this conscience accepted the Pill.[13] The executive committee of the AWP persuaded fifty-two priests working in the District of Columbia to attach their signatures to the statement. On August 4, the statement was delivered to O'Boyle.

The AWP centered its campaign in the Catholic Church's tradition of defending conscience against an overreach of law. In a second manifesto that followed quickly on the heels of its "Statement of Conscience," the group explained to the local media that it stood for the "long practice and tradition in the Catholic Church which respects the intelligently formed conscience of the individual."[14] It prided itself on recognizing both sides of the doctrine, objective and subjective. The directives published by Cardinal O'Boyle and Pope Paul VI championed the law but neglected conscience, distorting tradition. In contrast, an early AWP manifesto read, "Our public statements . . . while accepting with reverence the encyclical of Pope Paul on birth control, have also reflected our belief that this tradition of respect for the individual conscience need not be set aside."[15] These were the first salvos of the American Catholic 1968.

Conscience Rights and the Laity before 1968

To understand how the AWP found the courage to go public in 1968, it helps to listen to lay voices in the era's editorials, periodicals, and survey data. As early as 1963, amid the Vatican Council's second session, lay Catholics from across the United States demanded public recognition of the rights of conscience when it came to contraception. Laypeople like the man from the Bronx who wrote to *Jubilee* in response to the magazine's call for lay opinions believed that years of emphasizing obedience to laws had rendered moral life unacceptably rote and Catholic conscience tragically moribund. Noting that morality consists in following the demands of conscience, not law, he urged the church to finally let the conscience assume its proper position in moral decision-making on artificial contraception. Conscience, "man's practical moral judgment of a concrete action, atrophies with disuse," he insisted.[16] This Catholic, already a father, wanted authorization to keep his conscience in good condition by deciding how to answer the era's most pressing question: could responsible individuals decide for themselves on the matter of reproduction, or should they rely on church law? The magazine received similar letters from a physician in Chicago, a salesman from Texas, and a housewife in Cincinnati.

Laypeople grew increasingly assertive about conscience rights after Vatican II completed its later sessions. A May 1964 editorial in *Ave Maria* magazine suggested that showdowns between laity and clergy were becoming common as a thirst for self-rule spread into all aspects of Catholic life: the editors gloomily prognosticated that "conflict of conscience and authority [would] almost certainly become more and more of a problem for individual Catholics in the future, and on a very practical daily level."[17] They also predicted that struggles between subjectivity and law would soon appear in parishes, Catholic parent-teacher associations, and college campuses. Priests warned one another about what to expect. Penitents invoked the rights of conscience in the sacred confines of the confessional, daring the priest to violate their rights or downplay the lesson on subjective truth creation he and his colleagues had been feeding the laity for more than half of the twentieth century. "Much is being said nowadays about 'the primacy of conscience,'" a confessor observed in a letter sent to *American Ecclesiastical Review* in 1964. "I have heard that this principle is being applied by some Catholics who claim that their conscience declares that birth prevention is perfectly lawful."[18] The magazine's respondent—likely Father Francis Connell, a moral theologian—advised the confessor to stand his ground.

Yet the world's leading moral theologian, German priest Bernard Häring, encouraged the laity to make the shift to conscience in lectures he gave on a tour of the United States in 1965. The Catholic Church needed a response to the wide and rapid distribution of oral contraceptives (popularly known as the Pill) after their approval by the Federal Drug Administration in the spring of 1961.[19] Häring, a major influence at the Second Vatican Council and the onetime personal confessor to Pope John XXIII, came up with a solution. In a 1965 talk to a gathering of the Christian Family Movement, he argued that couples may make a "decision of conscience" to use birth control after serious prayer and dialogue. Catholic moral theology, as it understood God's judgment, respected the decisions reared in a subjectivity. It did not grant law the final word. In referring to Catholics who used birth control, Häring told his audience that "if their conscience [was] upright, sincere, God [would] judge their sincerity of their conscience and in view of the difficulties life presents to them."[20]

In a speech made a year later to a diverse group of Protestants and Catholics at Brown University, Häring extended the traditional Catholic prohibition against conscience coercion into the interpersonal relationship of marriage. He warned that one spouse should never coerce the other's conscience into banning birth control just to uphold a church law. "In such a deep relationship as marriage," he explained, "the covenant of love, the most basic condition of all is mutual respect for conscience. It would destroy the very essence, the very foundation of marriage . . . if one were to score a victory over the conscience of the other" with a forced observation of the artificial birth control ban.[21] Conscience, a "true conscience," contained "one's knowledge of the good." If the individual's inner sanctuary apprehended a good at loggerheads with official church teaching on birth control, the Catholic, Häring asserted in 1966, must follow the good as revealed in his or her inner nucleus. If a conscience conflicted with the beliefs of a husband or wife, the same thing was true. A Catholic had to act on internal cues.

The single most important source for conscience rights published before 1968 was the Dutch Catechism. Catechists from the Netherlands remade the genre in 1967, replacing the formulaic language of Thomism with existential dilemmas and florid prose. In the United States, the text sold well to a generation of American Catholics reared on Vatican II, the antiwar movement, and civil rights. *Time* magazine called the Dutch Catechism "one of the year's best religious sellers" in 1967 and reported that seventy-five thousand copies had flown off bookstore shelves that year.[22] Significantly, the catechism attempted to explain "the many reasons why at the present time greater stress is laid on the personal verdict of conscience."[23] The reasons were threefold. First, the church increasingly recognized the law's inability to anticipate each unique human person and the situations persons found themselves in. Second, Catholics found themselves in a time of transition in which values were being questioned and remade. Finally, Catholics increasingly relied on conscience as the law's penchant "to dive too deeply into details" became obvious. The law exceeded its mission statement and waded into the messy minutiae of life where it did not belong. Equally significant, existential desires and poetic phrases in the Dutch Catechism only served to amplify Thomas Aquinas's emphasis on conscience, not diminish it: "Medieval thought, which was very objective and strongly orientated to society, even laid stress upon this element . . . it remains the constant teaching of the Church that each man must be guided by the profound law of his conscience."[24] It became a popular intellectual move in the late 1960s to blend existentialism and medieval Thomism when making the case for conscience rights.

The Dutch Catechism applied the teaching on conscience to contraception in a manner that left its many lay readers with no doubt that they possessed a right to follow their subjectivity on the intimate question of sexuality. Each woman, the text concluded, must be guided by a self-asserting subjectivity, an entity that had legitimacy because of Catholic thought. "The last word lies with the conscience and not with the doctor or the confessor," it instructed.[25]

Married lay couples with children also encouraged the church to make the changeover from law to conscience. Patty Crowley, a founder of the Christian Family Movement organization, polled men and women on what they thought the church should do about birth control.[26] She wanted to take the pulse of public opinion before casting her vote as a member of the birth control commission at the Spanish College in Rome in 1966. Lay couples made the case for robust subjectivity in the qualitative section of Crowley's surveys and did so succinctly. A couple from Michigan thought the church should provide "guidelines" only for the use of oral contraceptives. After that, "it should be left up to the conscience of the couple to weigh the problem."[27] A couple from Los Angeles, married fourteen years and parents to six children, concluded, "Personal conscience seems to us the only answer."[28] A San Diego Christian Family Movement couple, ages thirty-seven (husband) and thirty-six (wife), married fifteen years and with five children, told Crowley, "Let this be a matter of conscience."[29] The law, and obedience to the law, no longer proved to be an apt guide for sexual behavior. The Catholic Church ought to let conscience break the impasse. Driving the AWP's public stand was the longing, often stated in public and in private writings, for an open acknowledgment that Catholic principles of self-governance did not cease to exist in the bedroom.

Rebellion in the Name of Tradition: Father Shane MacCarthy

Members of the Association of Washington Priests courageously preached the doctrine of prudent self-sovereignty from parish pulpits. AWP member Father Shane MacCarthy, just shy of his thirtieth birthday and only in his third year of priesthood, kept the flame of conscience rights lit at Assumption Parish, where he served as assistant pastor. MacCarthy finished five years of study at St. Vincent's Seminary in Latrobe, Pennsylvania, after earning his bachelor's degree in 1960 at Holy Cross College, a prestigious Jesuit liberal arts college in Worcester, Massachusetts. Inspired by the Second Vatican Council and the Civil Rights movement, the idealistic priest came to Assumption, a racially mixed parish in Washington, after requesting a transfer there from a cushy suburban parish in Silver Spring, Maryland.

On August 4, 1968, Cardinal Patrick O'Boyle's pastoral letter was being read from all Washington pulpits. MacCarthy prefaced his reading with his own exegesis on the doctrine of conscience. He told his parishioners that the pope's encyclical did not have a monopoly over a Catholic's selfdom. Indeed, no law from pope or state erased the authority of a conscience. Catholics formed subjectivities in a mature fashion and in their own circumstances. "I submit to you that our consciences must be formed not only by the encyclical itself but in the light of the mature response which it elicits," MacCarthy said.[30] Next, he explained another traditional plank of the theology of conscience: the law did not determine where a Catholic would spend the afterlife, whether heaven or hell. That individual ascended to glory or descended to eternal torture based on whether he or she followed conscience. "No statement, no matter how authoritative it may be can presume to dictate whether I will be eternally glorified or damned," MacCarthy preached. "Ultimately that posture of conscience has to be made by me and me alone."[31] He then proceeded to read the cardinal archbishop's statement "in toto," as O'Boyle had directed.

A diligent foot soldier in the campaign for conscience rights, MacCarthy elaborated on the many ways that church doctrine backed conscience in a second homily he gave in 1968, the notes for which he jotted down on loose-leaf paper taken from his parish's rectory (fig. 5). He knew his doctrine: he was taking full advantage of the continuing-education initiatives made available by O'Boyle and the discussion groups run by the AWP. MacCarthy attended seminars on the church's intellectual life at the Catholic University of America, where he came in contact with the oeuvre of Bernard Häring and the works of Charles Curran, a professor at the university who later became a famous dissenter from *Humanae vitae*.

As he explained to the congregation during his homily, there were moments in church history when law and conscience were in conflict, but the church supported not only law but the assured core of the person. MacCarthy, noting that conscience is the person's "ultimate subjective norm," told his audience that "conscience is so important that the Church says that

ASSUMPTION RECTORY
3401 NICHOLS AVE., S. E.
WASHINGTON, D. C. 20032

Conscience is so impt that
Ch says that "erroneous conscience"
is binding.

———————   ————   ————

For each individual man,
        his own conscience is the
                Norm of moral conduct

⟨ An ultimate subjective
    norm

                    .... always dependent
                        on a higher norm
                        — an Objective
                            Norm

The subjective norm of conscience must
always seek the obj norm

5. Notes for a homily delivered by Father Shane MacCarthy in August 1968 at Assumption Parish, Washington, DC. He takes note of the erroneous conscience, the conscience as ultimate subjective norm, and the obligation of conscience to seek an objective rule. The American Catholic History Research Center and University Archives (ACUA), The Catholic University of America, Washington, DC.

'erroneous conscience' is binding."[32] Dogma did not sit in the law's corner; it divided itself and stood behind the conscience. "Dogma of infallibility does not break the integrity of conscience," MacCarthy declared. "On the contrary, [the dogma of infallibility plays an important role in] safeguarding it [conscience] in the ultimate decisive questions thru the surest orientation toward truth."[33] He apparently felt the need to include the capacity of conscience to withstand infallibility, even though *Humanae vitae* was not considered infallible.

MacCarthy outlined the doctrine in a cut-and-dried manner, but he also envisaged sacrificing his priesthood in a blaze of glory to protect the rights of conscience. In early October, he was on the cusp of living out that dream: after private and public confrontations with O'Boyle over the role of conscience in sexual ethics, the cardinal censured MacCarthy. However, he received the lighter punishment of suspension and remained on the grounds of his parish merely as an observer. He no longer preached from his pulpit, educated his flock, or absolved sins in Assumption's confessional. In the name of conscience rights, the young priest had risked losing a clerical appointment that had required extended seminary training and gave him an emotionally meaningful ministry with the city's African American Catholics. This was a painful experience for the young priest, but he loaded it with meaning. MacCarthy dreamed about voluntarily enduring the public execution of his vocation in a Christ-like fashion to save Catholics from eternal bondage to the law. As an agent of Christ in the world, he would surrender his vocation to God if it meant preserving his flock's prerogative of self-sovereignty. As he preached from a local pulpit at the start of the public dispute, MacCarthy declared, "If I or any of my colleagues must offer our present functioning as priests on the altar of our Cardinal, then I can think of no better reasons, than in defense of the integrity of intelligently formed conscience of the individual which is none other that [sic] Jesus Christ speaking to each of us in the depths of our hearts."[34] Christ does not speak to Catholics through law but rather breathes his message into their sacred nucleuses. MacCarthy's pledging this sacrifice extended from his deep commitment to a socially active priesthood. Like his brother priests, he vowed to risk it all for the rights of conscience. He told O'Boyle in a personal letter that his service as a priest would be meaningless if the church forced him to disregard the importance of selfhood cultivation. "I could not live out my life or my service of others if were not to respect the intelligently and responsibly formed conscience of any people who follow a theological option which is in good standing with the Roman Catholic Church," he wrote.[35]

Cardinal Patrick O'Boyle's Stand

To get a full view of the American Catholic 1968, it is also necessary to see the events of that year from the perspective of Cardinal Patrick O'Boyle (fig. 6)—the chief supporter of law's authority over conscience. O'Boyle took discreet but confident steps to shut down the AWP's campaign. Appointed as archbishop of the newly created Archdiocese of Washington in 1947 by Pope Pius XII, he received a cardinal's red hat in June 1967, almost a year to the day before he published his seemingly innocuous *Guidelines*, the document that ignited the conscience rights crisis with its reminder that the use of artificial birth control entailed sin. As his first move in his theological chess match with the AWP, O'Boyle called together a crack team of specialists to help him formulate a response to the AWP's letter to him. The cardinal knew his limits. He ascended the ranks of the Catholic hierarchy in the twentieth century as an administrator of New York City's Catholic Charities and coordinator of the church's war relief services during World War II, not as a theologian. A smart tactician and accomplished policy maker, he spent much more time in the postwar period expanding the infrastructure of his archdiocese (earning the moniker "Cinderblock O'Boyle") than he did reading Thomas Aquinas.

In preparing to take on the rebel priests of his archdiocese, O'Boyle brought famous theologian John Ford and rising academic star Germain Grisez to Washington to serve as his consultants and aides, hosting them in a two-bedroom suite near the bishops' residence. Francis Connell, a close friend of O'Boyle's who served as his informal adviser at Vatican II, had passed away the year before, leaving Ford to serve as the cardinal archbishop's right hand. Ford was the moral theologian who had persuaded Pope Paul VI to publish *Humanae vitae*. Grisez, a specialist in the theology of Thomas Aquinas and at the time a professor at Georgetown University, was a close friend of Ford's and had written an influential book on contraception and the natural law in 1965. He was a father of four, and he spent the bulk of his career teaching Christian ethics at Mount Saint Mary's University in Emmitsburg, Maryland. Both men were profoundly committed to shoring up the power of the Catholic Church to convey objective truths to the faithful. Eric Genilo, Ford's biographer, distinguished the theologian's "standard mode" from his "crisis mode" when it came to how he wrote or thought. Ford arrived in Washington in deep crisis mode, ready to back the law. Mark Massa, a theologian and historian who has written on Grisez's storied career, notes that the young professor's early works backed *Humanae vitae* with a creative reinterpretation of law's obvious practicality.[36]

6. Cardinal Archbishop Patrick A. O'Boyle (*right*) upon delivering an address in Washington, DC. The American Catholic History Research Center and University Archives (ACUA), The Catholic University of America, Washington, DC.

Over dinner on August 2, O'Boyle and his team formulated a three-pronged response to the AWP: first, they planned to write a pastoral letter, to be read from each pulpit in the archdiocese, condemning the AWP's misinterpretation of conscience; second, each priest in the movement for conscience rights would receive a personal letter from the cardinal urging him to cease and desist; and finally, the group began drafting a pamphlet on natural law and birth control to win the theological argument.[37] O'Boyle's initial response had a dimension of discretion: the pastoral letter he required priests like O'Donoghue and MacCarthy to read from the pulpit on Sunday, August 4, urged obedience to *Humanae vitae* but did not mention the AWP by name. But that letter got right to the point even if it did not name names. Catholics, O'Boyle explained in his thesis statement, were "bound in conscience to accept and to follow the Holy Father's teaching."[38] He offered the AWP the opportunity to call off its campaign at an early hour.

O'Boyle's personal letter (prong 2 of the team's response) pursued a definition of conscience, widely available in midcentury teachings, as an input for the law and an output of following the law. The properly functioning Catholic subjectivity imported the ban on birth control into the self, grasped the law, and bound conscience to the pope's pronouncement. O'Boyle denounced the AWP's defense of Catholic married couples' conscience rights. "You put a lot of stress on conscience—the consciences of married couples that allow them to practice contraception," his letter stated, "even though your view is at odds with the Holy Father's teaching and your actions are at odds with my repeated instructions."[39] The only conscience that had rights *in the church* was a conscience properly formed along the lines of the law. The Catholic possessed a right to follow the truth as known in conscience but held no such right in the church to follow a false conscience. Both O'Boyle and the pope had issued clear and just laws banning the use of artificial contraceptives. A properly formed conscience thus aligned with the ban. "Conscience must be properly formed; it must be right conscience," the cardinal archbishop's letter stated.[40] A Catholic could not seek shelter behind an erroneous conscience.

O'Boyle thought that his office carried with it the responsibility to denounce false consciences that accepted artificial birth control. The AWP had to stand down, lest it risk creating a vast population of Catholics equipped with warped subjectivities. Ultimately, it was highly likely that these Catholics and their enablers among clergy would spend an eternity in hell, a fate the cardinal wanted them to avoid. He sounded the same themes in a private lecture given exclusively to the offending priests in early September at Washington, DC's Theological College, where many of the men had learned theology as graduate students.[41] O'Boyle's main point would not have been lost on his audience: the divine law set conscience free to import the truth, not misapprehend it. The distorted understanding of conscience promoted by the AWP, however, sent Catholics "into a quicksand of confusion and error where their spiritual life [would] be hopelessly smothered."[42]

The day after O'Boyle's lecture, the AWP clarified its position for the local press. It sought not to undermine the law but to uphold the long-standing rights of conscience.[43] O'Boyle quickly summoned the priests to his chancery, where the he offered them an opportunity to recant and set aside their misguided understandings of conscience. Nearly forty years of experience in the inner workings of church bureaucracy had taught O'Boyle to move gradually yet decisively—a combination of tactics he used to devastating effect in his series of clashes with the AWP. He had given stern warnings to the men for nearly two months, but in the back of his mind the cardinal knew he might have to bring the hammer of ecclesiastical censure down on a group of committed pastors he genuinely cared about. No members of the

AWP retracted their argument for the rights of conscience. Instead, the group sent O'Boyle yet another petition vowing to honor laypeople's traditional conscience rights: "The undernamed priests again state that we believe in the long practice and tradition in the Catholic Church which respects freedom of conscience and that without being unfaithful to the Church itself we cannot desert our position, namely, that we will respect the intelligently and responsibly formed consciences of the people we serve."[44] This statement carried the signatures of dozens of priests from inside and outside the District of Columbia, both parish priests and members of religious orders.

The cardinal archbishop decided not to waste his time negotiating with the rebel priests and went instead to the Catholic people of Washington, DC. In a Sunday homily given on September 22, 1968, from the pulpit of St. Matthew's Cathedral, the archdiocese's crown institutional jewel, he likened the spread of the AWP's ideas to a biblical plague. His closest advisers had urged him not to give the incendiary pronouncement, but Grisez, the homily's ghostwriter, persuaded him to preach fire and brimstone. O'Boyle imagined the Washington, DC, church as reenacting a scene from the book of Deuteronomy. "Then too," he preached, "a false idea of the freedom of conscience suggested that God's chosen people could set aside the precepts of His Holy Law, in favor of the dictates of their own hearts."[45] He associated the AWP's emphasis on conscience with the specter of "moral subjectivism," a favorite trope of critics of conscience rights and a caveat often offered by church authorities concerned about the excesses of subjectivity. Moral subjectivists, O'Boyle explained, elevated their own unique situation above the objective law.

Appointing himself as a Moses figure, the cardinal took it upon himself to deliver his people from a potential bondage in moral subjectivism. "My dear friends in Christ," he preached, "can you understand that I am impelled to act because I cannot stand by and let you be misled by an idea of freedom of conscience that could bring down on you so horrible a curse?"[46] The salvation of souls was at stake. But at that point in his homily, O'Boyle immediately discovered how his interpretation of conscience would fare among certain segments of the Washington, DC, faithful: nearly two hundred in a congregation of an estimated one thousand rose from their pews and walked out of the cathedral. After he finished his homily, the *Boston Globe* reported, the two hundred returned to their pews for the Eucharistic prayer.[47] But most of the people in the cathedral gave O'Boyle a standing ovation upon his completion of his sermon. He had critics, but he also had supporters.

Cardinal Patrick O'Boyle personified better than any other figure in modern American Catholic history the tendency to swing from one side of the law-conscience duality to the other. He dispensed several permutations of the church's teaching on conscience between the late 1950s and the late 1960s, placing law over conscience, and conscience over law, as the situation in political or ecclesiastical life demanded. He converged the two streams driving conscience language in the nation's public sphere: the campaign to protect conscience rights from a growing liberal state and, often uttered in the same breath, a rearguard action to contain assertions of self-governance in the church itself on the matter of sex. In 1957, as we noted in chapter 2, O'Boyle warned the US Department of Justice in a confidential memo not to force Catholic men to act against conscience and drop bombs on civilian targets. He also warned the state that government officials could not force Catholics to distribute condoms or take part in abortion and sterilization procedures. O'Boyle was also a committed defender of conscience rights in the political sphere. In 1971, he endorsed a pastoral letter from the National Conference of Catholic Bishops defending the conscience rights of Catholic men to object to the draft for Vietnam.

O'Boyle's journey from the law to conscience both implicated and challenged papal power. He pointed out how forced bombing runs or involuntary medical procedures stood as exceptions to the remark by Pope Pius in his 1956 Christmas address that "no Catholic could invoke conscience" to dodge a law. In the debate over artificial birth control in the nation's capital, O'Boyle moved to the law side, arguing that papal power, as expressed in *Humanae vitae*, leaves conscience no room to maneuver to avoid the brunt of objective church teachings. The twinned nature of shackling a conscience to the law or liberating a conscience from the law roiled church power at its highest levels.

Yet O'Boyle has an even longer history with the Catholic concept of self-rule that should not be buried by his defense of Rome in 1968. Three years earlier, in 1965, perched in the same St. Matthew's Cathedral pulpit from which he likened the spread of strong-willed subjectivities to a pestilence, he assured non-Catholics that the church respected its fellow Americans' freedom of conscience in matters of artificial birth control. In the wake of *Griswold v. Connecticut*, the 1965 Supreme Court case that established a "right of privacy" in matters of contraception, O'Boyle reaffirmed the well-worn lesson that non-Catholic conscience rested beyond the powers of civil coercion: "In great issues of this kind, where opinion is sharply divided, the first and most important consideration in searching for a solution is the preservation of the God-given rights of conscience."[48] He accepted that Catholics had "no right" to violate the internal orbs of non-Catholics with legislation. He even endorsed non-Catholics' conscience rights in a heated moment of national sexual politics: Massachusetts liberalized its restrictions of artificial birth control in the same summer of 1965. All the while, even as he noted these freedoms, O'Boyle held it as axiomatic that the church had the final say in forming the consciences of the Catholic faithful on these important matters, even if it renounced claims to its fellow citizens.

The tables had turned in 1968: O'Boyle found himself on the receiving end of conscience violation charges. He unsealed yet another letter from the AWP just five days after his book of Deuteronomy homily. Imagine his indignation when on September 27 he again read one of the AWP's key lines: "It is a time-honored principle of Catholic tradition and practice that the conscience is the proximate norm of morality."[49] O'Boyle was a cautious man—a gradualist by nature—but he was about to gamble with the future of the Washington, DC, Catholic Church. He was pondering whether to suspend thirty-nine dedicated shepherds as the priesthood itself edged toward a major institutional crisis. Already that year, men had begun leaving their vocation for marriage and new careers. Six hundred would leave active ministry each year from 1969 to 1972. Between 1968 and 1988, a total of ten thousand US priests resigned.[50] O'Boyle would be suspending nearly forty priests from ministry while also considering the possibility that his show of episcopal force could trigger an even larger wave of resignations.

The stakes were high, but O'Boyle had had enough after he read the AWP's September 27 letter: he concluded that the association, full of intransigents, posed a permanent threat to the orthodoxy of Catholic teachings in the District of Columbia. The purveyors of this overly subjectivist theology of conscience needed to pay a price for defending such a dangerous proposition. The ban on artificial birth control could not be communicated clearly to the faithful with the AWP parading about the archdiocese trumpeting a falsehood about the powers of subjectivity. These priests, the very men who transubstantiated bread into the Body of Christ during the Mass, had already disrupted the moral discourse of the district by connecting their flawed concept of conscience to tradition. Consequently, O'Boyle suspended thirty-nine district priests (members of the AWP and signers of the "Statement of Conscience") from active ministry in the last days of September 1968. Thirty-four (Shane MacCarthy included) were suspended from preaching, teaching, or hearing confessions. Five (Joseph O'Donoghue and John Corrigan included) were fully suspended from the priesthood and evicted from the rectories on archdiocesan property. In driving his point home, O'Boyle noted in his press release announcing the punishments that the encyclical, "even if it [was] not infallible, [was] binding on the consciences of all Catholics."[51] The AWP could no longer misconstrue the theology of conscience.

The suspensions of dozens of priestly vocations and an off-key homily must have seemed strange coming from a Catholic leader celebrated in the nation's capital for his defenses of the working classes and his strong stand for civil rights, but Cardinal O'Boyle embodied the contradictions of the Catholic Left as exposed by sexual politics at the end of the 1960s. He had pushed for civil rights in the public sphere yet denied the rights of conscience in the church's own orbit of authority. O'Boyle had grown up in the blue-collar town of Scranton, Pennsylvania, the son of a devout Irish Catholic mother. His youth in Scranton and his experiences managing expansive relief and orphanage networks in New York City only strengthened his commitment to fighting for working-class people. He defended unions in Washington, DC, and even made sure that the workers who expanded his cinderblock empire were well compensated.

It was O'Boyle's faith in the natural law that brought him to oppose conscience in Catholic sexual ethics, but that same faith in absolutes also fueled his decades-long commitment to the civil rights of African Americans. He began to systematically yet gradually integrate the Catholic schools of Washington, DC, in the 1950s, and he tore down the racial barriers of the Catholic Youth Organization in 1951 in a dramatic fashion by appointing three prominent African American Catholics to its board. He moved slowly in the 1950s so as not to offend the white laity, but O'Boyle grew emboldened by the Civil Rights movement. The cardinal could be seen offering public invocations at civil rights rallies, demanding open housing in the nation's capital, and conspicuously applauding Lyndon Johnson's Civil Rights Act of 1964.[52] He absorbed the church's idea of truth but not the racist views of many Irish Catholics or his own archdiocese's white southern Catholics. The cardinal saw no contradiction in his defense of objective truths in civil rights and his stand for ultimate norms in sexuality even if American progressives thought him contradictory.

The American Catholic 1968

The AWP, with so deep a faith in its cause, invested its movement completely in the defense of conscience rights after O'Boyle handed down censures of suspension and eviction in late September 1968. Not only did his censures fail to quell the broader turn to conscience in American Catholicism—his punishments helped transform a local theological dispute into a sixties-style rights movement that brought thousands of the faithful to the streets to demonstrate their dismay with authority. Father Corrigan vowed to take the cause of subjectivity on the road in October of 1968. If the AWP received support from laypeople and priests across the country, the group would gain leverage in the local showdown with O'Boyle. It pledged to write every bishop in the United States, rally American priests to its cause, and "continue to speak publicly as a group about defending the Catholic orthodoxy of our position on conscience."[53] Corrigan pondered why the rights of conscience—long discussed in confessionals and the classrooms of parochial schools—could not also be acknowledged by the AWP in public: "If we can follow this practice in private in accepting a person's responsible judgment of conscience, do not our people have a right to know that?"[54] These rights, like human or civil rights more broadly, were to be acknowledged openly in public discourse. No authority, even a cardinal, could simply suspend a Catholic's rights to form and follow conscience, even on the matter of artificial birth control.

The evicted T. Joseph O'Donoghue, one of the AWP's most dedicated rank-and-file members, took the theology of conscience to the streets in September 1968. He gave his first public elocution on conscience rights to a crowd of 250 parishioners who had gathered spontaneously to protest his suspension and removal. That was just the first stop, albeit impromptu, on his speaking tour. The *Washington Post* estimated that later that month, eight hundred Catholics descended on Sherman Circle Northwest to hear the ousted priest give an open-air address. O'Donoghue sounded the tocsin of conscience rights. That conscience was taking the limelight again is hardly a surprise—it was the rallying cry of the AWP's campaign and the central framing device for its stand against O'Boyle. O'Donoghue spoke into the microphones as cameras clicked: "You are saying what our brethren of other faiths have been long waiting for you to say, something that we have not clearly said since the Reformation. Namely that Catholics are men and women of faith who in conscience listen to the word and in conscience decide."[55] One can imagine that huge crowd of men, women, and children greeting O'Donoghue's ideas with applause and cheers. He then denounced the absence of due process in the Catholic Church, which allowed O'Boyle to simply suspend the priests without a tribunal or a judge. He accused the cardinal archbishop of trampling on "human rights, civil rights, and church rights."[56]

Lay supporters helped the movement for conscience rights become increasingly organized in the weeks following the suspensions and evictions. Lay benefactors bought a property a dozen blocks west of the Catholic University of America that became the Center for Christian Renewal (CCR), a command station for the AWP's movement. The National Association of Laymen and the National Liturgical Conference sent money.

Jane Briggs-Hart, daughter of Detroit Tigers owner Walter Briggs and a well-known Catholic activist, made one of the initial donations. Senator Eugene McCarthy also made a financial contribution to the CCR to jump-start the AWP's movement.[57] Laypeople and the AWP sent O'Boyle a serious signal of their resolve when they purchased the house. The area around the Catholic University of America is known as "Little Rome" on account of the preponderance of priests who attend the university and the many houses of study for religious orders built nearby. Since the university's founding in 1896, priests from across the nation had been enrolling there to earn master's degrees and doctorates. The founding of the CCR meant that a movement of rebel priests now had a stronghold right on O'Boyle's home turf and in the immediate proximity of "the Bishops' University." The cardinal archbishop was a trustee at the university; his claim to fame before his dispute with the AWP was having been the one to tell crowds of protesting students, in a classic moment of the Catholic 1960s, that theologian Charles Curran's tenure promotion would be granted. Curran was initially denied tenure on account of his critiques of the natural law.

The priests dismissed from archdiocesan property now had an official headquarters at the epicenter of the struggle between law and conscience. In the kitchen and living room of the CCR, they partook of the spirit of protest of the 1960s: they planned public demonstrations, orchestrated a letter-writing campaign, and garnered support from elite Catholic laypeople. Civil and canon lawyers visited the center frequently to offer the priests legal advice.

In November, the AWP pulled off Unity Day, a 1960s-style protest rally demanding that the bishops formally recognize the rights of conscience. Nearly three thousand Catholics packed into the auditorium at the Mayflower Hotel to celebrate what a poster from the event called a "dignified, prayerful, public witness supporting the principle of freedom of conscience in the Church" (fig. 7).[58] Catholic laymen and laywomen came to the rally after the late Mass, their children in tow. At the event, nuns and priests swayed, arms locked, as they sang "Mrs. Robinson." Senator Eugene McCarthy, the antiwar candidate in the Democratic Party's 1968 primaries, led the crowd in a rendition of "The Impossible Dream," a ballad about defeating one's enemies no matter the cost.[59] The senator brought the crowd to its feet. Jane Briggs-Hart then took the podium, reciting a long list of national bishops' associations that recognized the supremacy of conscience on the question of artificial birth control. The suspended and evicted priests milled about the crowd, shaking hands with the District of Columbia faithful and embracing supporters.

Unity Day Rally

Sunday, November 10, 2 p.m. — Sylvan Theatre (on Washington Monument grounds) Join Senator Eugene McCarthy, Mrs. Philip Hart, Father John Corrigan and the 54 "conscience statement" priests, and many thousands more . . .

IN THIS DIGNIFIED, PRAYERFUL, PUBLIC WITNESS SUPPORTING THE PRINCIPLE OF FREEDOM OF CONSCIENCE IN THE CHURCH.

PARISH GROUPS   ORGANIZATIONS

FAMILY GROUPS   INDIVIDUALS

ALL WELCOME!

Sponsors:
The 54 Washington Archdiocese "Conscience Statement" Priests
Washington Lay Association
Committee on Freedom in the Church
Center for Christian Renewal

Supporting Organizations:
National Association of Laymen
National Liturgical Conference (A voluntary association of laymen, nuns, brothers, priests and bishops)

7. Flyer for the Unity Day Rally planned by the Association of Washington Priests. The rally took place on November 10, 1968. The American Catholic History Research Center and University Archives (ACUA), The Catholic University of America, Washington, DC.

The rally had an element of strategy. The AWP had planned the drive for the same time that 257 American bishops would be arriving at the Mayflower Hotel for the annual meeting of the National Conference of Catholic Bishops. The bishops were crafting a response to the birth control encyclical, finally catching up to the other bishops around the world who had written national letters in response to *Humanae vitae*. The AWP rallied to convince the bishops to honor the traditional rights to follow conscience on all serious moral matters. The spirit of the Civil Rights movement, still lingering in the

8. Members of the Association of Washington Priests during the "Pray-In" at the Mayflower Hotel, November 12, 1968. The American Catholic History Research Center and University Archives (ACUA), The Catholic University of America, Washington, DC.

District of Columbia, electrified the collective and individual protests of the American Catholic 1968. Two days after the rally, John Corrigan—an AWP member still under suspension—led a march of one hundred priests up Connecticut Avenue on November 12 to stage a "pray-in" at the Mayflower (figs. 8, 9). The priests had appropriated the tactics of the civil rights marchers and 1968 dissidents. Clerics with guitars led their brothers in singing spirituals.[60] The pray-in reached its high point when Corrigan presented a two-point resolution to Archbishop John Dearden of Detroit, president of the bishops' council.

Its conflict with Cardinal O'Boyle made the AWP the incarnation of conscience rights and universalized its struggle. In a sense, the besieged priests battled for conscience rights in the nation's capital to make them real everywhere else. The oppressed were fighting the oppressors across the globe in 1968 in a universal struggle to emancipate all humanity. This hope appeared in explications of Catholic doctrine at the same time it appeared in anticolonial discourse and second-wave feminism. The AWP and its supporters joined the global movement for liberation and rights in form but not in content, however: Catholics demanded that the bishops recognize rights of conscience that echoed from the depths of a doctrine first articulated by

Thomas Aquinas in the thirteenth century; they did not seek existential self-realization in the culture of conformity or civil rights from a nation-state. "The priests in Washington, in taking the position they have, uphold the traditional teachings of the Church on conscience," a group of laypeople told Cardinal Lawrence Shehan, archbishop of Baltimore, in a letter. "We laypeople voice our concern on this matter because we, too, feel an obligation to follow a formed and informed conscience."[61] It was a common refrain for the American Catholic 1968: laypeople supported the priests because they wanted conscience to be liberated and tradition to be real in the world.

Conscience quickly gained champions across the United States and around the world after the AWP took its stand. Reflecting the global reach of the enthusiasm for conscience, a Dutch theologian noted in the *Clergy Review*, a British journal read by American priests, that Catholics "constantly hear it said nowadays, that man's conscience is the ultimate guide in the Moral order . . . it seems a happy feature of the present-day renewal that this old doctrine is being revitalized and ever more forcefully expressed."[62] Theologians accorded the law an off-centered, less authoritarian role in Catholicism after the Washington, DC, event exposed the law's overbearing nature.

9. The Pray-In featured songs during the priests' occupation of the Mayflower Hotel during the annual meeting of the National Conference of Catholic Bishops. The District of Columbia press took a strong interest in the events at the hotel. The American Catholic History Research Center and University Archives (ACUA), The Catholic University of America, Washington, DC.

A seminary professor from Chicago, as if to shrug his shoulders, wrote in the summer of 1968, "It seems that it can be safely argued that a Catholic possesses a genuine freedom of conscience in every area of his life."[63] After the breakthrough of conscience into the Catholic discourse during the struggle between the AWP and O'Boyle, Catholics became more willing to point out law's limits. The AWP raised a litany of questions about moral life and forced church authorities to respond. How far could the idea of conscience-following be pushed within the Catholic Church? To what ends could a conscience be followed? Did conscience take primacy over matters of sexuality just like it did over the matter of conscription? Is following conscience an end in itself? Priests like Claretian Gregory Kenny were ready to push the envelope: "Today we live in the age of the individual conscience," Kenny proclaimed in 1972. "This central truth of Christian ethics has re-entered the Christian spotlight."[64] But not all agreed that conscience belonged at the center of Catholic life.

The Revenge of Doctrine

Cardinal O'Boyle escalated his attack on the AWP's campaign after issuing the suspensions and evictions. He moved to win in the realm of ideas after clearing the field with the strong arm of his ecclesiastical office. He issued a second pastoral letter, "The Catholic Conscience," and John Ford and Germain Grisez placed copies of a pamphlet they had written, *Sex in Marriage*, in parishes across the city. O'Boyle continued to assert that the law, clearly articulated by church authority, binds a Catholic conscience to obedience.[65] Ford and Grisez's *Sex and Marriage* left Catholics no room to follow conscience in the arena of artificial birth control. "A Catholic forms his conscience in the light of what the Church teaches in the sense that he forms it in accordance with what the Church teaches," the pamphlet explained.[66]

The intensity of O'Boyle's critique does not diminish the importance of conscience to global 1968. In fact, the criticism only proves the thesis: conscience became such an important category in the church in 1968 that a number of prominent Catholics felt the need to respond. Dietrich von Hildebrand, William Buckley Jr., and Pope Paul VI joined O'Boyle in the effort to prove to the faithful that an intense investment in subjective truth-creation capacities does more harm than good.[67] Buckley, author of *God and Man at Yale* and the star of his own TV talk show, accused conscience rights advocates of failing to consider the consequences of their arguments. "It seems to me that the Church has an obligation to especially emphasize the fact that to follow one's conscience without a total consultation and a submissive consultation with the contending position as specified by the Church is an act of hubris," he maintained. "Those people who speak so confidently about the supremacy of the conscience haven't really faced up to the consequences of that supremacy."[68] That winter, the need to properly position conscience as an applicator of law reached the Vatican. Speaking to a public audience in February 1969, Paul VI offered his critique: "We must make one observation about the present-day concern to make conscience the supreme and exclusive guide of human conduct. We often hear it repeated, as if it were an undisputable maxim, that man's whole morality must consist in following his own conscience. . . . But we must stress . . . [that] conscience of itself is not the final arbiter of the moral value of actions it suggests. Conscience is the interpreter of an interior and higher norm."[69] What set O'Boyle apart from the other critics was his power and willingness to anathematize those lower on his local hierarchy who publicly called for recognizing traditional subjective truth-generating capacities. Critiques, and O'Boyle's assertion of ecclesiastical power, contributed mightily to the very idea he sought to silence.

But could O'Boyle deny the strong backing of conscience by Catholic doctrine? He, too, existed in the duality of objective and subjective. No official Catholic literature promoted the external completely at the expense of the internal. O'Boyle and the members of his team knew that authority figures did not simply program or engineer an internality to obey the laws. Catholics had two authorities, law and conscience, that fundamentally structured their thinking. Ford and Grisez—experts in moral theology and the cardinal's key theological advisers—could not deny the orthodox position that the individual forms his or her own conscience and then acts in the world on the reality created through subjectivity. Ford's consistent defense of conscience in the civil realm on conscientious objection or in his lectures on confession techniques could not be completely repressed in the dispute over artificial birth control. *Sex in Marriage* granted that in regard to artificial birth control, "each individual Catholic can and does form his conscience on this and every other subject."[70] Only after this sentence appeared did the authors of the pamphlet backpedal to make clear that a Catholic formed his or her own conscience—but exclusively with law.

Cardinal O'Boyle also had to qualify his definition of the Catholic conscience to avoid the appearance of undermining key teachings found in Catholic doctrine. The debate in Washington, DC, made the doctrine's twinning of obedience and emancipation a glaring contradiction. O'Boyle conceded that Catholics had to follow their conscience when they reached a conclusion—any conclusion—in these internal illuminations: "Conscience is our best judgment concerning what is right and wrong, and we must follow our judgment."[71] He also recognized that Catholics who followed an erroneous conscience remained within the Catholic fold.[72] His definition of conscience, he explained, "by no means contravene[d] the truth that every person is bound to follow his conscience."[73] Ford, Grisez, and O'Boyle could not suspend the radical side of the doctrine in the heat of 1968. The doctrine came with both a conservative side and a radical edge. It proved difficult to speak of one without mentioning its twin.

The priests who sided with O'Boyle diagnosed the District of Columbia's theological and institutional crisis as the logical outcome of doctrine itself. These conservative priests acknowledged that the teaching on conscience had built-in warring components. Father Robert W. Lawson of Bridgton, Maine, published an editorial in the *Boston Globe* in December of 1968 explaining how the church's "official sources" encouraged the following of conscience yet simultaneously made clear that conscience, prone to error, required authority and law to be set aright. "The present controversy within the Roman Catholic Church about family planning is due in large part to the ambiguous treatment of 'conscience' in official Catholic literature," he wrote.[74] The debate in the district played out in public the drama of a doctrine. The catechisms and religion classes of the twentieth-century Catholic Church made thousands of its laypeople and priests literate—through repetitions of the tradition—in the language of conscience rights. The church gave its own laity and priests conceptual tools to undermine authority. Lawson acknowledged that following conscience seemed plausible but concluded that only a strong assertion of law from O'Boyle could end the crisis in the proper fashion.

Another priest from Chesapeake Bay, also a supporter of O'Boyle's, yielded the same theological ground to the men of the association. Cardinal Lawrence Shehan, archbishop of Baltimore and the ranking member of the bishops' committee initially tasked with mediating the dispute between O'Boyle and the AWP, received a letter from a priest, William Kenneally, pointing out that the see-saw debate between law and conscience in the nation's capital emanated from centuries-old tensions. "A point which would seem to require re-emphasis is the fact that for the conscientious Catholic, the teaching authority of the Church [is the] norm for the formation of a true and right conscience," the Vincentian wrote. The AWP needed reminding that consciences were to be formed under the law. Then he pointed out to the archbishop that it was not so simple: "All readily admit—and have been doing so for centuries—that everyone is obliged to follow his conscience when it commands or forbids."[75] Kenneally backed O'Boyle; many lay Catholics did in fact possess faulty subjective perceptions on the matter of artificial birth control. As this was the case, the priest explained, clergy had the obligation to correct erroneous consciences with clear pronouncements of law. But the doctrine made clear that Catholics must connect conscience to the law with a self-directed process of formation. Kenneally, and the archbishop himself, set the context but could not forge the links between objective and subjective. Lay Catholics had to form the internal guide for morality with external sources. Then they had to follow the conscience they themselves reared with self-powered moral formation. "This delicate procedure requires the grace of God," Kenneally's letter concluded.[76] At stake in the debate about contraception and conscience was who in the Catholic Church could perform the "delicate procedure" of forming conscience—the individual or the church's laws.

The two wings of the debate had human forms in 1968. Cardinal Patrick O'Boyle and one of the priests he had suspended, Father Shane MacCarthy, were both ordained clergymen, and both possessed self-identities as men of tradition. Both were good Irish Catholics: the two men believed they were keeping coreligionists away from the fires of hell. MacCarthy remained on archdiocesan property after his suspension, though how his inflammatory sermons escaped the notice of O'Boyle is something of a mystery. When a reporter for the *Washington Daily News* caught up with him in early October 1968, MacCarthy was hopeful that the AWP would not be punished for "saying what it believe[d]."[77] He rejected the label "dissenter" and dismissed the notion that he was rebelling against church teaching. In linking himself to tradition, MacCarthy told the paper that the AWP defended "the right to respect conscience in matters where there are legitimate options" and that the group was not "dissenting from the encyclical or from the Pope."[78] He did not fancy himself as a radical priests fighting for the sexual emancipation of the laity but took himself to be a guardian of a traditional moral system that respected both law and conscience. O'Boyle, for his part, also understood himself to be a keeper of teachings hundreds of years old.

The divisibility of the doctrine and its resulting intellectual fission careened through the Catholic press. John Deedy, editor of *Commonweal*, a storied Catholic periodical meant for an educated laity, understood O'Boyle to be squashing a key plank of Catholic tradition that bishops and theologians feted at midcentury. "Current Church controversies have buried one pleasant Catholic concept," Deedy declared.[79] "Remember when churchmen used to speak of conscience and exalt Thomas à Becket, Thomas More, and Joan of Arc—especially Joan of Arc—as exemplars of the Catholic tradition on rights of conscience? Remember all the lectures and sermons?"[80] The church celebrated stands of conscience in midcentury pedagogy, and it offered many narratives of heroic stands of conscience against corrupt powers. "Then," Deedy wrote, referring to 1950s-era Catholicism and the political theology of conscience, "the witness of conscience was huzzahed unqualifiedly."[81] He accused O'Boyle of treason. Perhaps he hadn't realized that Catholic leaders like O'Boyle were remaining consistent in advocating conscience rights from the state even as they issued injunctions to crush subjective truth-generators in the church's own house. Conscience, men like O'Boyle thought, could only follow truth: the state-issued draft law was unjust, but the church's law on contraception was clear and just. Still, Deedy was right to comment on the dissonance created by the two postures and the cardinal's selective application of the doctrine. If doctrine holds in one area, it holds equally in another. Church officials who pumped these ideas into Catholic education and public debates about political power now wanted conscience instructed exclusively by church laws on matters of artificial birth control. O'Boyle could have his own cake, but he would have to eat it too.

The Ambiguity of Victory and Defeat

The continuity of doctrine proved to be a boon to individual liberation in some ways. But also, due to its transcendence of time and situation, the Catholic Church's teaching on conscience seemed to trap the AWP and O'Boyle in a debate that could never reach a satisfying conclusion. Both outcomes—law over conscience, conscience over law—seemed to carry the day. The rally and the sit-in, along with the constant campaigning and circulation of conscience letters, only earned the AWP formal recognition of the duality in the National Conference of Catholic Bishops document *Human Life in Our Day*, released on November 15, 1968. In paragraph 20, the bishops' statement affirmed the possibility that conscience formation could result in "responsible parenthood." The bishops contended that responsible parenthood accepts "the properly formed conscience of spouses in all the judgments, options, and choices which add up to the awesome decision to give, postpone, or decline life."[82] Here the AWP scored a victory for conscience rights: the formation of conscience allowed Catholics to use artificial birth control and kept them walking along the footsteps of tradition. Further down the line in paragraph 41, however, the statement made clear that *Humanae vitae* carried the authentic teaching of the divine law. The ambiguity was inscribed, and reinscribed, into the tradition.

The AWP could count a few intellectual victories. High-ranking members of the Catholic hierarchy dared not deny the rights of conscience in public addresses made in the wake of the AWP's struggle with O'Boyle. A month after publishing *Human Life in Our Day*, John Dearden, president of the National Conference of Catholic Bishops, explained the bishops' take on conscience at a press conference. Dearden appeared to accept, with verbal recognition, the AWP's argument about the importance of following a well-formed conscience. He recognized the long-standing teaching that conscience constituted a sacred space, closed off from the outside, where believers encountered God with candor. The encyclical and *Human Life in Our Day*, he explained, did not "seek to pass judgment on those who independently form their conscience contrary to the authentic church teaching. We are not qualified to judge. We cannot move in from the outside and say thus and so are right or wrong."[83] Dearden, in other words, accepted the limits of the law, the external benchmark for moral behavior, in shaping the conscience. Phrases like these were minor but symbolic victories for the AWP. Words, however, were small consolation for men still barred from preaching, teaching, and hearing confessions—the heart and soul of their calling as priests.

O'Boyle won an institutional victory by way of attrition. The methodical gradualism he had applied to civil rights issues proved effective as a method to wear down the AWP. Three members left the priesthood in October 1968 after the initial wave of suspensions and evictions in September. Nearly half the priests would leave the movement after November. Fighting for the rights of conscience inside the church itself—even if AWP members imagined themselves as purveyors of tradition—meant paying a hefty price. Some of these priests assumed positions in the secular world that resembled their priestly ministries, such as social work. Some started families. By August of 1969, only nineteen of the original thirty-nine penalized priests had chosen to maintain their status as priests.[84]

But the teaching and preaching of the theology of conscience remained a viable option, marking another stealthy victory for the AWP. Four priests—Fathers Raymond Kemp, Andre Bouchard, John Cunico, and Shane MacCarthy—sought an agreement with O'Boyle that would return them to their full-time responsibilities. All of them worked in inner-city Catholic parishes and respected the cardinal's commitment to civil rights. O'Boyle dropped his requirement of a public apology and asked only that the four priests teach *Humanae vitae* in accordance with the principles as laid out in the National Conference of Catholic Bishops' *Human Life in Our Day*. Only Father MacCarthy rejected the offer. The three other priests accepted, because the document, after all, provided a considerable loophole for the formation of conscience in producing "responsible parenthood."

In the spring of 1971—nearly three years after the dispute—the show-down between Cardinal O'Boyle and what remained of the AWP underwent two weeks of hearings in a special Vatican court in Rome, the Sacred Con-gregation for the Clergy. The court was headed by John Wright, bishop of Pittsburgh, a staunch defender of *Humanae vitae*, and, of course, a theorizer of conscience rights.[85] A few active members of the AWP took the dispute through the established procedures for mediating church arguments. The hearings considered the content of the group's "Statement of Conscience" as well as O'Boyle's response to it (suspensions and evictions). The Sacred Congregation opted for a pastoral solution, not a judicial or canonical rul-ing. Striking a blow against the AWP, the court found that O'Boyle's mea-sures were within the parameters of church law. He had the authority to sus-pend the priests. The court then affirmed that *Humanae vitae* was authentic church teaching.

But the traditional role of conscience also carried the day. The AWP con-vinced a court of canon law in Rome to concede yet again that Catholics had "inviolable" rights of conscience. The Congregation's ruling came with a five-point section on conscience. The fifth and final point acknowledged the side of the tradition laypeople inhabited when they made the choice to use artificial birth control: the document concluded that "in the final analy-sis, conscience is inviolable and no man is to be forced to act in a manner contrary to his conscience, as the moral tradition of the church attests."[86] Catholics could invoke the rights of conscience and follow conscience, but they might pay a price even in the church, as do rebels who engaged in acts of civil disobedience to critique race relations or war. All that the remaining priests of AWP were required to do for reinstation to full ministry was to of-fer a written or oral statement affirming these propositions. The ambiguity of doctrine remained.

MacCarthy—as he had dreamed of doing throughout the fall of 1968—sacrificed his priesthood on the altar of conscience rights. After enduring nearly seven years of suspension from ministry, he left the priesthood in 1975. That year he married Karen Nuebert, with whom he would have two children. He transformed his religious vocation and social concern into a long career working in global charities like the Peace Corps and the United States Agency for International Development. He moved from a global debate on conscience rights to appointments in Ghana, Swaziland, South Africa, and Egypt.

Cardinal O'Boyle clearly won the institutional battle. He ended careers and put those who wanted to return to the clerical fold through a long series of court proceedings. He earned a victory through tactics of gradualism and attrition: half the force that had fought for conscience rights in 1968 would leave the priesthood. But O'Boyle lost the battle for ideas: the language of conscience continued to proliferate in the Catholic Church itself.

Conclusion

In the summer and fall of 1968, a social movement led by Catholic priests coalesced around the defense of conscience rights in the area of marital sex and contraception. What began as a series of reminders to Cardinal Patrick O'Boyle to acknowledge traditional rights of conscience evolved into a set of marches, demonstrations, and letter-writing campaigns to forcibly claim these rights. These priests did not invoke conscience in a vacuum: not only did they have the backing of certain segments of the American laity, they were also tapping into the theologies promoted by scholars like Bernard Häring and key post–Vatican II texts like the Dutch Catechism. But the rebellious traditionalists came up against the strong stand made by Cardinal O'Boyle for *Humanae vitae* and the law. O'Boyle, as this book shows, pursued a legitimate interpretation of the doctrine. The tactics he deployed to uphold the law, however, were controversial. When he suspended priests like T. Joseph O'Donoghue, John Corrigan, and Shane MacCarthy, his actions sparked a 1968-style showdown between authority and "the people." The terms for this dispute were set by a unique Catholic teaching on the proper calibration of objective and subjective that originated in the thirteenth-century thought of Thomas Aquinas.

The debate over conscience rights never allowed Catholics to transcend the categories of the medieval doctrine. O'Boyle and his team of supporters never ignored completely the viability of following conscience, and some of their publications even acknowledged the importance of acting on an erroneous conscience. Both sides scored victories and incurred defeats in the official statements published after the debate and in the official rulings on the matter issued by courts at the Vatican. But American Catholics continued after the 1968 debate over *Humanae vitae* to seek solutions to moral problems in sources other than obedience to the law. The capacity of the law to define reality had been seriously curtailed by the Association of Washington Priests' stand for conscience rights. The next story to tell is how a generation of Catholics applied the tools of modern psychology and Jewish scholarship to conscience to make it strong enough to offer guidance in a world seemingly bereft of strong and clear laws.

FIVE

Psychology and the Self

Conscience has traditionally been understood as a judgment made by an individual regarding the moral licitness or illicitness of an act that one is considering doing. Today, however, while retaining this moral meaning, theologians generally incorporate it into the psychological meaning of conscience, namely, self-awareness and self-understanding.

—Robert J. Rigali, SJ (1975)

Modern psychology has contributed a great deal toward our understanding of conscience, its formation and malformation.

—Jeffrey J. Keefe, OFM (1977)

In June 1969, W. Norris Clarke, known affectionately to his fellow Jesuits as "Norrie," delivered a conference paper with characteristic panache. A popular teacher at Fordham University, he hooked his audience by describing philosophy as the effort "to take possession of our own experience in depth, and to situate it as a vision of reality as a whole."[1] The directors of the university's Pastoral Psychology Institute had invited Father Clarke, a Thomistic philosopher, to take part in an interdisciplinary academic panel, "The Mature Conscience." Clarke took the institute's mandate to heart. He deployed the insights of the behavioral sciences, especially psychology, to understand a theological concept. He peppered his paper with quotes from Thomas Aquinas's *Summa Theologica*. But he also uttered phrases during his presentation like "well-developed," "self-awareness," "self-possession," "motive force," and "inner dynamo." Conscience can be described as "mature," Clarke argued, "when the voice of my conscience is really the voice of my own deepest and most authentic self speaking out to guide my actions."[2]

In 1966, Jesuit philosopher Bernard Lonergan described the late twentieth century as the years when the Catholic Church and the rest of the world moved from a "classicist world-view to historical-mindedness."[3] In a classicist framework, truths exist outside persons and assume a timeless quality. The classicist world is structured, traditional, and inherently conservative. The laws that govern it are ironclad, and no human effort can change the structures that give hue and heft to the universe. With historical-mindedness arrives personalism, existentialism, and subject-centered thought. Truth emerges from the flux and chaos of the universe. It no longer exists outside persons but arrives within them. Psychology spread rapidly across the landscape of American Catholicism as the classicist world fractured into protean historical-mindedness. In the same moment, the traditional theology of conscience, renewed with the vernacular of psychology, also appeared incessantly in American Catholic life. Psychology—interspersed with existentialism, personalism, and developmental theories—transformed conscience, long a staple of Catholic moral thought, into an entity that grew and matured. Psychology enhanced a Catholic tradition with roots in the medieval world, allowing thinkers like Jesuit Norris Clarke to integrate maturity, authenticity, and self-awareness with Aquinas's teachings on the concept.

American Catholics, despite some attraction to psychology and the occasional priest who studied it against the wishes of his superiors, by and large managed to resist the allure of the discipline for most of the twentieth century.[4] When psychology did break into Catholic circles in the 1960s in the years surrounding the Second Vatican Council, it is understood to have produced unsettling results. Robert Kugelmann contends that humanistic psychology helped dismantle a hierarchical understanding of the church and replace it with person-to-person relationships.[5] Conscience is a natural object of interest for psychologists and psychoanalysis, because it is so internal and even mental. But American Catholic thinkers who adopted psychological lenses became preoccupied with the concept. They self-consciously built on the traditional lessons about conscience found in moral theology manuals, catechisms, and textbooks. They built twentieth-century individualism onto a thirteenth-century foundation.

This book has been recounting how the loss of law's moral authority facilitated the rise of conscience. The intense debate over contraception in the District of Columbia throughout the summer and fall of 1968 demonstrated the limits of ecclesiastical law, swinging moral authority over to subjectivity on matters of sexuality. The civil law lost authority over Catholic conscience when politicians and generals demanded participation in an immoral war. This chapter shows that law staggered after a concomitant blow from complexity. In a world suddenly understood to be in flux and full of pulsating energies, one slipping into Lonergan's historical-mindedness, law could no longer define reality. Psychology presented a solution from the depths of tradition: forming and following conscience.[6] With the authority of law jeopardized by its inability to anticipate situations and its failure to produce moral behaviors in the world, Catholics increasingly needed to be equipped with the mature conscience that helped them navigate a complex moral landscape rife with authority figures who yearned for political domination.

Priests deployed the tools of psychology to produce a new type of political and moral agent. This individual had to become a virtuous subject without relying too heavily on the law. A strict obedience to a code produced a pathological creature and a political liability: this person obeyed laws to please superiors. These craven automatons gladly remained under the thumb of local authorities and gleefully carried out destructive political programs to remain in an authority's good graces. To put it in the psychological language used by Father Clarke, these individuals had "immature consciences" that "allowed an external voice" to dominate their internal development. Catholics needed a mature conscience that drew from the law prudently, not exclusively. Actions had to enter the world from the inside to the outside, not from the external pressing down on the internal.

The political and moral urgency to strengthen conscience derived in part from a new openness to Jewish sources of psychoanalysis and developmental psychology on the part of American Catholics, particularly clergymen. Catholics had kept a distance from psychology for most of the twentieth century because of the discipline's Jewish roots. But the works of Sigmund Freud, Erich Fromm, and Lawrence Kohlberg suddenly became helpful to them in the 1960s and 1970s in their effort to understand how a subjectivity developed beyond an unhealthy dependence on the law. Jewish scholars like Fromm and Kohlberg, considering the lessons of Nazi Germany and the Holocaust, taught Catholics to free their internal orbs from the dominance of external figures and to manifest a conscience that truly spoke from within the self in the name of self-sovereignty. From Freud, priests learned that a nucleus lorded over by a parent or communal authority on the matter of sex produced unstable individuals who chained themselves to a parochial existence. In the same stroke, Catholics encountered major distinctions between their brand of modern and medieval Thomism and a Jewish thought much more amendable to secular American modernity. But, as this chapter shows, the effort to learn from Jewish psychoanalysts and psychologists on the part of Catholic priests and confessors marks a significant and creative ecumenical endeavor that shaped the intellectual and political trajectory of the conscience rights movement.

Conscience and Developmental Psychology

It took a European to break down the walls that American Catholics had raised between conscience and psychology. In 1963, German moral theologian Bernard Häring—a scholar of global repute after publishing his masterpiece, *The Law of Christ,* in 1954—gave a series of lectures on new trends in theology to a group of seminarians and their professors at Mount St. Alphonsus Seminary in Esopus, New York. He encouraged the future confessors to study psychology. For most of the twentieth century, American priests had heard the opposite message. Jesuit John Ford found psychological tools ill-suited to understanding conscience. His contemporary Francis Connell argued that psychologists study consciousness, not conscience, a term better understood by scholars familiar with natural law.[7] Fulton Sheen called Sigmund Freud's "relegating our mistakes to our irresponsible babyhood" a "prejudicial way of thinking" in his 1949 best-selling book, *Peace of Soul.*[8]

Häring urged priests to study psychology and sociology to better understand penitents, the main constituency priests served. A study of the mind—and societal structures—revealed what was possible or impossible for a penitent in a given environment. These realities could only be understood if Catholics seriously limited the law's ability to define morality. In fact, the Catholic Church's overextension of statutes formed the backbone of Häring's Mount St. Alphonsus Seminary lectures. A confessor might wrongly urge a penitent to abstain from sexual activity, although sexual gratification was easing a painful neurosis. It might not be possible for a penitent to simply obey the law. "In all things we must have some knowledge of psychology and sociology; we must continue to study these subjects," he warned the priests and future priests. "Otherwise we will make terrible mistakes."[9] Häring's lecture series foregrounded the call for the church to study sociology and psychology as promulgated by the Second Vatican Council in *The Pastoral Constitution on the Modern World,* a 1965 document that Häring helped draft.

Catholic writers remained skeptical about Freud's concept of conscience in the early 1960s, but they also challenged Fulton Sheen's wholesale dismissal of the Viennese doctor. Freud understood conscience as the individual's "superego"—a mental faculty created by parents and community members that injected pain when local norms were flouted or soothed with pleasure when dictates were obeyed. Catholics found the superego limited, because it could never be connected—through the process of formation—to the laws that transcended the individual's insular existence. The concept of superego only allowed for a modest restructuring of categories installed during infancy. A Dominican priest declared confidently in a 1961 article that "theologians and philosophers . . . rightly stigmatized Freud's concept of moral conscience as a caricature of the real thing."[10] Yet Catholics like this priest started to find this study of the concept intriguing. In light of Freud's findings, it could not be denied that authorities formed an individual's internal monitor in the very early stages of life. Catholic intellectuals ought to admit that "the superego . . . deepened our insights into the actual workings of the human psychism."[11] Belgian theologian Louis Janssens underwent this same debate in his 1965 book, *Freedom of Conscience and Religious Freedom*. Janssens, a professor of theology at Louvain University in Belgium, concluded that Freud did not properly grasp the nature of conscience, because his superego faculty left no room for educative training of reason, as undertaken by the church. Nonetheless, he thought Catholics could recognize clearly that "unconsciously the child guide[d] himself according to the example of his educators and he adopt[ed] the ideal of life which govern[ed] his environment."[12] Psychology and psychoanalysis established a beachhead in Catholic thought as thinkers like these accepted a number of Freud's insights.

In the mid-1960s, Catholic clergymen looking through a Freudian lens came to see the laws of their own church and its education system as creating superego lay Catholics. A generation of Catholics were thought to possess a conscience that reacted like the crack of a whip when a Catholic failed to observe laws. These faithful aimed to please authority with their obedience to rules. When a Catholic ignored the rules of the Eucharistic fast or ate meat on a Friday, his or her inner enforcer induced guilt. Such scrupulous superego Catholics found comfort in observing particular laws that forbade eating broth-based soups or limited the number of cigarettes that could be smoked before someone crossed the threshold into sin. A Benedictine priest who taught at Sacred Heart Seminary in Detroit thought that Catholics were not autonomous enough to form a conscience independent of authority. In Catholic life, he lamented, "the only conceivable function that conscience [could] have [was] to oblige conformity to the law."[13] The catechisms of the Catholic Church and the denomination's massive education system programmed the behavior of its rank-and-file members, rendering them docile. Its educators drummed into faithful pupils from a young age the duty to obey laws to avoid sin—and priests who had adopted psychological concepts thought that schoolchildren consequently struggled for the rest of their lives to overcome a punitive internal regulator. Catholic education often prevented "the emergence of a personal conscience," theologian Charles Davis observed, a remark that mid-twentieth-century Catholics would have found curious.[14]

The work of another important twentieth-century Jewish psychoanalyst, Erich Fromm, enabled Catholics to call on the insights of psychology to make a second, more optimistic intellectual move to defeat their legalistic internal censor. Fromm's 1947 book, Man for Himself, identified two strands of conscience. The Freudian superego conscience—which Catholic thinkers saw in their church's own members—Fromm dubbed "the authoritarian conscience." This conscience was captive to outside forces, so the self felt obligated to obey and please these external sources of authority. Key to understanding the authoritarian conscience was the notion that this internal faculty was operated as if by a remote control handled by an external, often corrupt authority.[15] But Fromm's research also led him to conclude that this was merely a preliminary phase in conscience formation, not a permanent destination—an argument Catholics were readily prepared to agree with, because they championed processes of subjective formation.

A superego could be further developed to become what Fromm called "the humanistic conscience." This internality was "our own voice, present in every human being and independent of external sanctions and rewards."[16] Fromm contended that attention to the self and a concern for listening to one's own voice develops a strong conscience, which serves as an individual's best moral guide in a dangerous world. The agent owns a humanistic conscience in the sense that it speaks from that individual.

Psychological frameworks identified conscience as both a problem and its solution. Conscience could be society's worst enemy (authoritarian) or the individual's best friend (humanistic). It was a tale of two cities—one internal and mature, the other under external influence and puerile. Both sides of the conscience were described in a 1966 article by a Redemptorist priest for the Liguorian, his order's American magazine. He admitted that conscience could be an authoritarian agent: "if external laws, commands, and even irrational whims of parents, teachers, priests, and others in authority [were] the foundation of your weak little voice in your conscience," then the individual could rightly conclude that he or she is being dominated.[17] But the clergyman held out hope that the conscience, if properly formed, could become an anthropocentric force that spoke from the person's core and guided that individual in each decision. For those possessing such a conscience, it meant "more than obeying laws" and became a "strong voice within" that "knows, feels, appreciates, and judges" a situation with the individual's interest in mind. Catholic writers included the humanistic conscience in their articles, a trend that augured the growing influence of psychology on their notions of selfhood.

Fromm's bifurcation of superego quickly underwent a trisection. Psychologists split conscience into three parts in the mid-1960s and Catholic thinkers followed their lead, strengthening theological notions with these fresh secular insights. Psychologists of the 1960s identified three drives in conscience: (1) logical choice, (2) unconscious feelings/desires, and (3) goals to achieve/projections. Freud's work continued to inspire the categories—his superego lurked in the unconscious, and his "ego-ideal" provided goals—but the arrangement into discrete functions was novel among scholars who dedicated their careers to studying the mind. Secular psychologists and Catholics remade into the first steps of a much longer developmental process what Freud had declared a permanent condition of submission and pain. The Catholic thinker most influential in diffusing the three-pronged theory of conscience in church circles was Jesuit Louis Monden. Monden spent his career at the borderlands of psychology and theology: he served as professor of religion and psychology at the John XIII Seminary in Belgium and held a concurrent appointment at the University of Louvain. In his book *Sin, Liberty and Law*, which was translated from French and published in the United Kingdom and the United States in 1966, Monden argued that conscience is characterized by three levels of orientation: instinctual, moral, and religious. His typologies of conscience made the rounds in US Catholic media in 1966 and 1967, appearing in articles published by the *Sign, Continuum*, and *St. Anthony's Messenger*.[18]

Labeling the distinct orientation levels of conscience—and propelling the movement of conscience to a higher plateau—was part of the broader effort to match the traditional faculty to a dynamic moment in history when laws seemed to have lost a grip on reality. It became morally and political imperative that conscience evolve from a superego demeanor into a posture of maturity. The first orientation of conscience was instinctual, and it resembled the superego. As Monden explained in his book, the law, which commanded the instinctual conscience, came "not from within but from without . . . [and] by means of prohibitions and taboos" curbed individual expression.[19] The instinctual conscience merely transmitted the inclination to obey laws. When kicking into the moral drive (level 2), conscience inspired the individual to realize that he or she possessed freedom. This mode of conscience spurred a drive for self-realization. On the moral level, conscience acted "as a power of discrimination deciding in every choice what [would] promote authentic self-realization and what [would] stand in its way."[20] Conscience appraised each and every action, taking the step when the move promoted the authentic self, and bypassing an action that did not. On the third level, the religious plane, the individual acted out of love and without any prodding from an external law. An internal nerve center, this third incarnation of conscience understood sin not as breaking a law but as "refusing God's love." This "religious conscience" was what Catholics often referred to as the "mature conscience"—and Monden argued that it should be the goal of all Catholic ethics and education to foster the mature consciences in the church's members. A mature conscience, explored in detail below, took the place of the law and directed the Catholic to a lifetime of extensive spiritual growth.[21]

The inroads developmental psychology made into Catholic thought can be seen most clearly in how Catholic writers conveyed the moral evolution of children. Catholic mothers deployed the tools of psychology—stages of development, types of conscience, and the neuroses generated by strict obedience to law—to describe the moral journey a child made from infancy to adolescence. Mrs. Fank Marbach, a mother of eight, called on fellow mothers to downplay obedience to the law so that children could develop a "love-infused" conscience. "In trying to form a God-loving rather than God-fearing conscience," she counseled (adopting Monden's terms), child rearing would be providing "a cocoon in which the child's instinctual conscience develop[ed] more easily into a moral one."[22] Good Catholic parents helped a subjectivity transition smoothly and organically from one stage to the next. If parents pushed obedience to the law too vigorously at home, it would distort a child's conscience. Felicitas Betz, a German Catholic educator, warned parents in a 1968 essay that "the greater the pressure [to follow law], the more difficult it [would] be for the conscience to free itself in later years."[23]

The Catholic parent who understood developmental psychology recognized the moment the child realized a higher form of conscience, affording a mom or dad a considerable advantage and offering reassurance they were successfully rearing a future responsible and autonomous Catholic subject. Marbach noted that children developed the first inklings of self-rule between the ages of six and eight by demonstrating an ability to make their own moral decisions apart from their parents. A child first identified the mother as his or her conscience, allowing an external authority to command internal life. Then on to school, where for the first few years of formal education the child recognized the schoolteacher as his or her conscience. Finally, early adolescence was about the time that the true conscience evolved by undergoing "a process which detache[d] it still further from the child's parents and teachers," Betz wrote.[24] The goal of Catholic parenting—like Monden's goal for the entire church—was to produce in children a well-developed subjective moral guide that encouraged prudent self-governance.

At the dawn of the 1970s, Catholic priests and educators made the destruction of superegos an explicit goal of religious education. A stunted subjectivity, entrapped in a cycle of anger and rage, finding comfort only in submission, perceived only the law; thus, those who possessed it could never see the total field of relations and realities unfolding before them. Jesuit John Glaser, a teacher at St. Mary's on the Lake, the major seminary for the Archdiocese of Chicago, celebrated the process by which abolition of superegos unfolded "a larger horizon" for the individual.[25] Glaser concluded that the destruction of legalistic internal censors "must be affirmed, encouraged, and fostered, just as any other discovery of God's will [was] the object of our benevolence and beneficence."[26] Catholics viewed moral training in the church through a prism of psychologically tinted glasses. "To help the child pass from the ruthless superego infantile morality to a healthy and positive mature conscience" should become a top catechetical goal of the 1970s, declared another priest.[27]

Catholics who distrusted the law faced an immediate question: how should a Catholic form a conscience in a context in which law had been repudiated? The church's priests and educators naturally turned to psychological ideas for answers. On the one hand, the work of shaping subjectivity occurred with or without the individual's effort: it occurred naturally as an individual aged and developed. On the other hand, the kneading of the self's internal core had to rely on multiple sources, secular and religious, due to the law's failures. Moral guidance moved, then, from the singularity of the law to the plurality of a range of social and cultural sources. Brother Gabriel Moran, a theologian at Manhattan College, recommended that conscience formation comprise reading scriptures, consulting the hierarchy, and "our own critical intelligence."[28] Another Catholic educator suggested that formation be guided by books, articles, and trusted authorities from inside and outside the church. Each Catholic must then "weigh the information [gathered] in consultation."[29] As the church was one of the sources of instruction as well as a source of self-cohesion, the institution's lessons deserved prolonged consideration. Catholic thinkers never advised the individual to neglect church sources in cultivating a refined moral subjectivity. That person could realize a correctly formed inner self only after consulting "the whole Church" for help in resolving the conscience.[30] Molding the person's nucleus with the full powers of the church meant listening to bishops, the pope, the law, and the church's theologians. It also meant giving attention to situation, emotions, institutional context, and relationships.

Sound conscience formation created the mature conscience. In turn, the mature conscience delivered to Catholics two valuable powers for navigating moral life in a context of exploding complexities. First, a seasoned internality understood why an act ought to be performed: out of virtue, not obedience to the law. "As the child reaches out toward the attainment of a mature conscience," a priest explained in a 1972 article, "he should be encouraged to see the wrongness of his faults such as lying, cheating, stealing, etc., in the view of the harm it does to another creature of God."[31] An act of cheating or stealing was not wrong because it violated the Ten Commandments but due to the fact that it transgressed against another individual's divine personhood. The mature conscience, developed beyond the parochial superego, apprehended this reality. Instilled in a Catholic child, such an attitude would carry into the adult years.

Second, the mature conscience was a highly refined internal guide strong enough to offer guidance after law melted away as a moral authority. Priests increasingly shifted the locus of moral authority from the external laws to the strong internal guide of the mature conscience during the 1960s and 1970s. "Because of the complexity of moral decisions in contemporary society . . . the Church is less inclined to give specific, detailed instructions as it did in the past," a Dominican priest wrote, capturing this sentiment exactly: "This approach is less directive and demands that Catholics develop a mature Christian conscience, imbued with the love of Christ and the spirit of the Gospels."[32] No longer should the Catholic Church rear men and women who followed law; instead, it should seek to equip each believer with an adult internality. The planners of the Fordham conference discussed earlier in the chapter had set aside time for an entire scholarly panel on the mature conscience, testifying to the importance of the concept and its interdisciplinary constitution. A paper delivered there by John R. Cavanagh, a psychiatrist who ran his own private practice and taught courses in pastoral psychology at the Catholic University of America, evaluated the maturity of a conscience by the individual's ability to assess facts and quickly appraise the moral surroundings of each situation. This well-formed internality confronted the particular data and integrated it with the person's emotions: "A mature conscience is well-informed concerning the facts and is molded in conformity to the individual's capacity to discern realistically and react emotionally to the requirements imposed on him by a situation."[33] Catholics considered a range of factors in addition to laws—but not completely without the clarity offered by a code. A proper formation of mature consciences: the greatest moral hope in a world without legitimate rules.

Personalism and Existentialism

Catholic writers, in moving conscience toward personalist and existential definitions, liked to tell readers what a conscience was not. A first step in establishing conscience as a key component of 1960s Catholic personalism or a core of the existential Catholic self was to make clear that it was not automated. A Franciscan declared in 1964 that conscience was not "some type of gadget attached to my soul."[34] Bernard Häring said that conscience did not provide a "mechanical application of general rules."[35] For laywoman Fank Marbach, conscience could never be a "red and green traffic light that blinks Go and Stop."[36] Conscience was not a machine that an authority planted in the self that signaled when to perform an action or restrain from that action.

Some of the old Scholastic definitions of conscience as an applicator of law seemed stuffy to Catholic writers and detrimental to the development of the individual. Reducing conscience to an instrument entailed a selective reading of the doctrine on their part, choosing to forget the more radical elements of the neo-Scholastic take on conscience, but the machine served as a powerful metaphor. Catholics of the mid-1960s worked to bring the age of subjective data processors to a close. In the recent past, external authorities with remote controls manipulated Catholic subjectivities. But conscience was not a machine, a database, or a computer. It belonged entirely to the person; the individual now had the responsibility to make his or her actions extend from the values held in conscience. Action entered the world after being transmitted from a self-refined nucleus. A Catholic subjectivity did not stop and go at the behest of an outside signal caller. "Conscience is not some mental filing cabinet which I can open and find answers," a priest wrote.[37] The conscience would provide answers—but none were ready-made by laws.

An existentialist conscience assisted the person in bundling multiple moral obligations into a single consolidated entity. In the late 1960s, an increasingly complex world was pulling individuals in several directions. Catholics had specific moral duties to God, spouse, society, family, and other persons. Conceivably, a different self could surface in each distinct situation, a painful prospect for Catholic existentialists. Conscience performed a task of integration, drawing all responsibilities into a nerve center and rendering the Catholic self consistent across the divisiveness of late-modern life. Häring identified the formation of conscience as a task that created an "integrated personality."[38] As it had done in the neo-Scholastic system, conscience linked understanding and action. But the existential conscience had a larger task before it: this whirling core of obligations consolidated a complex Catholic self. Personal responsibility, one's own actions in the world, the rules of the church, multiple relationships, and duty to authority—all competing factors that divide a personality—interlocked and blended in the person's conscience, "a harmonious production of man's personality."[39]

The transformation of conscience from machine to personalist and existentialist entity augmented its importance in American Catholic life. Conscience now contained a Catholic's unified self. It combined the drives of intellect, will, and desire. This internal node synthesized, totalized, and integrated a Catholic self. American culture engaged existentialism through the wildly popular works of Jean-Paul Sartre and Albert Camus; but in the American Catholic community the arrival of existentialism had the strange effect of bolstering a medieval tradition of conscience-following. Existentialism taught Catholics to let a sacred subjectivity understand the full package of the self, grasping all a person's many internal dynamics. "Conscience is an attitude which possesses an entire being," as Marbach put it.[40] Here as elsewhere, American Catholics followed in the footsteps of European theologians. Häring referred to conscience as the "totality of man," and according to Louis Janssens, conscience manifested the "total meaning of existence" as concrete actions in the world.[41] The conscience, because many feelings and ideas dwelled within it, guided the person to perform actions in the world that aligned with his or her whole being.

Catholics deployed the theology of conscience to achieve for the Catholic self what Sartre and Paul Tillich had accomplished for their Protestant and secular enthusiasts: a state of unity inside the self and a radical communion with the divine. A Franciscan cleric imagined conscience as "my whole soul acting as God intended it to act."[42] A Benedictine priest called the conscience a living and breathing space "that [told] the person whether he [was] interacting meaningfully with his environment in relation to the purpose for which he exist[ed]."[43]

Existentialism and personalism built on tradition. An earlier generation of twentieth-century Catholic educators, inspired by Thomas Aquinas, marked conscience as the person's proximate or immediate moral authority. Conscience held sovereignty in moral affairs because it resided closer to the person than did laws. Existentialists and personalists did not want conscience to be thought of as yielding this hallowed ground. Rather, they asked that the traditional prerogatives of the concept be built on and bear a heavier payload. A lay theologian from Manhattan College summed up much of the new literature on conscience when he declared, "To speak of personal conscience as the ultimate norm of morality is certainly not new; [but] to realize all the existential implications of this statement is new within the Catholic fold today."[44] He and other scholars added existentialism, personalism, and psychology to Thomas's classic teachings on conscience. Indeed, several long-standing tenets of the teachings appeared in the new literature. Louis Monden made room for the erroneous conscience amid his profoundly psychological take on the concept.[45] The Dominican editors of the *New Blackfriars* noted that while the self and the concept of conscience became ever more complex, "the circumstances [did] not indeed change the moral law."[46] Janssens did not want his book to be understood as a defense of excessive subjectivism. The Catholic Church still charged the individual with the duty to form a conscience in line with the law, a process not at loggerheads with psychological or existential definitions of conscience. When conscience manifested a "total personality," it brought law along with it. Ultimately, as a Jesuit priest wrote, Catholics simply synthesized the new and the old: "Christian conscience must be formed according to an existential and individual ethic as well as to the essential ethics of the universal moral law."[47]

Jesuit Robert Springer gave the psychological, personalist, and existentialist conscience a manifesto with his 1968 pamphlet, *Conscience and the Behavioral Sciences.* The pamphlet's appearance marked an important event in the intellectual history of psychologizing conscience. It is important to note that Springer had been inspired by the times: he was a theologian who picked up sociology and psychology to study conscience. He served as professor of moral theology at Woodstock College in Woodstock, Maryland, the oldest Jesuit seminary in the United States. The promulgation of *Humanae vitae* in July 1968 likely encouraged him to pen an impassioned defense of subjectivity later that year.

The tools of psychology and sociology could be used to destroy the superego conscience machine—a motor running smoothly in American Catholicism as of 1968 thanks to the pope's condemnation of contraceptives. Springer thought that a "computerized morality" dominated Catholic life: "you feed the data into the machine (object, purpose, and circumstances) and conscience selects the pertinent norm, whereupon out comes the answer."[48] Catholics were not automatons but persons, he argued. To be sure, they were persons in a society undergoing a transformation on a scale not unlike the shifts toward a heliocentric universe or evolutionary existence as described in earlier eras by Copernicus and Darwin.[49] Springer's pamphlet offered a solution to the problem of mechanical obedience and societal flux: develop new norms with modern tools of social science and link them to the conscience, the internal space that theologians had refined for centuries. Sociology captured the changing structures of society, and psychology provided valuable lessons about the internal dimensions of the person. Sociologists knew that society could change; psychologists spent their time studying subjectivity.

Catholics of the institutional church—trapped in a static moral universe—had become so focused on obedience to the law that they had become incapable of developing new objective norms and confirming those norms in the self's sacred inner chambers. Their Catholic conscience could not, Springer believed, "grow" or "mature." Springer designed an operation of calibrating conscience and changing norms intended to bust Catholics out of the holding pattern. To put it in simple terms: the Catholic studied the shifting structures of the environment; he or she considered the changing norms when forming a conscience; and this individual, growing and developing, created a new moral norm sensitive to both objective and subjective. Tradition would be upheld: Thomas had long argued that an objective rule only becomes truly objective if the conscience grants it authority.

Father Springer admired a Catholic's quest to confirm morality in conscience—to force the conscience to grow—and he criticized the church's outright ban of artificial birth control as an inhibitor of growth. "Since conscience is the person in his highest strivings, the perpetuation of this repression of growth and freedom is a sin against the person," he concluded.[50] Any morality of law not attuned to the changing moral structures and the subjective dimensions of the person, he added, "is bad psychology, bad morality, and deplorable formation of consciences."[51] *Humanae vitae* and other laws would only produce a new generation of superego-conscience Catholics. The church's own moral training seemed poised to rear a generation of mindless conformists, something Protestants and American liberals had fulminated against.

Conscience and the Behavioral Sciences was not merely a screed against the standing moral order. Springer constructed a new definition of conscience for his readers: "Conscience may be described in its several dimensions as the person acquiring a set of norms for determining good and evil, developing the ability to evaluate, experiencing feelings of satisfaction and guilt and moving toward an integration of his conduct with his sense of right and wrong and with his feelings."[52] Conscience, in both psychology and the institutional past, acquired norms in its effort to establish "good and evil." The "ability to evaluate" was already implicit in the long-running emphasis on conscience formation, which allowed the individual to identify just laws to be followed and unjust laws to be eschewed. The existential, psychological, and personalist conscience added new tricks to an old set of operations:

"feelings" and the "integration of . . . conduct" helped confirm that an action should be performed because it is good. Springer, rather radically when compared to *Humanae vitae*, did see the law as a category in motion; the American Catholic community would need to adjust norms in response to a new environment and the historical context. Still, as Springer conceived it, conscience was the subjective receiver of the objective norms, as it had been since the thirteenth century. The church must have law, he explained, but the objective rules must be seen in the response of the subject.

Lawrence Kohlberg and American Catholics

Many Catholic moralists embraced psychology around the time that Lawrence Kohlberg (fig. 10) revealed his stage-based model of moral development in the late 1960s. A secular Jewish intellectual who delayed attending university to help Jewish refugees arrive in Palestine (later the State of Israel) after World War II, he would come to exert a profound influence on how Catholics understood conscience and conscience formation. Kohlberg finished his graduate studies at the University of Chicago in 1962 and quickly thereafter became a leading figure in a generation of postwar psychologists who questioned Freud's findings. His career took off: he left the University of Chicago in 1968 to join the faculty at the Harvard Graduate School of Education, where he would remain until his death in 1985.[53] He and his contemporaries critiqued the parochialism of the superego conscience. Together they propounded new types of conscience and imagined new trajectories of conscience development beyond a communal- and familial-dominated subjectivity. As explained above, Catholics absorbed the new research on conscience into their traditional theology, seeking, like the developmental psychologists, a moral training that went beyond a simple obedience to rules.

Kohlberg identified three levels of moral development: a preconventional level, wherein the individual associated good or bad with punishment or its absence; a conventional level, when the individual followed the rules of the family, group, or nation and associated good or bad with the extent to which the group was pleased or displeased; and a postconventional level, achieved as the individual "assert[ed] values" distinct from ideas held by authority figures. Each of the three levels of Kohlberg's model has two stages within it. In the postconventional level, the individual arrived at his or her destination: stage 6, "The Universal Ethical Principle Orientation." In this stage, Kohlberg wrote, what was right was defined not by laws or contracts with society but by a "decision of conscience in accord with

10. Harvard professor Lawrence Kohlberg, 1971. UAV 605 (Kohlberg1-71), OLVwork350870, Harvard University Archives, Cambridge, Massachusetts.

self-chosen ethical principles appealing to logical comprehensiveness, universality, and consistency."[54] The level 3, stage 6 individual broke society's civil laws to assert higher claims of human equality, dignity, and justice. The individual arrived at this stage after the requisite time spent obeying orders (preconventional) or conforming to the group (conventional). The pinnacle of moral life found in Kohlberg's model of moral development—an act of conscience in accord with one's values—dovetailed nicely with the aspirations that Catholic moralists held for the people of their church.

Kohlberg's theory spread rapidly across the landscape of US Catholic media in the 1970s. The outline of his schema of moral development appeared in periodicals such as *Communio,* the *Journal of Religious Education,* the *National Catholic Guidance Conference Journal,* the *Living Light, U.S. Catholic,* the *Catechist,* and *Horizons.* A Dominican complained that since its debut, "the moral development theory of Lawrence Kohlberg ha[d] received wide and largely uncritical acceptance."[55] But Kohlberg was not accepted uncritically so much as embraced enthusiastically, because his work provided Catholic thinkers with empirical evidence of moral development and pinpointed for them exactly how an internal moral orb evolved in sync with a Catholic's life stages. "Kohlberg's findings have valuable implications," wrote Father Jeffrey Keefe, a Franciscan priest with a doctorate in clinical psychology from Fordham University, in summing up the Catholic reception.[56]

Kohlberg made Catholic educators aware of the limits of moral evolution: conscience *had to move through all the stages* to become postconventional. Keefe found Kohlberg's thought valuable because it showed that moralists had to "find out where people are, as moral philosophers, in order to draw them along, if they are stuck at early stages."[57] By exposing the ironclad stage-based trajectory of growth, Catholic educators could use Kohlbergian lenses to gauge the real pace of a moral subjectivity's evolution. This would help them identify a student's level of moral growth and then allow Catholic moralists to inspire the conscience to reach the next stage. As students could not skip stages and only see one stage down the line, Keefe explained, "exposure to the next higher stage of moral thinking" would help them "see aspects regarding a moral question of which they were not aware, and [spur] them to move toward that level."[58] A Jesuit priest told a reporter from *US Catholic* that during college, he watched students move from conventional morality to postconventional morality. He claimed to have spent an entire month on the task of selfdom cultivation with the students in his moral theology course at Creighton University to prepare them for the new stage of life as postconventionals. Catholics grow up with strict rules, he explained, and in college they "encounter others and realize their way is not the only way to behave."[59] The well-formed internality of Kohlberg's postconventional became a student's premier moral guide in a context where laws ceased to provide easy answers.

The movement from stage to stage clarified the task ahead for Catholic educators: left to its own devices, conscience would merely absorb its surroundings. A subjectivity stalled in conventional morality could become the uncritical reproducer of lessons learned from television, peers, movies, music, and magazines. Kohlberg's scheme strengthened the Catholic proposition that following a properly formed conscience enables individuals to transcend the directives of immoral authorities. "Should we tell the young to follow their conscience? Yes, but show them how to form a conscience," a Jesuit high school teacher concluded. But, he pointed out, offering a parting warning to his readers, it was important to "remember that 'following one's conscience' means different things to different people. To Kohlberg's post-conventional, it means doing the right thing no matter the cost."[60] Kohlberg redoubled a long-standing tradition: conscience must be properly formed to grasp transcendent norms and followed upon realizing the existence of such norms. His psychological stages charted a new course to reach the familiar destination.

Kohlberg shared Catholics' distrust of the law. This refined conscience, for him and for Catholics alike, refracted values and principles. Both were more abstract than laws, and they offered a flexibility that postlegal Catholic thinkers craved. Kohlberg's stage 3, level 6 individual acted out of principles like justice and equality. He or she, Kohlberg explained, did not follow "concrete moral rules like the Ten Commandments."[61] Twentieth-century history made it abundantly clear to Kohlberg, as it did to Catholics, that laws did not define right or wrong. The state sanctioned segregation with the law, he consistently noted in his writings, but the law could never make moral the specific acts that propped up the system. Acts, he explained in a 1970 lecture, could not be made good or bad with law; "only knowledge of the good that lies behind them" could "give them virtue."[62] Performing acts on the highest moral plane entailed carrying them out in full knowledge of the principles that informed each act. Catholics agreed with this argument even if their values were more supernatural than Kohlberg's democratic principles. If equality, justice, or the dignity of personhood frame the act, Kohlberg argued, the act can be called virtuous. One freely chose these principles and acted, often against prevailing norms, in their name.

In the vast corpus of Kohlberg's writings, it is difficult to find a concrete definition of *conscience*. Despite mentioning "decisions of conscience" in the sixth and final stage of his developmental schema, Kohlberg rarely paused to dwell on the term. We can infer that he meant something different by the word than did American Catholics. But we need not extrapolate too much: he advanced a modest definition of *conscience* in "Moral Stages and Moralization," an essay published in 1984, just one year before he died by suicide. The word *conscience* could hold great meaning, or it could hold very little; it depended entirely on the individual. The word gained meaning in relation to the principle the individual held behind the act of following conscience. "Orienting to the morally right thing, or following conscience as against following the law," did not immediately indicate the achievement of stage 6 development.[63] A Jehovah's Witness, Kohlberg explained, "has gone to jail for 'conscience,'" and "conscience may mean God's law as interpreted by his or her religious sect or group rather than the standpoint of any individual oriented to universal moral principles or values."[64] The individual Witness acted in a conventional vein in following conscience because the directive to act on one's inner light derived from the group, not universal morality.

Kohlberg's concept of conscience challenged the Catholic notion that the individual's conscience rights derived from the church's own strong defenses of confident subjectivity in its doctrines. If the catechism told the Catholic he or she must follow conscience—then that individual who followed such a subjectivity simply exhibited conventional (level 2) behavior. Kohlberg, demonstrating his distaste for doctrine, argued that for words like *conscience* to evince mature behavior, "such ideas or terms must be used in a way that makes clear that they have a foundation for a rational or moral individual who has not yet committed him- or herself to any group or society or its morality."[65] Catholics and other religious groups might have identified Kohlberg's total rejection of organizational affiliation as an extreme position: he believed that the church would need to be abandoned before an individual could act on rational and universal principles. But Catholic moralists ignored these tensions and concentrated far more on the common ground shared with Kohlberg.

Kohlberg was a progressive educator in the tradition of American liberalism. His main intellectual inspirations, in addition to French psychologist Jean Piaget, were American philosophers John Dewey and John Rawls. Historian John McGreevy has shown that the relationship between American Catholicism and American liberals coalesced on certain issues (state intervention into the economy, unions) and diverged on others (abortion, euthanasia).[66] The commingling of Kohlberg's liberalism and Catholic moral theology is another chapter in this modern history of attraction and repulsion. Catholic moralists and Kohlberg agreed on the existence of universal principles and the evacuation of law's moral authority in modern America but broke sharply from one another on the utility of religious doctrine and the realness of supernatural phenomena. Kohlberg, of course, shared with Catholics an abiding concern for the formation of conscience and a belief that following it constituted the highest form of moral behavior. But like his intellectual hero John Dewey, he was hostile to doctrine, and he followed Dewey's lead in rejecting transcendent truths in favor of inductively arriving at conclusions only through measurable empirical data. From Dewey and his progressive notions of education, Kohlberg drew the lesson that educators ought to move individuals through a series of stages that culminated in the "attainment of a higher level or stage of development in adulthood, not merely the healthy functioning of the child at a present level."[67] The student would attain knowledge while passing from one stage of development into the next, each graduation marked by the active restructuring of thinking habits. Each cognitive restructuring, Dewey argued, entails a deeper recognition of democratic ties to other members of society. Kohlberg defined progressive justice as the "reciprocity between the individual and others in the social environment."[68]

The focus on justice as a recognition of the ties among individuals in society marked the democratic component of Kohlberg's thought. John Rawls provided this other secular drive in Kohlberg's work. The principles that one acted on as a level 3, stage 6 were derived largely from Rawls's 1971 book *A Theory of Justice*. Individuals should act on abstract values to build up what Rawls called "the justice structure."[69] Such a structure distributed rights and advantages to society's members, who were charged with determining how those rights could exist—and how they could be maximized—while preserving societal cohesion.[70] The question Kohlberg asked was how individuals could learn to act on principles that secured rights and equality for all society's members. How did the individual act ethically to help create a functioning justice structure? Kohlberg's moral schema aimed to create individuals who became active democratic citizens. He believed that assertions of conscience were moral because they expanded democracy and opportunities for others. He was not overly concerned with how the individual could make it to heaven with a good conscience.

Catholics appreciated Kohlberg's concept of conscience-following as an assertion of values, but they took issue with the secular underpinnings of his theory. He certainly helped strengthen the imperative of conscience-following and conscience formation in American Catholic life, but Catholic writers offered the occasional caveat that he made little room for doctrine, faith, or the supernatural power of grace. Level 3, stage 6 individuals were imagined by Kohlberg to be in the vanguard in modern democratic culture. They followed a conscience informed by equality and dignity to challenge laws that made other members of society less equal. A Dominican, noting the inherent secularism and absence of transcendence in Kohlberg's concept, stated his dismay forthrightly: "Kohlberg's entire moral structure rests upon a conception of morality and of conscience which is exclusively concerned with a universal prescriptive system of resolving claims of distributive justice."[71] Jeffrey Keefe—a psychologist who promoted Kohlberg's work among fellow Catholics—reminded readers of the *Catechist* that Kohlberg's theory of moral growth was incomplete. Kohlberg argued nobly for "the principle of justice—giving each person his or her due, and the basis of equality of every individual"; but for Catholics, "conscience is informed not only by ethical principles, however lofty, but by relation to the living Lord."[72] They did not form their conscience exclusively with justice and democracy in mind. "The Christian ethic goes beyond enlightened humanism," Keefe maintained.[73] Hence Catholics formed conscience with the guidance of Christ, the Holy Spirit, and the magisterium.

For all his secularism, Kohlberg aligned with Catholics on the crucial issue of universalism, a commitment that landed him in hot water in the 1980s when his work was critiqued for its failure to acknowledge gender. His research indicated that his stages of moral development started or ceased at different points among members of different demographics—rural or urban, upper or lower class—but *all children (male or female) went through these stages* as part of their development. As early as 1968, Kohlberg could confidently assert that "our data show no differences between Protestant, Catholic, Moslem, and Buddhist children—all go through the same stages at much the same rate."[74] Catholics could, in certain ways, support the claim that all people everywhere evolved morally to the point where conscience expressed assertions of universal values. An enthusiastic Catholic theologian thought that Kohlberg had disproved ethical relativism: "As a result of his extensive research Kohlberg concluded that ethical relativism, or the position that moral values and judgments of right and wrong are entirely relative to culture in which a person lives, is absolutely erroneous."[75] Catholics may have downplayed the secular and democratic nature of Kohlberg's principles—but they rejoiced upon reading his major premise: values were universal. Values transcended local cultures, religious sects, gender, race, and other particularities to be universally true for all people. In turn, Catholics and Kohlberg agreed that individuals could understand and live out the universal principles through the choices they made. People everywhere—if guided properly through the stages of formation—could become principled decision-makers.

Kohlberg did eschew doctrine, but he was not opposed to the existence of eternal or natural laws. In an essay in which he addressed his affinity for religious thinkers like Martin Luther King, Jr. and Jesuit priest Teilhard de Chardin, he hinted that the universality of stage-based growth indicated the existence of a natural law: "Stage 6 moral principles enjoining and uplifting human personality are 'eternal and natural law' in the sense that they are the universal outgrowth of the development of human nature. On the side of a psychology of human nature, my theory says that human conceptions of moral law are not the product of internalizing arbitrary and culturally relative societal norms. They are, rather, outcomes of universal human nature developing under universal aspects of the human condition, and in that sense they are 'natural.'"[76] The conscience needed to be formed by educators in church and society to the point where the individual connected his or own conscience, after stage-based formation, to the eternal and natural laws that govern all men and women. These eternal laws, according to Kohlberg, governed not only Christian existence but democratic societies.

Conclusion

Three factors explain the rise of Catholic conscience rights in the 1960s and 1970s: a debate about sexual morality, a dispute over the citizen's duty in wartime, and the concept's smooth adaptability to preexisting secular and Jewish psychological frameworks. In all three areas, Catholics stressed the deleterious social and political effects of strict obedience to the law. It is important to recognize that the psychological turn fed off the wider changes in the areas of sexuality and war and contributed to the broader unrest in church and society. Priests speaking a psychoanalytical and psychological language aimed to transform power dynamics in the intimate social spheres of life: between child and parent, penitent and confessor, and student and teacher. These changes, stressing the mature conscience rather than legalism, proved to be the prologue to new sexual moralities and modes of citizenship.

The psychological infusion into the conscience rights movement proves again one of the arguments pursued throughout this book: that the movement had both modern and medieval elements. Conscience began to perform a wide range of psychological functions in the 1960s and 1970s, but it never outgrew its longtime task to serve as the individual's immediate moral guide. This chapter has argued that psychology enhanced the core mission set for conscience by the teachers and scholars of the institutional and the medieval Catholic Church. The breakdown of law opened a space for a deep tradition, the formation and following of conscience, to spread widely throughout the church and modern American life. Catholics weaved developmental psychology, existentialism, and personalism into the conscience—making it the total sense of the self and a developed agent of moral maturity. Conscience then took on the workload of moral guidance previously borne by the law. Psychology, in other words, helped conscience assume its own mantle. Now this book swings back out to the political realm. The Vietnam War compelled Catholics to go public and to fight for conscience protections from a diverse set of political authorities at the federal level: in the Senate, the House of Representatives, and the Supreme Court.

SIX

The Conscience Lobby

During these last years we have all become a good deal more sensitive to the claims of the individual conscience, and I think this is a good development and one that it is important to emphasize in many areas where moral decisions must be made.

—Richard Cardinal Cushing, Archbishop of Boston, to Gordon Zahn, August 8, 1968

Conscience rights advocates tasted victory in February 1972. That month, after nearly eight long years of US involvement in the war in Southeast Asia, the American bishops published a strong statement on traditional self-determination. "In light of the Gospel and from an analysis of the Church's teachings on conscience," the document read, "it is clear that a Catholic can be a conscientious objector to war in general or a particular war because of religious training and belief."[1] A Catholic could reject all war, and a Catholic could reject participation in wars judged unjust. President Richard Nixon may have been winding down US involvement in the war with his Vietnamization program, devolving responsibility for the war to troops from South Vietnam, but the words were a significant victory for the conscience rights movement.

The bishops finally spoke the language of conscience in an unambiguous and conspicuous fashion after enduring seven years of petitioning, criticism, and goading from activists in the Catholic Church. Laypeople, scholars, and magazine editors began inviting the powerful clerics to join their cause when Lyndon Johnson escalated the draft in 1965 and launched Operation Rolling Thunder, which pounded military and civilian targets as well as the Ho Chi Minh Trail with a medley of explosives and defoliants. This chapter examines the rise of what effectively became a kind of conscience lobby, its successes in the church, and its broader failure in the US political system. Conscience rights advocates wrote articles, published books, gave speeches, ran petition campaigns, and sent hundreds of private letters to people of influence in the church and the state. As the war machine drew in thousands of men, spitting them out in the jungles of Vietnam, the movement's mission increased in urgency. What the conscience lobby lacked in smooth backroom diplomacy it compensated for in dogged determination.

The lobby's first goal was to bring the bishops over to its side. The pressure group managed to capture this objective late in the war. Its second objective was to secure formal conscience protection measures from the federal government, whether legislation or court rulings. Ideally, these Catholics would bring the state to recognize that no person could be dragooned into an army against the dictates of conscience, making real a medieval church doctrine and upholding Catholic traditions on responsible self-rule. Moreover, legislators and judges would authorize just-war Catholics to form and follow deeply held truths regarding each war, making it possible to become a selective conscientious objector. Lobbyists offered these two propositions at presidential commissions, the House of Representatives, the Senate, and the Supreme Court. Each attempt failed in its own unique manner, some with a landslide vote in opposition and others with the turn of a legislator's cold shoulder. But the lobbyists dusted themselves off and pled their cause at venue after venue in the 1960s and 1970s. The endurance of the grassroots movement for Catholic self-sovereignty brings into focus a central finding of this book: in a historical moment when law fails to direct individuals to moral ends, Catholics stopped at nothing to secure protection for sacred subjectivities.

That Catholics became the most dedicated special-interest representatives for the legal recognition of conscience rights is an unlikely development in twentieth-century US history. The rise of Soviet communism after 1945 inspired them to support the US government and its quest to contain the Red Menace. Their opposition to philosophical and political materialism ran deep. Since the late nineteenth century, Catholics in the United States and across the world had warned their fellow countrymen about the dangers of communism. American Catholics responded enthusiastically to the 1917 request of Mary, in one of a series of apparitions to peasant children in Fátima, Portugal, to pray for the conversion of Russia. Well into the 1950s, they clutched their rosaries, asking the Blessed Virgin to bring the Russians to their senses. Catholic anticommunists like Tom Dooley laid the intellectual groundwork for the invasion of Vietnam, convincing millions of Americans that the "Reds" had massacred hundreds of innocent Christians. Late into the 1960s, due in large part to their anticommunism, Catholics understood conscientious objectors to be cowards or perhaps even psychologically disordered.

The bishops' complete endorsement of conscience rights in February 1972 thus signaled a dramatic parting of the ways between cross and flag. They turned their back on the Selective Service System and the anticommunism of American democracy. In the early 1970s, inspired by laity, activists, and theologians, they deployed the theology of conscience to criticize the state. With their 1972 statement, these prelates marked the law as an oppressive instrument that destroyed the inner moral cores of the nation's citizens, and they made a central contribution to the spread of late-modern autonomy and the culture of democracy.

The rise of conscience claims must also be understood as a logical conclusion of the Catholic Church's centuries-old just-war doctrine. Because the church taught for over a millennium and a half that some wars were just and others were not, determining whether it was right or wrong to support a particular war was quite difficult. The bishops were sympathetic—or became sympathetic over the course of the Vietnam War—to the challenge laypeople faced in forming their conscience on the matter of war. The church pursued a complex view of state conflict, and it stood to reason that some military struggles might become unjust. This tradition, refined centuries before by Augustine and Thomas Aquinas, made conscience rights more palatable with the American bishops in the early 1970s.

Gordon Zahn and Franz Jägerstätter

No individual better embodied the dialectic of persistence and failure in the fight for Catholic self-governance than Gordon Zahn (fig. 11). At the February 1967 meeting of the American Pax Association, a key conscience lobby surrogate, Zahn became Pax's chairman. He was already well known to the Pax rank and file on account of his two books, a 1957 study of the Catholic hierarchy's support for the Nazi Party and a theological biography of Franz Jägerstätter, an Austrian peasant who claimed conscientious objector status against the National Socialist movement and lost his life for it. In his acceptance speech, Zahn announced the first major initiative of his chairmanship: the Pax Rights of Conscience Campaign.[2] Pax wanted conscience protections written into the rules of the draft, which was up for congressional renewal in 1967 even as the Selective Service System was bringing thirty thousand men into the military each month. Under Zahn's leadership, Pax began to advocate on behalf of the men who evaluated each war on its own

11. Gordon Zahn. University of Notre Dame Archives, Notre Dame, Indiana.

merits—forming their internal voices—before deciding to take up arms or declining to fight. Zahn, an intellectual gadfly who embraced controversy, was not shy when it came to making radical arguments in public.[3]

Only six months after the Rights of Conscience Campaign began its efforts, a Who's Who of the American Catholic Church had given the campaign their blessing. Bishop John Wright of Pittsburgh, Monsignor George Higgins of the Bishops' Conference Social Action Department, and Thomas Merton, the famous monk of Gethsemani Abbey, pledged their names. Priests from the Jesuit, Marianist, Josephite, and Passionist orders also attached their signatures to Pax's initial call. Sister M. Brendan, president of Marymount College, joined the cause, as did Dorothy Dohen, sociologist and author of *Nationalism and American Catholicism* (1967), a stinging critique of church-state comity. Publishers, attorneys, magazine editors, and professors rounded out the list of early petitioners.

The form that all these men and women signed and circulated promised to deliver the lobby's message loud and clear to the nation's political authorities: "The progress of the PAX RIGHTS OF CONSCIENCE Campaign [emphasis theirs] will be made known to Congressmen and other leaders as the petitions are signed."[4] Pax never planned to discuss traditional subjective truth-creation capacities as if they were a theory detached from reality—its members aimed to carve out a sphere for subjectivities in the official laws of the land. By the summer of 1967, the movement had gathered significant momentum at the grass roots.

Near the end of his stint in the Civilian Public Service during World War II, Gordon Zahn realized that both church and state needed to be pushed on the matter of conscience rights. The US Army called Zahn up in 1942, but he gained official conscientious objector status, a designation that kept him off the front and placed him in a New Hampshire work camp and later at a state-run hospital. He knew his Thomism and his moral theology manuals, so he began to press the Catholic Church on its silence regarding conscience rights before the end of the war. A radical proposition on this matter could be found in basic texts, but the bishops hesitated to mention the idea in public. But in July of 1945, Zahn angered Joseph Nelligan, chancellor of the Archdiocese of Boston, with a letter suggesting that the unjustness of the war meant that Catholics must follow conscience. "Of course you may state your own conscience tells you this war is wrong," Nelligan responded, as if to wave his finger at him. "We can only reply that your conscience is in error."[5] Zahn assured the chancellor that he did not intend to speak for the entire church. But he knew his own conscience: he had formed it to the point where he obliged himself to reject the law.[6] In a letter to a priest friend sent later that year, Zahn wondered about the Catholic Church actually owning up to its own teachings on conscience. God, he wrote, "gave us the voice of conscience" and an "obligation to follow the dictates of that conscience," and yet the church proved to be a stumbling block to following conscience in the world.[7] Zahn concluded in private in the 1940s what he made public over fifteen years later: more had to be done to convince the bishops to back traditional modes of self-sovereignty. Without activists in the church calling attention to the matter, the hierarchy would leave the teaching on conscience unsaid.

Between his brief consignment in a labor camp during World War II and the dawn of the sixties, Zahn's career took flight. Eugene McCarthy, his undergraduate mentor, offered Zahn a staff position after being elected to the Senate in 1959; Zahn held that position as he completed a doctorate in sociology at the nearby Catholic University of America. He secured a postdoctoral fellowship at Harvard University in 1952 and won a Fulbright scholarship to do research in Germany. Zahn practiced what theologian Benjamin Peters called a "supernatural sociology."[8] The young sociologist matched a deep commitment to moral truth as taught by the Catholic Church with his profoundly empirical methods. Zahn mined data and consulted primary source documents with an eye toward sharpening the church's theology. The spiritual side of analysis and divine revelation matched his commitment to modern politics and sociological analysis.

By the early 1960s, with his first book in print, several fellowships on his vita, and an assistant professorship at Loyola University Chicago, Zahn was ready to launch a public writing career. He came out swinging for conscience rights. In a 1962 *Commonweal* article provocatively titled "The Private Conscience and Legitimate Authority," Zahn urged the church to adopt a strong stance on conscience to break with its dark history of collaboration with totalitarian regimes. The Eichmann trial and early Second Vatican Council sessions showed that the Catholic Church should put its political programs where its doctrine long stood. Zahn pointed out that Adolf Eichmann understood obedience to authority to be a virtue and simply transferred his crimes onto his leaders as a result.[9] Among his long list of horrors, Eichmann had broken a fundamental teaching of Catholic ethics: he admitted to placing his subjectivity into the hands of an authority figure. But the problem of obedience went far beyond Eichmann. Zahn considered his own Catholic Church complicit in the mass violence of the twentieth century due to its calls for obedience to "legitimate authority."[10] The church clung to a mode of modern politics that divinized civil law, making it a moral obligation to obey secular state authorities.

Conscience was the antidote. The church should start readying its members by the millions to follow internally known truths in response to the unjust commands of modern political authorities. The conversion would begin in the realm of ideas: "We need a moral theology," Zahn declared, "which would require that every exercise of authority be exposed to the test of the enlightened moral conscience of the individual subject to it."[11] The individual with an enlightened self-core, following the protocols outlined in tradition, could identify a law as unjust and refuse obedience. Zahn's argument was well timed. He likely did not realize it when his *Commonweal* article went to print, but the Catholic president elected by the American public in November of 1960 had been escalating the war effort in Southeast Asia, increasing the number of "military advisers" in South Vietnam exponentially. By 1963, sixteen thousand of these advisers would be stationed there, up from eight hundred in 1960.[12]

Zahn's article mentioned but did not name an Austrian peasant beheaded by the Nazis for refusing to serve in the German army. Attentive readers of Catholic periodicals may already have heard of him, however: Zahn had discussed the intriguing character, Franz Jägerstätter, in a piece published four years earlier in *America*.[13] Jägerstätter served as Germany's anti-Eichmann and the perfect biographical vehicle to promote the rights of conscience. He told the Nazis he could not in conscience join in the state's unjust military campaigns—and in 1943, the Germans executed the father of three because of his refusal. Zahn explained his plans to write a book on Jägerstätter to his friend Thomas Merton. The Trappist monk encouraged Zahn to conceptualize Jägerstätter as a heroic witness to the moral potency a Catholic gained from a confident subjectivity. Merton called Jägerstätter a "moving symbol of a lonely isolated Christian who was faithful to his conscience" and withstood tremendous pressure to conform.[14] Zahn had spent years collecting Merton's writings, so the endorsement must have been encouraging as Jägerstätter commanded more and more of the sociologist's research agenda at the start of the Second Vatican Council. Both men agreed that Jägerstätter's witness to conscience might break the church's lazy conformity to the modern state. If members of the conscience rights lobby identified a martyr who incarnated its cause, a pitch to the bishops and the state might be made in a powerful narrative form.

A prolific and indefatigable writer, Gordon Zahn furnished the movement with a major manifesto in 1964. He published *In Solitary Witness: The Life and Death of Franz Jägerstätter* with Holt, Rinehart and Winston, a trade press. Zahn reserved his sociological analysis of "holy deviance" for the book's final chapter, choosing to narrate Jägerstätter's life in a highly accessible style for the first 135 pages. The rhetorical strategy paid off: the book became popular immediately upon its publication. Zahn brought to life a conversion akin to the one described by Augustine in his *Confessions*. Jägerstätter, as was well known to his neighbors in the small village of St. Radegund where he had grown up, sowed his wild oats. The Austrian liked to drink in the local pubs and enjoyed the company of women. A premarital affair yielded a child, resulting in Jägerstätter's self-imposed exile from the village. But he returned home a few years later after his conversion to a strict version of his Catholic faith. Neighbors took note of the former playboy's sudden devotion to the church. Jägerstätter prayed the Rosary as he strode the town's paths. He became the sexton of the local church, zealously caring for the sacred structure. He married and became a father to three daughters. In sum, his conversion created what Zahn called "Jägerstätter 2"—a devout and well-read Catholic who was a steady writer of commentaries and letters.

Jägerstätter wrote most frequently about the meaning of Christ's bodily resurrection and the deep wounds of sin. One of the lessons he especially took to heart was his church's teachings on conscience.

In Solitary Witness offered more than a conversion story. The book delivered a stinging indictment of the Catholic Church for failing to support a highly orthodox follower of conscience, one of its own, reared by the church and faithful to its teachings. Jägerstätter manifested the depth of his conversion not only as the parish caretaker, Zahn wrote, but by becoming a critic of unjust war and an open resister of the Nazi regime. His faith had consequences for his citizenship, one of the main convictions held by members of Pax. Yet as Zahn learned from interviews while researching for the book, a number of churchmen had pleaded with Jägerstätter to set aside his conscience and simply obey the Nazis' call for war. Representatives of the church—a pastor, a chaplain, a bishop, and an attorney—unanimously suggested that Catholic faith had little to do with political behavior. And the prison chaplain tried to convince Jägerstätter that "he had no responsibility as a private citizen for the acts and policies of the government."[15] In other words, Nazi law was legitimate and to be obeyed by faithful Catholics. Jägerstätter responded with a textbook rendering of the rights of conscience to rebut his lawyer's claim. He "justified his stand by insisting that this was the kind of moral judgment that has to be made by the individual conscience."[16] The Catholic had to make it out of this world, and up to heaven, with a good conscience. Jägerstätter could not stifle his longings and join the Nazi army and expect to remain in God's favor.

Zahn became a one-man self-sovereignty advocacy operation. There was no one more intent on securing clauses on Catholic autonomy in the documents produced by the Vatican Council. Too impatient for group organization, Zahn took matters into his own hands. His weapon of choice was a personal letter to a man of power. He sent one such missive to Father François Houtart, a framer of key Vatican II documents and a fellow sociologist, to underscore the importance of the council's recognizing the legitimacy of following conscience.[17] As Zahn explained in a similar letter to the archbishop of Liverpool, George A. Beck, the council ought to back the subjectivity of conscientious objectors with the same enthusiasm it granted Catholic soldiers. "What is needed, I feel, is a clear statement by the Council that the Church is to give the same recognition and respect to her children whose conscience obliges them to refuse military service as she has always given those who accept service," he wrote.[18]

Never one to back away from a theological dispute, Zahn wrote publicly in American Catholic periodicals what he had written for private eyes. He understood his move toward conscience rights as the maximization of tradition and the recovery of a teaching created by Catholic medievals and tragically buried by Catholic moderns. Zahn argued in a 1965 article that the duty to follow conscience should be stated clearly at the Second Vatican Council for all to understand. Teachings on the importance of conscience weighed down by recondite language needed a fresh elucidation: "The obligation to obey even the invincibly ignorant or erroneous conscience is not to be relegated to some dry and obscure theological treatise. It must be made a matter of common knowledge and public declaration so that there may be no further misunderstandings."[19] There should no longer be any confusion after the bishops held their global meeting: Catholics could follow a well-formed inner nucleus, even a mistaken one, and the church should stand behind any member exercising responsible self-rule.

The Nazi movement collapsed two decades before Vatican II (and no Western states executed conscientious objectors in the 1960s), but Zahn believed that Jägerstätter's bloody sacrifice held meaning for the conscience rights struggle in the church. He lobbied the council members with narrations of Jägerstätter's life and death. His letters were miniature exercises in supernatural sociology: empirically sharp yet saturated with theological passions. Zahn held that Jägerstätter died so that other Catholics may follow conscience. Like Christ, Catholics went to their death to set others free. Jägerstätter sanctified the teaching on conscience by putting his body on the line. Zahn's letters carried the pain he felt as he repeatedly prayed about Jägerstätter's final days. He explained to Cardinal Leo Suenens, one of the council's leading figures, how Jägerstätter tormented himself in the weeks leading up to his execution out of a fear he might have sinned in refusing to obey superiors.[20] Yet according to Zahn's reading, it was the institutional church that had sinned, not Jägerstätter. The church would again fail this saint, who followed the church's teachings at a great cost, if it backslid on the matter of conscience. It had grown too comfortable in encouraging obedience to civil laws. A weak statement on conscience rights from the Second Vatican Council, Zahn told Houtart, "would be dishonoring the sacrifice made by this man and others who gave priority to the call of their conscience."[21] Americans who attended the council, like John Wright and George Higgins, received similar exegeses of Jägerstätter's martyrdom. A complimentary copy of *In Solitary Witness* often accompanied the letters.

The movement for conscience rights scored a major breakthrough at the end of the Second Vatican Council because of Gordon Zahn's blazing typewriter: British Jesuit John T. Roberts, one of his many correspondents, took to the council floor on November 12, 1965, to give a crackling address on the Austrian peasant and the theopolitical meaning of his sacrifice. (Roberts had retired as archbishop of Bombay in 1950 out of his conviction that the Catholic population would be better served by a pastor from India, not a British colonizer. The official rules, however, allowed retired bishops to participate in church councils and even made them emeriti voting members of the assembled body.) Roberts, adopting Zahn's arguments, blasted the council's previous statements on war as "lamentably weak and insufficient."[22] Jägerstätter had suffered alone in silence—in both body and spirit—and the church not only failed to protect one of its devout, it all but handed him over to his Nazi executioners. With a memorable turn of phrase, Roberts addressed his fellow bishops: "What we must do here is to give clear testimony that the Church affirms the rights of the individual conscience to refuse unjust military service, and assure those of the Faithful, who bear such witness, that they will always have her fullest support. Once this has been done, martyrs like Jägerstätter will never again have to feel like they take their stand alone."[23] The church must renounce its practice of encouraging Catholics to follow the unjust laws of secular states—a point made frequently by Zahn—and instead convince civil authorities to make laws defending the rights of conscience. "Let us break with this tragic past," Roberts concluded, "by making a clear and unambiguous affirmation of the right and obligation of each Christian to obey the voice of his informed conscience before and during a time of war."[24] Roberts sent a copy of his speech to Jägerstätter's widow, still living in St. Radegund, Austria.

Letters arriving in Zahn's Chicago mailbox from around the world radiated joy for the future that *In Solitary Witness* had opened up to its many readers. The book made clear to them that healthy societies would be built by those responsibly exercising self-governance, not pliable and obedient servants. Jägerstätter's sacrifice removed the scales from one Italian woman's eyes: "The implications for Catholics are enormous. One's comfortable feeling that by a vague sort of extension of infallibility the clergy and general Catholic opinion can provide the right guidance in any situation is shattered. There are some situations in which individual conscience alone can be relied on, and it seems all too possible that such situations may arise for many of us in the future, that is if they haven't already."[25]

A Canadian man predicted that the book would become a "foundation stone" for the growing antiwar movement.[26] A British sociologist thought that the tale of Jägerstätter's death would spur the church into a prophetic mode. Because of the Austrian's legacy, the church would not merely manage political situations but actively critique them.[27] John Wright, bishop of

Pittsburgh and an active member in the Catholic Peace Fellowship, congratulated Zahn on a job well done: "It is a most important work and you have done the cause of conscience and peace a great service."[28] In *Solitary Witness* persuaded Catholics from all over the world to focus on achieving safe spaces, in church and society, to act on subjective perceptions of the world.

Lobbying Church and State

Vatican II certainly increased the frequency with which conscience language appeared in print. The *Tablet*, an international Catholic newsweekly produced in London, covered a 1963 speech by Cardinal Augustin Bea, a German Jesuit, on "man's right to decide on his own fate in complete freedom and according to conscience," and American publications reported on the curious remark by Joseph Ritter, cardinal archbishop of St. Louis, about "the dignity of the human person and his inviolable conscience."[29] Men like Ritter and Bea applied the doctrine of conscience to religious freedom but stopped short of considering the idea's implications for the realm of civil law. Persons could follow subjective truth on the matter of denomination or faith (as Protestants had long argued) but perhaps not in response to inner divinations regarding sex and war. In the context of the Vietnam War, however, American Catholic magazine editors took it upon themselves to apply Vatican II's ruminations on subjectivity and rights to the era's pressing political question about conscription. In the spring of 1966, the editors the *Catholic Mind* reviewed the *Declaration of Religious Freedom* issued by Vatican II in December 1965 and found that the document did not clarify the relationship between conscience and civil authority. Vatican II captured a portion of the theology by noting that Catholics are bound to follow conscience "to come to God." But, the editors asked, "do we have the right to follow our own judgment when it conflicts with the judgments of legitimate authority?"[30] That became the crucial question of the Catholic 1960s.

The conscience lobby, one wing of which could be found in the Catholic press, favored an expansive interpretation of the doctrine that applied the medieval teaching liberally to civil law, even "legitimate" civil law. The *Catholic Mind* concluded that the conscience, in every instance, "frees [the individual] from obedience to men."[31] Just as his inner sanctum unburdened St. Peter from abiding by the injunctions placed on his preaching and just as these mental judgments liberated St. Thomas More from taking the Oath of Supremacy in 1534, so, too, the conscience freed modern American Catholics, an increasing number of whom faced the draft, from obedience to civil laws in 1966.

Lobbyists found a sound explanation of the need for self-sovereignty in the example of Nazi Germany. Perhaps the loudest single voice for conscience rights during the Vietnam War was Paulist priest John B. Sheerin, heir to James Martin Gillis as editor of the *Catholic World*. In a series of editorials between 1966 and 1968, Sheerin applied the "primacy of conscience," the story of Thomas More's stand for conscience, and the lessons of Nuremberg (never abdicate your conscience to a political authority) to the draft for Vietnam. He made sure to limit the church's ability to mold the subjectivities of its members: his *Catholic World* editorials made clear that the church could appoint no official spokesman to decide for the individual Catholic's response to the war; conscience had to be given a primacy, and individuals were to be left to their own private deliberations.[32] In many of these Catholic writings, Eichmann, the Holocaust, and the ability of the Nazi Party to control individual minds lingered as a specter, a conjuring initiated by Gordon Zahn. *Ave Maria*, a popular devotional magazine headquartered near the University of Notre Dame in South Bend, Indiana, printed a thirty-page special report on conscience formation in 1967. The default position of Catholic political theology for most of modern history, despite a flurry of subjectivity talk in the 1930s and 1940s, had been to trust the state to make big decisions about security and violence. *Ave Maria*, a magazine with well-worn anticommunist credentials, suddenly promoted the "integrity and responsibility of conscience" and trumpeted the need for each citizen to remember that despite what the powerful say, "no one can abdicate his conscience to another."[33] Because Catholics had to consider "the Nazi horrors which were accepted in obedience to civil authorities," the task of conscience formation during the Vietnam War carried a new moral urgency.[34]

After 1965, American Catholic activists and writers began to demand that their bishops complete the global church's unfinished work and do away with competing clauses on conscience found in Second Vatican Council documents. Both the conservative and the radical components of the doctrine appeared in the texts, and the council's statement on conscience rights in the civil sphere was in reality quite weak, even after Zahn's heroic efforts and Roberts's rhetorical fireworks in the council's final hours. The lackluster statement on conscientious objection in the *Pastoral Constitution on the Church in the Modern World*—that it "seems right" for states to "make humane provisions" for those "who refuse to bear arms"—was far too moderate for the men and women in the movement to emancipate conscience.[35] State coercion began to bear down on Catholics and their fellow citizens: the defense of conscientious objectors seemed morally imperative as president Lyndon Johnson sent the first wave of conscripted troops to Vietnam in 1965 and US planes dropped crater bombs and Agent Orange on the Vietnamese.

Tensions surfaced immediately between an anguished laity forced to confront the state's draft for the Vietnam War and a taciturn body of American bishops. Catholics were obliged to follow subjective certitudes, on war as well as other matters like contraception, but lay Catholics could use the boost offered by an official statement from the American hierarchy authorizing them to follow this preexisting right of conscience in the public sphere. But did this not defeat the purpose of teaching on conscience? The conscience lobby not only faced the formidable task of addressing the Second Vatican Council's legacy of ambiguity, it was forced to confront the tensions between official pronouncements of doctrine and the individual formations of one's own internal sphere. Could the bishops issue a statement on conscience that did the thinking for the individual Catholic? Could individual Catholics follow conscience during the war without strong backing from the bishops? Was a declaration that "one must follow conscience" not also a rule from an authority figure? A Catholic rule of conscience-following would have to be announced, but the rights of conscience, because of the doctrine itself, were to be claimed by the individual.

The tension between liberation and obedience permeated a poignant letter sent by Catholic economist Franz B. Mueller to Leo Binz, archbishop of St. Paul and Minneapolis, in July of 1967. The sixty-seven-year-old Mueller was well past the age limit for induction, but he wrote his local bishop because his son had become eligible for the draft. By the time Mueller's letter arrived in Minneapolis, just over twenty thousand American men had died in Vietnam. More and more Americans began to question the war; fifty thousand marched on the Pentagon in 1967 in the first of many mass antiwar rallies that took place in the nation's capital. Patriotic Catholic parents like Mueller confronted a terrible proposition: a son may be sacrificed to win a war against global communism as the need to halt the Red Menace seemed to be declining. Mueller had been teaching economics at St. Thomas College in St. Paul for over twenty years and was just one year away from retirement at the time he wrote the letter. He had spent his career thinking in the neo-Scholastic mode, writing his dissertation on the socioeconomic teachings of Thomas Aquinas and going on to write several books on Catholic social teaching.[36]

It would be safe to conclude that Mueller read Vatican II documents with a trained eye. The manuals of moral philosophy made clear to him that Catholics could fight only in just wars. He wondered, however, whether statements on conscience strewn throughout Vatican II documents applied to the just-war teaching. Did they amount to a heightened sense of urgency to follow conscience? Mueller posed a knotted set of questions to his local archbishop. "Are we justified in assuming that the teachings of Vatican II regarding the rights of conscience apply to this area [war] as to any other?" he asked Binz.[37] Stated another way: Vatican II made clear that persons were free in conscience to approach God from the faith of their specific callings or relative upbringings, but could the same documents justify selective conscientious objection to war? Could the Catholic citizen approach the question of service to the state from the perspective of his conscience? Mueller then deepened his question: "Can those young men who, after a careful examination of 'casus belli' [the causes of war] and of their own consciences come to the conclusion they must not serve in that war (in any capacity), hope that they will be supported morally, legally, and constitutionally in their stand? Will the ecclesiastical authorities back them up?"[38] This task fell to the American bishops, who as of the summer of 1967 remained mum on the matter of conscience.

Mueller took a step back. He admitted to Binz that the church could not think for individual Catholics. Such an action would place conscience into the hands of an external ecclesiastical authority, a flagrant violation of the church's own teaching on conscience. "I am also aware of the fact that the Church cannot relieve us altogether of making our own decisions of conscience," he wrote, offering Binz a way out.[39] Still, the question lingered as to whether the American hierarchy would back Mueller's son if he decided not to fight. Mueller sent carbon copies of his letter to Senator Eugene McCarthy, Representative Clark McGregor, and Monsignor Roland Bordalon, the Secretary of World Justice and Peace at the National Conference of Catholic Bishops. The problem necessitated a top-down response.

If conscience rights went unheralded, activists of the American Pax Association warned, the bishops and the US government stood in violation of the Nuremberg ruling, the 1946 decision which held that individuals could be held culpable for carrying out unjust laws. Pax ramped up its campaign for conscience rights as Congress debated draft renewal. The draft, on the books since 1941, expired on July 1, 1967, and the House and the Senate considered amendments to the Selective Service Act throughout the spring and summer of that year. The bishops were set to play Judas in the Vietnam War drama: if they remained silent on subjective potentialities, they were preparing to hand Catholics over to the state and allow distant civil authorities to determine the morality of all actions, large and small.[40] The shepherds made a grave mistake by not recognizing the fact that destructive group activities began by usurping individual subjectivities on a mass scale, rendering individuals into crude implements of the political system. As it stood in the summer of 1967, a Pax letter noted that a Catholic man "must give his conscience into the keeping of the state."[41] "Twentieth century history gives much proof that the state is not a reliable keeper of the human conscience," the letter explained, using the example of Nazi Germany.[42] The bishops needed to stand up in favor of subjectivity to reverse the wave of destruction unleashed by Leviathan states. The US Cold War state appeared to be metastasizing into such a political beast at that very moment. In 1967, stories of men ordered to burn down entire villages and reports of wayward bombs striking civilian targets began to leak into the US press: Pax understood these to be the logical consequences of the mindless bondage so prevalent in a modern society. Conscience broke this spell. "Silence by the American Bishops on this issue would be interpreted in different ways," Pax wrote, as if to shrug. "By some it would be taken to indicate that Catholics could depend on their government to make moral choices for them—resulting in the abdication of conscience that was condemned at the Nuremberg Trials."[43] If the bishops wanted a church that produced Jägerstätters rather than Eichmanns, they had better fully enunciate the rights of conscience from a nationally visible pulpit.

Rumors circulated among Catholic activists and intellectuals in the fall of 1968 that the bishops planned to address conscience rights in a pastoral letter. The curates would consider the matter in November 1968, at their annual meeting in Washington, DC. There, activists hoped, the leaders of the church would issue a clear statement on conscience rights that laymen from across the United States could cite at draft boards and in courtrooms. In the correspondence the bishops received about the annual meeting could be found a tense letter for Joseph Bernardin, general secretary of the Bishops' Conference, from Jesuit Peter J. Henroit, a Washington, DC–based Jesuit priest. Henroit laid bare a desperate situation. Despite the optimism that came with the replacement of General William Westmoreland in the summer of 1968, many young Catholics remained critical of the draft. Every Catholic male across the United States thus faced a painful choice: either "obey conscience" and go to prison or "violate conscience" and participate in war.[44] It was a lose-lose situation that jeopardized the eternal fates of a generation of young souls. Henroit pleaded with Bernardin to issue a clear statement on the vigor of subjectivity to alleviate the tensions pulling Catholic men in different directions. The Jesuit reminded him that he had at his disposal several statements by theologians, including one by John Courtney Murray, which upheld the legality and constitutionality of acting on internal light in response to an unjust war. And yet, Henroit observed, despite the prodigious corpus of conscience theology, a body of thought that had expanded considerably in the 1960s, lay Catholics faced the draft without any clear backing from the bishops. Henroit entered the same field of contradictions as the father from Minnesota who queried his local prelate. Only the bishops, for better or worse, could provide the needed guidelines to laypeople. "Whether or not one agrees with their views on the Vietnam War," Henroit wrote, "one must recognize that many men face serious decision of conscience without any positive, explicit, and clear guides being offered by those who should be helping them to form maturely their consciences in this matter."[45] Would the bishops back up lay Catholic conscience rights in the civil sphere?

The November 1968 meeting was not the conscience rights campaign's salvation. The pastoral statement the bishops issued, *Human Life in Our Day*, failed to meet the high standards of clarity set by the lobby's stalwart members. As a prime example of the interstitial nature of war and sex in the modern United States, the statement addressed both the priests in Washington, DC, who called for recognition of subjectivity in the bedroom and the antiwar activists who wanted conscience affirmed as young men faced the draft. The American prelates repeated the Vatican II style of affirming both sides of the Catholic Church's teaching on subjectivity: *Human Life in Our Day* upheld the rights of conscience, after formation, to reject unclear law, and the bishops simultaneously supported the law's ability to bind the conscience to obedience, especially the rule on contraception. But subtle changes were occurring among prominent clergymen amid a brutally unpopular war. The bishops dedicated paragraphs 135 to 155 of the statement to the Vietnam War, with the section's latter half briefly exploring the role of conscience. The bishops acknowledged themselves as heirs to "a spiritual tradition which accepts the enlightened conscience, even when honestly mistaken, as the immediate arbiter of moral decisions," and they celebrated the "decline of uncritical conformism to patterns."[46] They even advanced a moderately revisionist view of conscientious objectors, who, they suggested, might not be cowards but genuinely principled. But in paragraph 152, the document disappointed in the same fashion as Vatican II. There the bishops suggested that the state make it "possible but not easy" for Catholics to reject participation in a war judged unjust.

Bringing the bishops into the conscience lobby proved to be a difficult task. Gordon Zahn learned from an extended correspondence with the archbishop of Boston, Cardinal Richard Cushing, that powerful clergymen were men of affairs with many loyalties. A strong stand in the name of conscience would antagonize the considerable number of Catholics who supported the war effort. Zahn sent Cushing a letter on March 1, 1968, the twenty-fifth anniversary of Jägerstätter's execution, suggesting that he "alert" the Boston clergy to the fact that certain Catholics in their flocks "might feel obliged in conscience to refuse participation in what they believe to be an unjust war, just as Jägerstätter did twenty-five years ago this very day."[47] But Cushing—no matter what iteration of the theology Zahn elucidated in his letters—could not assert the rights of subjectivity in the unequivocal style the activist demanded. He thanked Zahn for the letter (and the enclosed donation of fifty dollars for Boston's Newman Centers), but the cardinal, considering the field of responsibilities before him, anticipated that an endorsement of self-rule on such a matter might hobble his efforts to recruit Catholic priests to the military chaplaincy. "I don't understand how I can come out with a statement that you recommend concerning the rights of religion and conscience at the present time," Cushing wrote, "when I am trying to get Chaplains to follow the troops wherever they go."[48] Catholics interacted regularly with the government, the military, and the Selective Service System—and public support for selective objection might damage all these relationships.

Cushing understood just how subversive conscience rights could be, even if Zahn truly believed that the Catholic's duty to follow and form conscience marked a traditional theology that deserved to prophesy from a high pulpit no matter the political consequences. But the cardinal simply thought his hands were tied on the matter. He told Zahn at the outset of their exchange that he could "never assume leadership in telling young men here or elsewhere that the war in Viet Nam [was] unjust and that if they sincerely believed [the war unjust] that they should not serve."[49] War, he argued, is the oldest institution of mankind (Cushing traced its roots to Cain and Abel), and Catholics all over the world had the duty to serve in their nation's armed forces. Prelates like Cushing were pulled in multiple directions. He probably knew very well that supporters of the war effort could be found in Boston's many ethnic neighborhoods and burgeoning suburbs. The Irish mothers on the South End and the Italian fathers on the North End likely had sons fighting in the jungles of Southeast Asia.

The pressure program for conscience rights still managed a series of small and symbolic victories as the war pushed on. The campaign—long the preserve of dedicated activists—watched a steady stream of bishops offer their endorsements. It began as a trickle in the late 1960s and expanded to a steady flow at the opening of the 1970s. The perduring of the war, the surging death toll, and the thousands of Catholic men graduating from the nation's universities pressured the bishops to speak out in the name of conscience rights. In 1967, Atlanta Archbishop John Paul J. Hallinan, a civil rights crusader, wrote a public letter for Pax proclaiming that "the nation [had] no intrinsic right to keep the individual's conscience, no matter how benignly," and he denounced the government's case that it and it alone decided on the morality of war, as "in the totalitarian, not the American tradition."[50] Pax reprinted the letter and circulated it widely.

But in January of 1969, Richard Nixon took the presidential oath of office and immediately expanded both the draft and the bombing campaigns. He ended graduate school deferments and made the paperwork for conscientious objection even more complex. Consequently, individual members of the hierarchy took it upon themselves to keep up the pressure on the state to grant concessions to Catholic conscience-followers. Albert Fletcher, the bishop of Little Rock, Arkansas, wrote J. William Fulbright, a US senator and chairman of the Foreign Relations Committee, to make the case for legal recognition of the rights of conscience.[51] Edmund S. Muskie, a senator from Maine, received a similar letter from Peter Gerety, the bishop of Portland, Oregon.[52] Joseph Brunini, the bishop of the Natchez-Jackson Diocese in Alabama, sent his congressmen a theological excursus on conscience in August 1970. Catholics encountered God on the sacred grounds of conscience, Brunini explained, and God revealed his plans during this one-on-one meeting. The state could promulgate laws, Brunini conceded, "but, in the last analysis, each young man makes his judgment for himself in the court of the last appeal, the forum of his own conscience where he is alone with God."[53] John J. Russell, bishop of Richmond, Virginia, endorsed the powers of subjectivity in June of 1970 with a letter published in the *Catholic Virginian*, his diocese's official newspaper.[54] A year later, Russell sent a character letter directly to Dr. Curtis W. Tarr, the national director of the Selective Service System, championing a young Catholic's right to self-governance in response to the draft. As he explained to the federal official, "The teaching of the Catholic Church with respect to participation of Catholics in war is quite clear. . . . The guiding principle has been one of adherence to the individual's carefully formed conscience."[55] The Catholic activists—and the pressure of a long war—brought a contingent of bishops into the conscience lobby by 1970.

Conscience Rights at the Supreme Court

To be sure, the conscience rights movement seemed to fail and succeed at the same time. Recognition from the state proved elusive even after a few bishops joined the cause. Jesuit political philosopher John Courtney Murray joined Yale president Kingman Brewster in casting a vote in favor of selective conscientious objection on a special presidential commission that convened in 1966. But the commission's eighteen other members voted against the measure. The vote was the first in a string of political failures; the House Armed Services Committee rejected the notion of selective conscientious objection only a month later. Moreover, conscience rights never came up for an official vote on the floor of the House or the Senate. Then a bit of luck: a test case fell into the hands of the Catholic conscience rights campaign, bringing new voices and influential people into the movement's center and offering a concrete political means, the courts, to secure protections for divine subjectivities.

In February of 1970, a judge from the Northern District of California delivered his verdict on a case that had been making its way through the Golden State's legal system for two years. Judge Alfonso Zirpoli, a critic of the war (with a draft-age son), concluded that a refusal to allow Catholics to follow conscience violated the Establishment Clause of the First Amendment.[56] The law exempted certain groups, Quakers and Jehovah's Witnesses, offering them a special establishment status, and discriminated against the arguments offered by Catholics. The most noteworthy part of the case was its victory: a powerful judge accepted a controversial defense of selective conscientious objection. Success was unexpected, given the conscience lobby's failures in Congress, and it marked a precedent.

The other astonishing aspect of the case was the extent to which courtroom arguments relied on Catholic doctrine. Richard Harrington, a seasoned draft lawyer who represented the eleven Catholic priests and two Catholic laymen who were suing the State of California, made a mixture of medieval and modern the crux of his winning argument. He portrayed Vatican II statements as the most recent in a long line requiring Catholics to follow conscience. The council's defense of conscience had roots in the work of Augustine and Thomas Aquinas, Harrington explained, and could be drawn as well from the early modern writings of Robert Bellarmine and Jesuit Francisco Suarez. The duty to act according to one's inner light also could be found in the books of Matthew and Romans, Pope Innocent III's decretals, and "the great treatise on theology" written by Alphonso Liguori.[57] This vast corpus of works, Harrington argued, "unequivocally placed upon [each of] the plaintiffs . . . the duty to examine and act in accordance with his own conscience."[58] All of a sudden, the campaign's provocative position on subjectivity and its generative capacities echoed in courts of law.

The rights of conscience finally found a point of entry into the legal system: a California court. But the celebration was short-lived: the federal government sued immediately, sending the California case to the US Supreme

Court. Federal officials moved quickly to close any loopholes opened by the rogue California judge. Curtis Tarr, director of the Selective Service System, told a House subcommittee on the draft in February 1970 that should the California ruling be left to stand, the Selective Service could not continue to draft men into the military. Two months later, Tarr warned of even direr consequences: selective conscientious objection, he told the Armed Services Committee, "would tend seriously to undermine the considered judgement of the country to wage war."[59] The Supreme Court agreed to hear a single case, *Gillette v. United States*, which bundled three selective conscientious objection suits.[60]

The bishops looked as if they would take over the conscience lobby as the date for opening arguments in the case, October 1970, drew nearer. They began making the moves necessary to file an amicus brief with the court in support of Louis Negre, a French-born Catholic from California and a self-proclaimed selective conscientious objector who cited just-war theory to make his case. John Noonan, one of the brightest legal minds in the United States and a famous Catholic author of important scholarly studies on doctrinal development, responded positively to the bishops in April of that year when approached about writing the brief. In June, Noonan submitted a draft to United States Conference of Catholic Bishops (USCCB) staffers. Though he was a law professor at the University of California–Berkeley, his legal take on the matter was leagues away from being a technical legal document.

In dramatic fashion, Noonan's memo retraced all the classic components of the doctrine of conscience. His argument was traditional: forcing a Catholic to act against realities disclosed in his or her inner sanctuary— the internal space where an individual listens to God—entails coercing that person to disobey God, violating his or her religious freedom. The state set Catholics against their God when it required them to fight in a war known in conscience to be immoral. "No command of secular authority may relieve the Catholic of his obligation to obey his conscience," Noonan wrote.[61] He explored the just-war sequence in church teachings, which, he argued, made ample room for the formation of conscience. Conscience formation and conscience-following signaled responsible moral behavior, not a perverse assertion of self-will. Shaping a subjective moral world with church teachings and consideration of the moral consequences of following a civil law was therefore an objective undertaking and not a political process. "Large latitude is given to the individual Catholic conscience to determine the character of a war," Noonan wrote. "In any moral action, [a Catholic] will consider a variety of factors—but this normal way of forming his conscience will not make his judgment merely personal or political."[62] The conscience formation process connected a Catholic to the objective external truth. Noonan's final layer of analysis placed the California plaintiffs on the doctrinal footpath hewn by the original apostles, early modern hero Thomas More, and Nazi resister Franz Jägerstätter. The blood splashed on the doctrine over the centuries made it self-evident that Catholics were obliged to follow conscience during the Vietnam War. "In the context of this teaching of some nineteen hundred years, sealed by the blood of martyrs, it is plain that for a Catholic to refuse to do an act because it is against his conscience is for him to fulfill the most basic duty of his religion," Noonan maintained.[63] The words of the amicus brief carried a Catholic imagination of sacred duty and blood; Noonan stressed church doctrine and tradition more than the US Constitution's Establishment Clause or due process clauses.

The Catholic movement for conscience rights in the nation's political life, like the Association of Washington Priests' case for conscience rights in the church itself, drew a sizable coterie of critics. Writers for *Jubilee* and the *Social Justice Review* slammed the lobby's central arguments in 1968, dismissing conscience as "unverifiable" and conscience rights as profoundly negligent of the church's rich political thought.[64] But the most damning critique came from William Consedine, the general counsel for the Bishops' Conference, in response to Noonan's June 1970 memo. The USCCB had created the Office of the General Counsel to monitor the legal system and the press for the church's interests in a wide range of areas. Consedine, the office's director, unleashed a scathing denunciation of Noonan's near-total investment in the theology of conscience and his neglect of constitutional and political considerations. Yet again, Catholics would be squaring off against fellow Catholics on the implications of the church's teachings on conscience. In a memo sent to Joseph Bernardin, the general secretary of the USCCB, Consedine warned that Noonan's brief was built on an irresponsible interpretation of recent church teachings.[65] The bishops had merely suggested that following conscience was to be an option; Consedine believed that they did not make it incumbent on all Catholics to follow conscience.

Three weeks after sending the first memo, having studied the *Gillette* case more fully, Consedine sent out a second one more critical than the first. He pointed out the inherent myopia of a doctrine that encouraged Catholics to transcend politics and neglect the law. Doctrine bound Catholics to follow conscience, but it did not oblige the state to recognize the claim. "So far as Catholic doctrine is concerned," Consedine wrote, "it is elementary both that Negre must obey his conscience and that the government is not bound by Negre's conscience." State law "is not subject to individual veto," the lawyer concluded.[66] He argued that the church's recent history worked against conscience rather than in its favor: both *Human Life in Our Day* and the Second Vatican Council placed considerable limits on it. Consedine reminded the bishops that Vatican II "was careful to specify that the individual's rights of conscience do not override the just requirements of public order."[67] All things considered, he suggested that the Noonan brief was not only politically obtuse but dangerous. Adopting Noonan's arguments might create friction between the Catholic Church and the Selective Service System; it might jeopardize the exemption for seminarians. If the bishops let Noonan write the amicus brief, priests and brothers might be forced to serve on the front as chaplains rather than as volunteers. Consedine, a lawyer in a specialized practice, advised his clients to remain silent as Supreme Court justices considered arguments in favor of and against Catholic conscientious objectors.

The leaders of the Catholic Church, persuaded by Consedine, decided not to help the campaign for conscience rights at the Supreme Court. Leaders in several committees at the USSCB quietly backed away from filing the paperwork after considering what Consedine had to say in his memos. But the lobby's failure to convince the prelates again contained seeds of victory. Several groups and individuals, including Noonan and Harrington, filed their own briefs. The amicus briefs and writs filed by other Catholic parties inscribed the rights of conscience into the Supreme Court's permanent record. In addition, Catholic defenses of subjectivity had a strong showing at the trial. Priests gave the justices an unrequested tutorial in the Catholic manual tradition. Documents filed for Louis Negre, the Catholic plaintiff, featured an eleven-page portion of a Jesuit priest's 1957 ethics manual, replete with lengthy discussions of error, certainty, doubt, formation, and "reflex principles."[68] A character letter from Jesuit James E. Straukamp accompanied the formal document. In it, Straukamp frankly informed the court about the advice he offered his spiritual mentee: "I counseled Private Negre that he was obliged to form his own conscience after giving all deference to the information and advice of the duly constituted government authorities and other persons, and that under Catholic doctrine he would be in religious duty bound to act in conformity to his conscience, even though it might err through invincible ignorance."[69] Negre had acted on the advice of his priest in objecting to the Vietnam War.

The most powerful defense of conscience came from the Executive Board of the National Priests Council. The board, which represented 127 local priest associations and thirty-three thousand clerics across the United States, explained that all Catholic priests have the sacred duty to help laypeople properly form their conscience. Under no circumstance, and with no exceptions, should a priest ever tell a layperson to contravene a deeply held subjective truth. That priest would be telling a Catholic man, who concluded in conscience that the Vietnam War was wrong, to go out and commit a mortal, potentially soul-damning sin. The priest's duty to instruct laypeople to form and follow their inner sanctum held the same stature as the laypeople's duty to follow conscience: it was sacred and unbreakable. The duty was universal and consistent. Priests, by their sacred vows and vocation, were free to ignore civil law and instruct their penitents to follow conscience. "For the Catholic religion unequivocally requires priests to counsel the faithful to follow conscience in respect to military service," the Executive Board explained, "whether or not civil law makes any provision for following conscience."[70] The Church and its priests could stand in judgment of civil law, and if they deemed it necessary, priests could advise laypeople to transcend the law and tip moral truth over to their conscience. Priests could not, however, tell a layperson to ignore or silence conscience. In other words, the priests refused to send Louis Negre to hell.

The Supreme Court disagreed. The justices voted 8–1 against selective conscientious objection. But once again, the conscience lobbyists did not quit—instead, new activists in the cause for conscience rights joined in the wake of the Supreme Court's ruling. The bishops, after refusing to support lay Catholics at the Supreme Court, came roaring into the ranks of the conscience lobby in 1971 and 1972. Joseph Bernardin, a top official at the USCCB, wrote a private letter to Senator Philip Hart, a Democrat from Michigan whose wife, Jane Briggs Hart, was active in the debate about birth control, asking him to bring up legislation on selective conscientious objection for a vote on the Senate floor.[71] Hart, a willing participant, set an amendment to the Selective Service Act in front of his colleagues on June 4, 1971. He translated the doctrine of conscience into broader American terms, but the Catholic vibe of his statement was readily apparent. The Michigan senator, in one of his more incendiary lines, made the case that the individual—and the individual alone—decides whether a war qualified as moral or immoral from the comfort of his own subjectivity. "The individual determination of what is a just war must be made by the individual in obedience to his personal perception and his own conscience," he wrote.[72] Downplaying the Supreme Court's decision, he celebrated the "proud element of a free society" that recognized responsible self-sovereignty.[73] Hart pleaded with the Senate to make a Catholic reality an American reality as the Vietnam War pushed into its near-final stage in the summer of 1971. But the senator, like other conscience rights advocates that came before him, failed. His colleagues ignored his recommended changes to the draft system.

Conclusion

As conscience rights suffered a stinging defeat in the Supreme Court and quiet dismissal in the Senate, the idea in its political incarnation entered its finest hour in the Catholic Church. The Supreme Court issued its opinion on *Gillette* in March of 1971, and just seven months later the bishops approved of a document asserting that the gospel and the Catholic Church's teaching on conscience made clear that a Catholic can be a total conscientious objector like a Quaker, or a selective objector in the just-war tradition. The bishops had received an advance draft of this statement in the spring of 1971 and were encouraged to offer amendments and suggest changes in language in the months leading up to their November meeting. Jesuit priest Patrick McDermott, assistant director of the Division of World Peace and Justice, a subcommittee of the United States Conference of Catholic Bishops, shepherded the statement through layers of church bureaucracy that spring and summer. Ballots came pouring into the USCCB mailroom in June and July, just two months after the *Gillette* decision. Most bishops favored the statement even if many expressed anxiety about the excesses of subjectivity. The final document earned the required two-thirds majority needed to pass it without much controversy. The general secretary of the USCCB, Bishop Joseph Bernardin, informed a fellow curate that 217 bishops voted in the affirmative for the statement, and just 31 in the negative.[74] The text became available to the public in February 1972. The Catholic Church and the Selective Service System, which had shared a comfortable relationship since World War I, diverged sharply during the Vietnam War over the question of conscience rights.

With this statement, the bishops stood alongside activists, theologians, priests, and laypeople in declaring that the law was "not perspicacious enough," "not just enough," "not deliberate enough," "not total enough," and nowhere near "moral enough" to guide Catholics and their fellow citizens in a time of war. The highly placed prelates, often conservative on many matters regarding war during the twentieth century, straightened out the ambiguous theology of conscience created by the Second Vatican Council and later texts. No Catholic or other person, it seemed, could be forced to violate conscience in wartime. The bishops' willingness to subvert civil law is stunning. Their statement signaled a dramatic move away from a church that had loyally followed the American flag during World War II and the Cold War. The bishops hesitated to apply the rights of conscience to conscription out of fear they would jeopardize friendly relations with the Selective Service System. But in 1972, they gambled with national security and risked their comity with the state: if the bishops backed conscience, one episcopal supporter of the statement rightly concluded, "the whole foundation of the authority of the state could be compromised." The doctrine legitimated acting on subjective cues, as it always had, but now the bishops gave conscience rights a stronger possibility of creating a new reality in the world. "It must be admitted," the bishop wrote, pushing aside security concerns, "that if the judgment of an individual conscience to a particular war is unjust, the conscience of the individual should be respected."[75] Perhaps the authority of law really would evaporate and the state's ability to coerce would be seriously curtailed.

Multiple state actors positioned at various rungs of power found conscience rights preposterous. No order could be upheld without law. No security could be secured without a draft that sent civilian soldiers abroad. Commissions, congressmen, senators, and Supreme Court justices shot down the concept of conscience rights time and again. Nearly a year after the bishops published their statement, the United States completely withdrew its military forces from Vietnam. The North Vietnamese rushed toward Saigon (which they would later rename Ho Chi Minh City), prompting a massive refugee crisis felt across the South Pacific and on the US West Coast. Conscience rights were a failed political project as of 1973. The deep irony of the story is that the conscience rights struggle became moot almost overnight when Congress ended the draft. No evidence can be found to responsibly claim that the Catholic conscience rights campaign helped end the draft. But a rebellion against state law that made its way from local draft boards all the way to the US Supreme Court could not have helped keep conscription on the books.

The bishops became defenders of conscience at a fortuitous moment in US history. The law was about to stride from one crisis into the next, out of war and into the realm of sexual politics. When the Supreme Court struck down the state laws that restricted abortion in 1973, the infrastructure of the conscience rights movement was still in place. The bishops, assuming the lobby's mandate, immediately transferred the idea from soldiers onto doctors, nurses, pharmacists, and hospital administrators who, it was believed, might be forced to perform abortions. The next story to tell is how the pro-life movement borrowed concepts from the antiwar movement.

SEVEN

Beyond the Catholic Church

The drive for conscience rights in the Catholic Church and in civil society yielded, at best, ambiguous results. Many of the priests who served as the public face of the campaign in the important realm of artificial birth control did not remain in the church after enduring suspensions from teaching, preaching, and hearing confessions. The strategy of attrition deployed by Cardinal Patrick O'Boyle, archbishop of Washington, wore down his opposition. Claiming the last word, however, was the Association of Washington Priests—an official organization of Catholic clergymen created to pass judgments on relevant issues in the church—as conscience language spread among American Catholics, and the breakdown of the authority of law generated creative syntheses of modern psychology, Jewish thought, and medieval theology. The fate of the political arm of the conscience rights movement was also quite mixed. Draft board officers responded stoically to lay Catholics' seemingly endless incantations of the doctrine of conscience. Paeans to subjectivity and its expansive powers left congressmen, senators, commissioners, and US Supreme Court justices unmoved. Then in 1973, the battle to legalize selective conscientious objection became moot immediately after Congress scrapped the Selective Service System in favor of an all-volunteer army.

But Catholic conscience language flourished in the United States and around the world as it seemed to enter fields of fierce theological conflict in the arenas of marital sexuality and conscription. Catholic debates about sex and war injected a new vocabulary of subjectivity into wider national political and religious discourses. The Catholic Church, in fact, was the launching pad for a particular post-1960s iteration of conscience rights, an idea and a language that became common in late twentieth-century American life. The enduring legacy of the two-pronged movement for Catholic conscience rights in sex and war is a series of contests, fought in the nation's courts and in the realm of ideas, about when a law should command obedience and when it should yield to conscience, the individual's own truth creator.

Catholics found allies and enemies in this struggle. Protestants became unlikely partners. Secular human rights activists discovered that they shared with Catholics a passion for protecting individual dignity. Then the faithful conflicted with the liberal democratic state again as the central moral issue of the times moved from war to abortion. Legislators who expanded the state's commitment to providing medical care often forgot to provide conscience protections for doctors who wished to decline participation in the program on account of its facilitation of abortions. Catholic priests were quick to remind the state to honor such freedoms. Catholics also objected to the fact that the United States Commission on Civil Rights understood conscience protections as inhibiting the spread of civil rights (accusing morally fastidious Catholic doctors and nurses of prohibiting the realization of reproductive rights), and so they pushed back to make sure that subjective freedoms to follow one's own moral vision became politically mainstream. Ironically, where Catholics failed on the question of war, they succeeded on the matter of abortion; the state, feeling the grassroots movement of the pro-life religious right, changed its position and supported conscience rights regarding reproduction. In the end, Catholics doomed themselves to repeat the same paradoxical intellectual trap they had constructed during the debates over contraception and conscription: as they pushed for rights of conscience from the liberal democratic state on the matter of abortion and as a broader human right to seek truth, Pope John Paul II and Cardinal Joseph Ratzinger (future Pope Benedict XVI) clamped down on the rise of moral subjectivity in the church itself. The seemingly insoluble debate over law and conscience became one of the primary legacies of the church's turn to Thomas Aquinas in the modern era.

Liberal Protestants

Literary scholar Farrell O'Gorman found a fear running through nineteenth-century Protestant thought that Catholics, aliens to a democratic culture, threatened to collapse the important distinction between self and society.[1] Mainline Protestants carried that anxiety into the twentieth century. The institutional Catholic Church was the conscience of its members; a Catholic self apart from the hierarchy's power did not exist. Thinkers like Paul Tillich and Paul Blanshard, as explored in chapter 1, noted casually that Catholics could not possess a conscience because the word *conscience* meant making a direct connection to God.[2] Priestly mediators stood in the way of any parishioner seeking a straight approach to the divine.

In the 1960s, mainline Protestants abandoned this interpretation and became public promoters of Catholic conscience language. They made this dramatic reversal after entering what historian David Hollinger calls "a mood of self-interrogation."[3] The view that subjectivity stood on its own and that God beamed commands into it suddenly seemed naïve. "The voice of conscience is never unambiguously the voice of God," a writer for the *Christian Century* warned readers in 1968.[4] When Protestants undertook this act of self-critique, one of the intellectual roadblocks preventing a wider diffusion of Catholic concepts of self-rule—and any reconciliation between mainline Protestants and Catholics—came tumbling down. They began to study the Catholic theology of conscience, and they encouraged one another to recognize Catholics as authorities on the matter.

Part of the turn was pragmatic: Catholics had undertaken a great deal of research on the formation of internal moral regulators, Protestants quite simply had not. The irony of a group who over the entire span of US history had been calling for freedom of inner religious light without having done much serious research on the concept was not lost on Yale Divinity professor David Little, a presenter at the 1969 conference at Fordham University. "Roman Catholics need no reminder that it is important to think about the conscience," his paper began. "They have been pondering it with a good deal of sophistication for a long time."[5] Protestants, on the other hand, "have not of late engaged in much systematic reflection on the subject of conscience." This is strange, Little observed, "because Protestants are usually eager to claim 'freedom of conscience' as one of the great contributions of Protestantism to the rise of modern society."[6] Protestants could claim Roger Williams, Anne Hutchinson, and William Penn, but the terms of the conscience debate changed in the twentieth century. Protestants were taking the term for granted, whereas modern Catholics were not. Catholics nurtured a tradition of conscience and deepened their understanding of the term through extensive research—producing studies that became highly relevant in the 1960s and 1970s. Eric Mount, a professor at Centre College in Kentucky and former student of Richard Niebuhr, concluded that Protestants' deficiencies on the question of self-sovereignty could be remedied with a study of Catholicism. After a period of neglect, he wrote in a 1969 book, Protestants were "beginning a dialogue concerning the concept of conscience with Roman Catholic thinkers, in whose tradition conscience

has generally remained an important term."[7] The Catholic language of conscience came to prominence in American life in the 1960s and 1970s as a
group of critics suddenly became supporters.

Protestant theologian Paul Lehmann prepared the way for mainline
Protestants to see the Catholic idea of well-formed subjectivity as more de-
sirable than the autonomous conscience. Without placing too much faith
in the law, Lehmann, an intellectual journeyman who taught at Harvard,
Princeton, and Union Seminary, admitted that subjectivity required training
under external sources, conceding a point that priests had maintained for
centuries. His breakthrough 1963 book, *Ethics in a Christian Context*, argued
that individuals should form a conscience in the framework of community
and interpersonal relationships. He struck the balance between internal
and external after offering a series of critiques of both autonomy and law.
"Conscience may once have been a clear and certain interpreter of the will
of God . . . but it is no longer," he told colleagues at Princeton.[8] Protestants
became like Lehmann critical of autonomy, but they were not ready to grant
laws complete power over conscience. Ordinances did not provide refuge:
"The consciences of Catholics and Protestants alike have been bogged down
by the deadening gap between the strident certainties claimed for moral
insight and counsel and the daily occasions and responsibilities of decision-
making."[9] Law, in other words, could never provide guidance in the messi-
ness of day-to-day existence.

Where does one turn for moral guidance if both the law and the autonomous conscience are unreliable moral guides? Lehmann admitted that
institutions and communities might play an important role in forming conscience, moving the subjective guide for moral life into a conversation with
objective norms. Catholics had been splitting the difference between objective rules and subjective perceptions in a sophisticated and suddenly enviable
manner. Protestant thinkers like Lehmann celebrated the Catholic concept
of well-formed subjectivity as they abandoned Reformation-era autonomy.
A Catholic theologian noted the change in tune: Protestant theologians suddenly "emphasize[d] the necessity of avoiding the kind of individualism that
would make conscience a God."[10]

Prominent among the critics of autonomy was Carl Ellis Nelson, a Texan
whose intellectual talents earned him a faculty position at Union Theological Seminary in New York City in 1957. Freudian psychoanalysis convinced Nelson, as it did a generation of Catholic thinkers, that the profound
influence of familial and communal authorities on conscience means that
the internal faculty does not begin its life as an autarchic entity. Psychology
proved to be his gateway to Catholic theology. A Presbyterian who once

served as his denomination's national director of youth work, Nelson secured a grant from the Farmington Trust in 1972 to visit famous Catholic
seminaries and catechetical centers across Europe. He first visited Catholic
schools and colleges in Manchester, England, the institutions nearest to Oxford University, home base for his fellowship. Then he traveled to Brussels
to meet with Jesuit Andre Godin, a pioneer in the effort to blend psychology
and religion. The two men discussed moral theology and religious education.[11] Nelson next sat down with Father Antoine Vergote of the University
of Leuven to discuss the Catholic notion of conscience formation.[12] And he
also paid a visit to the Dutch Catechetical Center in Nijmegen, the very institution that produced the famous 1967 Dutch Catechism.

Nelson's adventures in Catholic Europe and the prodding of a Catholic
editor convinced him to assemble a 1973 volume of essays entitled *Conscience: Theological and Psychological Perspectives*. Robert Heyer, an editor at
Paulist-Newman Press, a prominent Catholic publishing house, asked him
to select several essays for publication. Nelson, who had been teaching a
seminar on conscience for over a dozen years at Union Seminary, had a sea
of literature at his fingertips. His choices are telling of the late twentieth-
century migration of Catholic conscience language into new territories. Six
of the thirteen essays making it into the volume were from Catholic contributors. These communicated the flexibility of the Catholic notion of conscience, and they conveyed the concept's high status in Catholic theology, an
importance dating to the thirteenth-century world of Thomas Aquinas. The
essays from Protestant contributors, on the other hand, continued the assault
on the autonomous conscience. Nelson bluntly summarized one contribu-
tor's essay as having proved that Luther never advocated for an autonomous
conscience. "Rather," he noted, it was modern Protestants who, in creating
a myth that conscience is free from authority, "have created a problem to
which they have found no satisfactory solution."[13] The entire volume suggested that Catholics had a better grip on the formation and development
of conscience than did Protestants. With such a confession, mainline Protestants flipped one of the guiding assumptions of the Reformation on its head.

Nelson, though a Presbyterian teaching at one of the nation's foremost
Protestant seminaries, was producing a book for a Catholic audience, and
this became a source of pride for him. In a letter written several years later
to a contact at San Francisco Theological Seminary, he claimed his book
was "widely used in courses on moral theology in Catholic colleges."[14] In
the acknowledgments, Nelson thanked Jesuit Robert Springer, author of the
important 1968 pamphlet *Conscience and the Behavioral Sciences*, for helping
him select the essays.

The Vietnam War compelled Protestants and Catholics to find common ground on the question of conscience and its formation. In 1967, Daniel Berrigan and John Sheerin attached their signatures to the "Statement of Conscience" issued by Clergy and Laymen Concerned about Vietnam. They joined Protestant luminaries like Martin Marty, Harvey Cox, and Robert McAfee Brown in publishing a statement that contained twenty-one mentions of the word *conscience*.[15] The absolute prohibition of abdicating conscience to a state authority figure and the spirit of Nuremberg Agreement, signatures of a Catholic influence, permeated the document.

Roger Shinn, a colleague of Nelson's at Union Seminary, announced in a statement to the Senate Armed Services Committee that the Second Vatican Council and the Nuremberg verdicts, more than any other statements available, proved that "men have no right to hand their consciences over to the state." Vatican II inherited the mantle of the Nuremberg outcome. Both pronouncements made clear that "men had a responsibility for the exercise of conscience" and could never blindly obey civil authorities.[16] Shinn had the personal integrity to make the case: war and death were prominent features in his many writings, but he also fought at the Battle of the Bulge in World War II, earning a Silver Star for valor. He arrived at Union Theological Seminary in 1960, first as a professor of applied Christianity and later promoted to a chair in social ethics named for his mentor and Union's most famous scholar, Reinhold Niebuhr.

Sifting through Shinn's personal papers tells a story of a speaker who presented at a full circuit of academic conferences in the heady ecumenical days of the early 1960s. The Jesuits of Woodstock College in Maryland, among them John Courtney Murray, invited Shinn to give an address in 1963. He also gave lectures alongside Catholic thinkers like John Tracy Ellis, Walter Ong, Dorothy Day, and Daniel Berrigan. Shinn's intense engagement with these thinkers during the Vietnam War perhaps explains his recognition of the Catholic political theology of conscience in a radio address given as the draft reached deeper into civilian life in 1966. As he ruminated on how "men had no right to turn over their conscience to their government," Shinn told the audience he always recalled a sentence written by a Belgian Jesuit, Father Piet Fransen: "Nothing is so sacred and final as the human conscience."[17] Shinn's mentioning this sentence encapsulated the major breakthrough of the Catholic teaching on conscience into mainline Protestantism and beyond. Shinn had not turned to Martin Luther or the Westminster Confession for a declaration on the autonomy of conscience. He had turned instead to a European Jesuit.

Mainline Protestants replaced their antebellum and even modern fear that Catholic confessors destroyed the conscience with the notion that Catholics were the most articulate and committed defenders of the person's sacred internal chamber. Jesuits had been regarded as the most notorious destroyers of conscience since the Counter-Reformation of the sixteenth century. Protestants long believed that Jesuits promoted the sacrament of confession in a concerted effort to snuff out the subjective dimensions of moral decision-making. But by the 1960s, mainline Protestants like Shinn and Nelson asked Jesuits for advice on the nature of conscience and quoted European Jesuits in public addresses on the topic. Shinn was hardly alone in applying the Catholic doctrine of conscience to the draft: Edward LeRoy Long of Oberlin College, Ralph Potter of Harvard Divinity School, and Paul Ramsey of Duke University all tipped their respective caps to the Catholic Church's strong stand for conscience rights.[18]

Amnesty International

Mark Philip Bradley, a distinguished historian of human rights, observes that for Amnesty International, "the idea of individual conscience inflected all of its work." Conscience stood as "the emotive watchword of Amnesty's engagement with human rights."[19] Conscience long occupied a central conceptual ground for that organization, from the 1961 editorial Peter Beneson wrote announcing its conscience rights campaign to the creation by 1980 of about two hundred letter-writing groups in the United States who took pen to paper to free "prisoners of conscience."[20] Beneson, a British solicitor who converted to Catholicism in 1958, coined the phrase "prisoner of conscience" in his editorial, which publicized the formation of Amnesty International and outlined its intentions to free nonviolent men and women from jails worldwide. Over a decade and a half later, the organization was awarded the Nobel Peace Prize, and its phrase had become a fixture in the global lexicon of human rights.

Beneson took conscience from its home in Catholic theology and circulated it around the world. Amnesty International secularized that theology, translating the doctrinal duty to follow conscience into a human right. It believed that as a law became unjust, the individual's inner resources were to serve as his or her leading moral guide. Farmers, laborers, doctors, parliamentarians, teachers, students, journalists, poets, playwrights, scientists, psychologists, students, and teachers followed conscience when critiquing a state or organizing a protest of an unjust law. The importance of conscience rose as a law became unjust; but from the standpoint of Amnesty International, all people followed conscience: individuals need only critique the state and find themselves in jail to act on their inner light.

Indeed, the organization pursued a broad definition of *conscience*—a 1977 Amnesty International flyer called it "a knowledge or feeling of right or wrong, with a compulsion to do right"—but the dilemma of law and conscience central to Catholic thought permeated the group's campaign.[21] A 1977 pamphlet, *Trade Unionists in Prison*, called attention to the plight of Sipho Kubheka, a South African union organizer placed under permanent house arrest for demanding labor rights.[22] Another 1977 pamphlet, *Lawyers in Prison*, named Cuban attorney and writer Angel Cuadra Landrove a prisoner of conscience after Fidel Castro imprisoned him for critiquing communism.[23] In both these situations, conscience, not law, was the premier moral guide. Prisoners of conscience like Kubheka and Landrove—and the tens of thousands like them across the world—acted on holy self-sovereignty and yet still saw the inside of a prison cell. The Catholic Church long held that the individual was obliged to follow subjectivity, and Amnesty International expanded and secularized that duty to encompass a wide variety of political dissents.

Scholars like philosopher Charles Taylor and historian Lincoln Mullen have taught us that secularization is the relocation of religion, not its end.[24] Belief endured in the late twentieth century, even as it became one choice of many to create a worldview. Amnesty International went to great lengths to make religious believers an important constituency of its outreach. It defended priests, nuns, preachers, ministers, laypeople, worshippers, and supplicants from all faiths and across all continents. In other words, it made religion a category, not a doctrine with access to a transcendent truth. Priests followed conscience the same way that a parliamentarian, journalist, union leader, or educator followed conscience. Despite this unwillingness to see religion as a special category, it retained an important ideological role in Amnesty International's campaign. Christian symbols called activists to arms to defend prisoners of conscience: an Amnesty International ad from the mid-1970s portrayed Jesus, Martin Luther, and Martin Luther King as prisoners of conscience.[25] A 1977 magazine ad depicted Christ being whipped by Roman soldiers above the statement "He was a prisoner of conscience, hated and persecuted."[26] The rest of the text assured readers that Christ was not the first prisoner of conscience and that many would suffer a similar fate in the contemporary world. The Soviet Union proved to be a particularly fertile breeding ground for religious prisoners of conscience at the end of the 1970s. "Over the years Amnesty International has also adopted prisoners of conscience from among the Lithuanian Catholic, Uniate Catholic, Russian Orthodox, True Orthodox Church, Jehovah's Witnesses, Jewish, Muslim, Buddhist and Georgian Orthodox religious groups," a 1979 report read.[27] The prisoner of conscience framework entailed an even deeper move into the landscape of religious diversity by defending not only people of faith and secular dissidents but also prisoners of conscience motivated by any faith tradition or none at all. Universalizing conscience entailed the translation of a doctrine into a program useful for the entire world, secular and religious.

The Catholic Church's defense of conscience anticipated the explosion of interest in human rights in the 1970s studied famously by historian Samuel Moyn.[28] Catholics laid the groundwork and readied hundreds of churches to welcome Amnesty International's linkage of conscience-following and human rights. Amnesty shrewdly exploited the opportunity. In a stroke of organizational brilliance, Amnesty International USA's California branch created an Inter-Religious Urgent Action Network, a pipeline that connected specific religious prisoners of conscience (priests, ministers, laypeople) to parishes and congregations on the West Coast. A memo sent to those churches offered their members the opportunity to write letters on behalf of Catholic priests in Spain, Seventh-Day Adventists in Rwanda, or Jewish activists in Argentina.[29] A group of Catholic laypeople also could write letters on behalf of ordained members of their church suffering in prison. In the mid-1970s, Amnesty distributed cards to Catholic churches featuring the image of South Korean Bishop Kim Chi Ha (in jail for criticizing the state), deliberately created to resemble the holy cards held by the faithful when praying to the saints for intercessions.[30] American Christians sent Amnesty long testimonials about the rewarding experience of defending conscience rights abroad from the comfort of their own religious sanctuaries. For reasons like these, Pope John Paul II could attach his signature to Amnesty's 1983 "Universal Appeal for Amnesty for All Prisoners of Conscience," even as he oversaw a Congregation of the Doctrine of Faith that rejected theologians' claims to conscience when it came to doctrinal disputes.[31]

Christians infused the precious theology of conscience into Amnesty International's infrastructure. The organization became a conduit through which the idea flowed into the world. The editors of *America*, a Jesuit magazine, thought Amnesty had been "touched by the spirt of the Lord," because it was "dedicated to freeing those who are unjustly held captive."[32] They applauded its efforts to liberate religious prisoners, such as a Serbian Catholic and church organist tossed in jail for distributing literature on the Fatima apparitions. They understood Amnesty as walking in the footsteps of the Catholic tradition of protecting conscience-followers. Christians, the editors wrote, "must go beyond appeals to human authorities. They recall that Thomas More, one of history's most famous prisoners of conscience, used to ask for prayers that he might not grow fainthearted."[33] Amnesty protected thousands of More-like figures suffering in jails worldwide. For their part, Catholics forged the links that created a sacred chain of conscience-followers, from the apostles of the New Testament, to the early modern plight of Thomas More, to the execution of Franz Jägerstätter in Nazi Germany. They authored the intellectual genealogy that stretched from late medieval Thomas Aquinas, to Enlightenment confessor Alphonsus Liguori, to twentieth-century American Catholic thinkers like John Ford, Francis Connell, Paul Marx, Patrick O'Boyle, Robert Springer, Thomas Cornell, James Forest, Eileen Egan, Sister Mary Brendan, John Noonan, and Gordon Zahn. Amnesty International stepped into the deep flow of this tradition and invited Christians into the stream to join the cause for conscience rights.

Abortion and Religious Freedom

In January 1973, the same month that president Richard Nixon and secretary of state Henry Kissinger pledged the withdrawal of US forces from Vietnam, the US Supreme Court decided *Roe v. Wade*, striking down the state laws that made abortion illegal. The campaign for conscience rights had gained traction during the 1960s in the debates about contraception and conscription before gliding out of these realms and into the brave new world of abortion politics, in which Catholics replaced the young men who faced conscription with the doctors and nurses who faced the specter (real or imagined) of being forced to provide abortions against their will. In other words, Catholics found themselves on familiar terrain in the early 1970s. During World War II and the Cold War, they lobbied for the conscience rights of military doctors and nurses who might be forced to provide sterilizations or abortions; they also advocated for quartermasters tasked with distributing contraceptives to soldiers. But now the threat to the conscience in operating rooms and physicians' offices expanded to include the entire nation. Two crucial shifts in the history of conscience rights occurred in the early 1970s: first, the conscience rights campaign moved gracefully from the causes of anticonscription and antidraft to the pro-life cause of protecting doctors and nurses from involuntary participation in abortion procedures. Second, the bishops and their staffers at the Washington, DC–based United States Conference of Catholic Bishops (USCCB) replaced the activists, laypeople, parish priests, and theologians as leaders of the movement. The latter shift stems from the fact that the Catholic bishops, led by Pope John Paul II, became profoundly committed to defending and promoting modes of traditional sexual morality.

The bishops came late to the assistance of conscience-followers during the Vietnam War but arrived early to defend the conscience of doctors, nurses, pharmacists, and hospital administrators who, it was believed, might be forced to perform abortions. Their emphatic endorsement of conscience rights at the end of the Vietnam War paid unexpected dividends when Nixon signed the Health Programs Extension Act in June of 1973. Dubbed the Church Amendment after its sponsor, Frank Church, the Democratic senator from Idaho, the bill allowed hospital personnel to refuse to perform abortions. This "conscience clause" prevented federal authorities from forcing individuals to carry out medical procedures that violated moral commitments fiercely held in the confines of a person's internal chamber. Historian Sara Dubow has shown that the Catholic Church was the most consistent supporter of the conscience clause in the months after *Roe v. Wade*.[34]

The Catholic language of conscience and the theological concept itself set the terms for the debate over reproductive freedom in the United States for the remainder of the twentieth century. The Catholic Church had long argued, appealing to a doctrine with roots in the medieval world, that no political authority can force an individual to violate conscience. This theological proposition finally found political backing from the liberal democratic state in the summer of 1973, when Nixon made the Church Amendment into law. Suddenly, the doctrine possessed real political power: the state actively protected conscience-followers. The Catholic campaign for conscience rights that emerged from church doctrine, world wars, totalitarianism, the invasion of Vietnam, raucous congressional debates over contraception, and the psychological notion of moral growth achieved its most stunning political victory in the realm of biopolitics. By the end of 1974, twenty-eight states had passed conscience clauses. As Ronit Stahl and Ezekiel Emanuel have shown, these loopholes proliferated in the United States after the 1970s.[35] The conscience clause, in effect, translated traditional Catholic theology into federal law.

When the Supreme Court struck down state laws prohibiting abortion in January of 1973, Catholics feared that state governments might require all hospitals to provide abortion services. Only four days after the *Roe* decision, Father Edward D. Head, chairman of the USCCB's Committee on Health Affairs, proclaimed that Catholics stood against "anything which might require health care personnel anywhere to participate in abortion procedures in violation of their consciences."[36] Priests and activists openly discussed their plans to tell the faithful to follow conscience and challenge the law. The newly formed Ad Hoc Committee on Pro-Life Activities called on nurses, doctors, and scientists to prove, with scholarly studies, that life begins before birth. It also began to apply the traditional teachings on self-governance and self-preservation to the budding moral crisis. Studies should go beyond science, an early memo noted, and "include the bases for conscientious refusal to participate in abortion procedures." By way of auguring the expansion of conscience rights, it then stated that the studies "should emphasize the freedom of conscience of non-Catholics as well as Catholics."[37]

Father James T. McHugh, a rising talent in the USCCB bureaucracy appointed to serve as the bishops' first director of pro-life activities in 1967, encouraged hospitals and health care personnel to stand strong against abortion laws. McHugh specialized in the defense of the unborn, a commitment nurtured in his theological training at Immaculate Conception Seminary in New Jersey and sociological studies at Fordham University and the Catholic University of America. He tracked with interest the rise of conscience clauses in the courts and legislatures. He praised the Supreme Court in February 1973 for not striking down conscience clause legislation passed in Georgia. And while he was optimistic about the rise of conscience clauses, McHugh believed that mobilizations to defend individual inner sanctuaries had to occur at the local institutional level. He encouraged each Catholic hospital to formulate its own conscience clause. Such a provision ought to state in plain language that "no physician, nurse or health care personal [would] be required to perform or assist in abortion procedures when it violates his/her conscience."[38] All hospital personnel called on to take part in abortion procedures, McHugh advised, should alert administrators and superiors to an impending involuntary transgression against subjectivity.[39]

On one hand, the conscience rights campaign during the Vietnam War sharpened the strategy Catholics put in place to achieve recognition of those rights, and on the other, the strong push for conscience rights in the area of reproductive health revealed fresh contradictions. Steve Bossi, a staffer with the USCCB's Division of Rural Life, wondered in a memo whether the program would become a selective instead of a consistent ethic. Church officials could not maintain a logical stance if they supported conscience rights on the matter of abortion without calling on the state to grant full amnesty to conscientious objectors to war. The rush to defend the inner sanctuaries of doctors and nurses threatened to slight other followers of conscience. "A denial to amnesty to those who could not in conscience serve in Vietnam is totally inconsistent with a pastoral instruction to commit civil disobedience in the case of abortion," Bossi argued.[40] Could the Catholic Church create a consistent ethic of disobedience to the state that became an integrated, all-encompassing defense of conscience rights across the realms of war and abortion? The doctrine of conscience rights served its contradictory revenge yet again. Bossi contended that doctrine cannot be applied selectively. If both sets of laws were truly unjust, then it became valid to follow conscience on both grounds. Nor could the church waver in one area if it wanted to stand strong in another.

Bossi's memo expressed desires for the realization of what activist Eileen Egan had described two years prior as the "seamless garment of life."[41] In the 1970s and1980s, the Catholic Church moved toward an ideal of offering a consistent response to life issues in the realms of abortion, capital punishment, euthanasia, war, and capitalism. In theory, all these affronts to human life merited a strong response from the church to protect the dignity of the person; and Bossi, operating in this headspace, entreated his fellow USCCB staffers to treat soldiers who objected to war and doctors who objected to abortion with the same respect. The phrase "seamless garment of life" became a conspicuous idea in 1983 after Cardinal Joseph Bernardin of Chicago used the words in a speech condemning nuclear war and abortion. He would later stretch the garment to include protection of poor, elderly, sick, incarcerated, and military people. The Bossi memo is a piece of bureaucratic minutia that likely went unanswered, but it spoke to a mode of public Catholicism that became a preferred approach (in rhetoric if not in practice) at the end of the twentieth century. Catholics emerged from the Vietnam War into the abortion controversy with an aspiration to protect all modes of life along with the bureaucratic agents (soldiers, doctors, and administrators) who sought exemption from participation in organizations threatening the sanctity of life. In the case of conscience rights, however, the issue of abortion came to the forefront when war faded as a primary concern after the termination of the draft in 1973 and the birth of the all-volunteer army.

McHugh gleaned a different lesson from the Vietnam-era quest for conscience rights. On the matter of war, lay Catholics who followed conscience seemed to have a more fastidious morality than the church itself. McHugh believed that the nation's bishops needed to emerge at the outset of the debate on abortion, calling for a strong defense of conscience rights. Lay Catholics had made statements about the immorality of war for several years before the bishops finally caught up with them in February of 1972. Thus the state, aware of the gap, questioned whether the church did in fact support Catholics selective conscientious objectors. McHugh wrote, "Our problems with conscientious objection to military service have taught us that the individual's personal conscience has been questioned if his personal views were stricter than the position of the church."[42] Lay Catholic doctors and nurses could follow the hierarchy's lead if the bishops spoke out strongly for conscience rights in regard to abortion. These efforts fortified subjectivity against the state.

Conscience entered mainstream political discourse in the 1970s as Catholics made conscience-following a right that could be possessed by all citizens. When the Catholic doctrine of robust subjectivity entered the discourse of religious freedom in biopolitics, the idea remade the long-standing American principle into a right to live out one's own moral vision. Catholics spoke less about medieval doctrine and more about the First Amendment. Theological ontologies were abandoned for the more capacious and more widely known language of "freedom of conscience." No references to Thomas Aquinas, Thomas More, Alphonso Liguori, or Franz Jägerstätter appeared in the pro-life memos.

The Committee on Pro-Life Activities believed that new freedom of conscience legislation should be made with both Catholics and non-Catholics in mind. This approach would "[broaden] the base for conscientious objection, and . . . not make it exclusively a religious question," McHugh explained.[43] Catholics translated a medieval concept into a public language during the initial phases of the debate over abortion, joining Protestants and secular liberals in becoming defenders of conscience. Conscience rights, while promoted during Vietnam to protect the men who followed Catholic doctrine, were remade by their new promoters at the USCCB to bring non-Catholic objectors, whether secular or religious, under their auspices.

Catholics turned the post-1970s United States into a series of proxy wars between law and conscience. James Rausch, a Minnesota priest appointed general secretary of the USCCB in 1973 who would later be accused of sexually abusing a seventeen-year-old boy, campaigned for conscience rights as abortion entered the areas of welfare policy and pregnancy benefits. In late 1973, the US Department of Labor published "A Proposed Revision of Guidelines on Sex Discrimination," which called on government contractors to insure charges incurred from pregnancy, miscarriage, and early child care. Rausch did not object to providing benefits to pregnant women; he questioned why the Labor Department allowed the insurance money to be spent on abortion. He protested the policy on the grounds that certain government contractors would have to violate conscience when insurance covered the cost of an employee's abortion. "The proposed guidelines would have the effect of coercing Government contractors to violate their consciences in order to retain or receive a Government contract," he wrote.[44]

Rausch called the Labor Department's attention to the conscience clause, signed into law by President Nixon in January 1973. The rule made it illegal for the department to enforce the new mandates: "the inclusion of abortion in this guideline directly contradicts the religious belief of many citizens, and forces them to violate their consciences."[45] The legislation—which the Catholic Church had championed—was not anchored in theology or doctrine, so it covered all Americans with conscience convictions, religious or secular. No stranger to national politics, Rausch regularly visited Capitol Hill in the 1970s and 1980s to discuss world hunger, civil rights, human rights, housing, and health care. Conscience rights, in response to the law's approval of abortion, became another one of his causes. Although a well-known social justice warrior, Rausch personified the double identity of certain Catholic priests during the church's sex abuse scandals of the late twentieth century. His own lawsuit was settled in 2002. His accuser, who claimed to have incriminating photos of Rausch, said Rausch "passed him on" to two other priests.[46]

Catholic conscience rights advocates clashed with fellow Americans who understood access to abortion as a civil right. After the United States Commission on Civil Rights (USCCR) issued an April 1975 report, *Constitutional Aspects of the Right to Limit Child-Bearing*, the august body received a scathing denunciation from the bishops for critiquing the conscience clause. According to the commission, conscience provisions undermined the rights to abortion as guaranteed in *Roe v. Wade*. They were unconstitutional because they allowed hospitals to refuse to provide abortions. Staffers who worked for the bishops created a rebuttal memo they called "A Critical Analysis of the Report of the U.S. Commission on Civil Rights on Abortion." The document portrayed the need to protect religious self-governance as a consensus on Capitol Hill. Freedom of conscience was a cornerstone of American democracy, and the USCCR threatened to set aside an American and a Catholic value in the name of providing abortions. In other words, according to the memo, the commission undermined the very traditions it was designed to uphold. As the bishops' staffers wrote, "An arm of government specifically concerned with the maintenance of civil rights has allowed its preoccupation with abortion to override any sensitivity to the rights of the unborn, or for the freedom of conscience of those individuals and institutions opposed to participation in abortion procedures because of conscience."[47]

The bishops and their Washington, DC–based organization became a watchdog for conscience rights because of abortion. Terence Cooke, who as a young auxiliary bishop of New York and Vicar Apostolic for the US Armed Forces, gave an official seal of approval to Catholic Peace Fellowship leader Jim Forest's pamphlet on conscience rights, sent his own letter to Dr. Arthur S. Fleming, chairman of the USCCR. Cooke had become an important figure in the US Catholic hierarchy in the years after the Vietnam War; he wrote to Fleming in 1976 as both the archbishop of New York and a cardinal. Catholics like Cooke simply expected fellow defenders of rights to understand the need to protect rights of conscience. In his estimation, it was profoundly strange that a commission dedicated to securing rights would criticize the conscience clause. He wrote, "The Churches will be faced with the strange anomaly of protecting themselves from attacks based on theories promoted by the U.S. Commission on Civil Rights when they have expected that Commission to protect the freedom of conscience and freedom of exercise of religion that is part of our tradition and that would ordinarily be invoked in their behalf."[48] The commission, by its nature, ought to be interested in protecting conscience rights.

Conclusion

The history of an idea like conscience rights is a story about the interpretations and misinterpretations of a concept, about applications and contradictions in a discourse. This method of writing history follows ideas as, in the words of Daniel Rogers, they "jump the tracks" of the institutions "that spawn them."[49] This specific mode of traditional religious self-sovereignty leapt out of its home in Catholic theology and into the wider world in the 1960s and 1970s. Thomas Aquinas, Dominican priest and theologian extraordinaire, placed a conceptual bomb in Catholic thought in the thirteenth century that went off in the second half of the twentieth century. Individuals, he argued, must be prepared to follow conscience, or face eternal consequences. Conscience advocates found antagonists in the church and the state, and they discovered unexpected bedfellows among Jews, liberal Protestants, and secular human rights advocates. The liberal democratic state moved from outright rejection of conscience rights during the Vietnam War to passing laws in the name of protecting moral selfdoms in the aftermath of the Supreme Court's decision in *Roe v. Wade*. The discourse of conscience rights spread around the world by way of these creative and sometimes combative relationships.

A conservative position on conscience rights, which grew out of the anticonscription movement and in opposition to the procontraception position of the Association of Washington Priests, took control of the Vatican in the 1980s and 1990s. Pope John Paul II and Cardinal Joseph Ratzinger, prefect of the Congregation for the Doctrine of the Faith, argued assertively that Catholics possess rights only to follow truths as relayed by laws and absorbed into consciences. Their position attempted to iron out the contradictions of the neo-medieval position, with its interplay of resistance and acquiescence: Catholic doctors should followed inner convictions to escape being coerced to aid in an abortion (an endorsement of conscientious objection), and lay Catholics should submit conscience to the authority of the church on all moral matters, especially contraception (an argument for obeying just and clear laws). Catholics, as understood by John Paul II and Ratzinger at the end of the twentieth century, had to be disobedient subjects and obedient subjects simultaneously.

Ratzinger gave addresses on conscience in which he aimed to correct the conclusions millions of Catholics had arrived at in the 1960s regarding the potency of moral subjectivity. He joined a long line of critics, including Cardinal Patrick O'Boyle, Pope Paul VI, and William Buckley Jr., but the future pope's treatises stood out among those of his peers as the most eloquent and sophisticated takedowns of the conscience movement. In a keynote address given to a group of bishops gathered in 1984 in Philadelphia at the National Catholic Bioethics Center, Ratzinger observed that while Catholics appealed to a medieval tradition, they incorrectly understood conscience to be "a deification of subjectivity, a rock of bronze on which even the magisterium is shattered. Conscience appears finally as a subjectivity raised to the ultimate standard."[50] He claimed that conscience does not justify dissent in the church; the term itself implies openness to training under the church's sacred laws. Ratzinger returned to the same center seven years later to expand on his remarks and close the case of conscience rights. He divided conscience into two levels: the ontological, which heard God's truths, and the "medieval tradition" of decision-making. Where the entire defense of Catholic self-rule went wrong was to argue that conscience, in making a decision, shields the individual from an obligation to seek the truth. In other words, Ratzinger accused the entire intellectual, moral, and political project of twentieth-century Catholic subjectivity of hiding behind protections granted to erroneous consciences. Error, always and everywhere, must be replaced with truth.[51] It could not be permitted to exist for the sake of its own existence. Both lectures, however, considered almost exclusively the moral wing of the movement and the theologians who promoted it, failing to address the political arm of conscience rights developed by Gordon Zahn and the bishops' defense of conscientious objection in the winter of 1972.

John Paul II denounced both the liberal moral flank of the movement and the psychological interpretations of conscience in his 1993 encyclical, *Veritatis Splendor* (*The Splendor of Truth*). The text offered insight into the ambiguity of the ascendant conservative position. The Vatican embraced some of the insights that came with the modern movement for conscience rights in the realms of politics and its increased sensitivity to the intricacies of personal development. This intellectual move allowed the pontiff to embrace the rise of sensitivity to conscience as a positive development because it reinforced the importance of respecting human rights, which he believed that communist and other violent states continued to violate. John Paul II commented on how the respect accorded to the rights of conscience, extending from a widespread recognition of the dignity of the person, "certainly represents one of the positive achievements of modern culture."[52] But modern Catholics had gone too far in enfolding themselves into society: "There is a tendency to grant to the individual conscience the prerogative of independently determining the criteria of good and evil and then acting accordingly. Such an outlook is quite congenial to an individualist ethic, wherein each individual is faced with his own truth, different from the truth of others. . . . These different notions are at the origin of currents of thought which posit a radical opposition between moral law and conscience, and between nature and freedom."[53] For Pope John Paul II, the Catholic turn to conscience signaled the faithful's tragic embrace of secular modernity's "individualistic ethic."

Individuals possess inherent rights of conscience and freedoms as persons made in God's image, but subjectivities must be made to submit to church authority. John Paul II also attacked what he called the "'creative' understanding of conscience," that is, the psychological take on conscience, which he believed broke from tradition, not built on it as many of its advocates thought. The promoters of the personalist and existentialist inner nucleus stressed "the 'creative' character of conscience . . . [and] no longer call[ed] its actions 'judgements' but 'decisions': only by making these decisions 'autonomously' would man be able to attain maturity."[54] Autonomy did not lead to maturity; obedience to church law realized a well-developed individual. The pope called for a clarification of the relationship between freedom and God's law in an effort to remove the flaws in the psychologized and psychoanalyzed takes on subjectivity and its formations.

As in the case of Cardinal O'Boyle, that of Pope John Paul II and Cardinal Ratzinger only proves the thesis that this book has been pursuing over the course of the preceding chapters: conscience became such an important category in the church and modern society that prominent thinkers, sensing danger and a threat to power, felt compelled to respond. On one level, the critique is devastating: John Paul II and Ratzinger claimed that the entire push for conscience was based on a misreading of theology. But perhaps more to the point, both the pontiff and his leading cardinal wished to repudiate the Thomistic inheritance of the twentieth-century Catholic Church. Thomas did, in fact, provide a robust system of protections for conscience, and his work demonstrated that even erroneous consciences produced truths worthy of respect. The denunciations, then, are actually quite flattering: conscience, whether properly understood or not, had become one of the key political and moral terms of the twentieth century. The movement merited considerable attention. The pope and a top-ranked cardinal bore witness.

CODA

From the founding of the Massachusetts Bay Colony in the 1630s to the rise of collectivism in the 1930s, Protestant reformers, republican states- men, Enlightenment doyens, and secular rebels defined the central tenets of American individualism. Influential thinkers and activists from these tradi- tions imagined Catholicism as an obstacle to the realization of liberty. This book is a chapter in the long story of American freedom, but it is an install- ment during which Catholics joined Protestant and secular thinkers as pro- moters of conscience and subjectivity. The Catholic campaign for self-rule inverts the prevailing narrative of the nation's history, showing how Ameri- cans built a late twentieth-century democratic culture on Catholic ideas of conscience and subjectivity rather than against Catholic notions of self and authority as in previous eras.

The barbarity of modern war and a spillover of its ethical quandaries into the realm of sexuality moved a radical suggestion by thirteenth-century the- ologian Thomas Aquinas to the center of US political and intellectual dis- course. Thomas laid out a case in the 1250s that individuals should be free to act on subjective perceptions of the world as crystallized in conscience. The medieval theologian offered an influential provocation: individuals, in the confines of a sacred nucleus, determined the moral legitimacy of an authority figure's rules, deciding whether to assent or dissent, to comply or resist. A fierce campaign launched by American Catholics to allow these medieval rights of conscience to influence moral reality, and to diminish the power of law, expanded the terms of modern of American democracy. Laws reduced soldiers and doctors to crude instruments of policy imple- mentation during both World War II and the Vietnam War as well as after the legalization of abortion. Modern Catholics claiming conscience rights helped individuals seize more space for self-sovereignty when confronted with a prescription. As a direct gain of the modern church's movement for a liberated modern self, leaders in the state had to assert authority with the moral capacities of the individual in mind. Catholics broadened twentieth-century democracy and pluralism by making clear that laws must be just and applicable to lay hands on a person's subjectivity.

Whig narratives of progress have long held that the expansion of freedom marks improvement for society. Increased liberty and wider latitude for the mind, so the story goes, spread reasonableness and rationality. But the Catholic struggle for conscience rights cannot support a case for a link between the rise of individual freedoms and the extension of tolerance. The quest for self-governance sparked a succession of political and intellectual contests in the church and the state that ended in bad blood. Thomas is partly to blame. The antimonies he built into the theology locked liberal and conservative antagonists into a recurring debate about restraint and freedom that has never been solved. Taking the side of either law or conscience, priests challenged bishops, bishops contradicted popes, archbishops undercut state bureaucrats, soldiers pushed back against officers, laypeople pressed confessors, citizens undermined courts, conservatives admonished liberals, and conscripts told off draft officers. The Catholic struggle for recognition of a robust subjective capacity to determine truth also expanded democracy and pluralism by making modern America and its largest denomination increasingly fractured and intellectually combative.

The theological drama has been rehearsed on a global scale. The enduring contribution of the 1968 contraception contest to the global Catholic Church's debates over sexual ethics is a constant seesawing of conscience over law and then objective above subjective in rounds of theological argumentation. Despite the best efforts of Pope John Paul II and Cardinal Joseph Ratzinger to diminish the influence of Thomas's subjectivism on modern Catholic thought, the thirteenth-century theologian's radical take on self-rule resurfaces on occasion with crisis-inducing venom. In 2016, Pope Francis conjured traditional subjective truth-creation capacities in paragraph 303 of his apostolic exhortation on family life, *Amoris Laetitia* (*The Joy of Love*). Francis's letter reads like a twentieth-century confessor's rule book. The Argentinian, like earlier generations of priests, encouraged Catholics to form conscience along traditional lines of church teaching and obey standing moral statutes. He held to the notion that a well-formed subjective guide helped Catholics follow the letter of the law in the name of achieving eternal salvation. "Yet," the pontiff added, "conscience can do more than recognize that a given situation does not correspond objectively to the overall demands of the Gospel." An assertive subjective perception could, in other words, see beyond a need to simply follow the rules. Francis made space for the conservative interpretation of conscience before swinging the doctrine decidedly to its emancipatory end. Conscience, he continued, "can also recognize with sincerity and honesty which for now is the most generous response which can be given to God, and come to see with a certain moral security what God himself is asking amid the concrete complexity of one's limits, while not fully within the objective ideal."[1] Francis also held to the idea that a well-oiled subjectivity could create its own truth, rest assured it is a proper path of action, and enable the individual Catholic to live out the perception in a messy world. Applying this to issues of twenty-first-century life, he argued that following conscience can make divorce and remarriage a reasonable act and keep a Catholic who chooses these ends in the good graces of the church.

Conservative cardinals and theologians the world over denounced the expansive freedom *Amoris Laetitia* offered conscience. It seemed that Francis diluted the power of law to guide individuals to a proper end. Liberal theologians believed that the pope acted in continuity with the church's high medieval theology when he accorded subjectivity a power to see alternatives for moral behavior. Both sides, oscillating the church between the two long-standing poles of the theology, grasp aspects of its truths.

The conscience clause that provides doctors and nurses with the right to refuse cooperation in abortion procedures has also spread around the world. Abortion has become legal in countries like Ireland, Italy, Germany, the Netherlands, Sweden, Austria, France, Canada, and England. The protections for the moral subjectivities of health care professionals have risen alongside these liberalizations at both national and supranational levels. The European Court for Human Rights, a body whose conservative roots have been explored by historian Marco Duranti, recognized the conscience rights of a French pharmacist who refused to stock and sell intrauterine contraceptive devices to his female customers.[2] The modern United States proved to be a launching pad for this crafty legal creature, which has its genesis in the Catholic struggle for self-sovereignty against the Selective Service System. The Catholic bishops have found a political ally in president Donald Trump, who pursues conscience clauses with help from officials in the Office for Civil Rights, housed in the Department of Health and Human Services. Conscience clauses gained an increasing number of supporters in the twenty-first century and at the highest levels of the US government. Supreme Court decisions issued in this century have protected the subjectivities of bakers and florists who, if forced to sell products to same-sex couples, claim their conscience would be violated.

The successes of Catholic theologies of responsible self-determination in the realm of reproductive rights show that democracy contracts as it expands. Democracy, and self-rule, can spread in more than one direction at the same time. Progress for some marks regression for others. As the right to refuse in conscience gained legitimacy from courts and legislatures, it chipped away at other genres of rights, particularly autonomy in reproductive and gay rights. An individual can follow his or her own moral vision and refuse to become part of a larger mechanism of distribution or a bureaucratic structure of procedure; but this moral freedom simultaneously limits the liberties of others to act on their deeply cherished ideals and constitutional guarantees. It is important to recognize that the roots of this dilemma are in the draft for military service. American Catholics desired to act on subjective truths that would come at the expense of the state's vision to achieve security by containing communism. The languages, politics, metaphors, and theologies of Catholic self-driven truth creation rose in response to conscription, starting in the 1930s and ending in 1973 with Congress's termination of the draft—the very moment that biopolitics entered a new phase with the legalization of abortion. War, the twentieth century's original pro-life issue and the phenomenon that motivated Catholics to fight for self-rule, has left its imprint on debates over abortion, health care, and gay marriage in the form of the conscience clause. Professionals in these areas have legal access to a mode of self-determination denied to potential conscripts into the military. But these rights would not be available if it had not been for the rise of conscience language in the antiwar movement. Contemporary sexuality and sexual politics cannot be understood without reference to the history of dissent against the modern military state.

The pontificate of John Paul II embodied the twists and divergences that launched conscience into the center of political and moral debates. The pope joined the fight in the 1980s and 1990s to earn conscience rights official recognition from secular governments. The burgeoning respect for freedom of conscience signaled a healthy regard for human rights, a cause John Paul II embraced on his own terms.[3] These sentiments explain why, as we saw in the last chapter, the pontiff signed a 1983 Amnesty International petition to free prisoners of conscience languishing in jails around the world on account of their moral stand against secular states. He embraced the spread of conscience rights if such rights guaranteed that the individual could pursue particular truths in the civil sphere, especially in religious education. Yet John Paul II, with the Prefect of the Congregation for the Doctrine of the Faith Cardinal Joseph Ratzinger at his side, worked tirelessly to stop the spread of self-governance in the Catholic Church on the matter of sexual ethics. His 1993 encyclical *Veritatis Splendor* made an unequivocal case: Catholics cannot hide behind erroneous consciences but must seek the truths as disclosed by law. Thomas was too generous to flawed selfhood; a firmer hand would be needed in the church to align objective law and subjective personhood.

In John Paul II can be seen the paradox of modern Catholicism as brought to the surface by the proliferating calls for conscience rights. Catholics cannot place conscience into the hands of state authority but are always obliged to entrust their inner sanctum entirely to the keeping of the church. A modern Catholic, then, is both subversive and submissive. A constant shuttling back and forth between these two postures, in realms of citizenship and sexuality, proves extremely difficult. This modern split personality is also a legacy of the 1960s and 1970s conscience rights movement. The church's dissent against the state carried over to dissent against the church. Church authorities like John Paul II and Cardinal Patrick O'Boyle promoted the former but pushed back against the latter. Then lay Catholics and theologians set the argument for conscience against bishops and popes on the matter of sex. The circular nature of the debate propelled the doctrine's rise, and it has also generated an endless loop of intellectual and political contestation.

Priests have been overrepresented in every phase and iteration of the modern conscience rights movement. Clergymen, long cast as opponents of independent thought, revealed themselves as liberators of conscience and subjectivity throughout twentieth century. They aimed to lift the intellectual, spiritual, and political constraints placed on everyday people. The story of American freedom will need to include a much larger role for men of the cloth as creators and sustainers of the nation's central values. This book has upended the narrative of priest-dominated Catholics that had gained credence before the Civil War, set the boundaries for secular liberalism, and still influences discourse on the current sex abuse crisis. For three hundred years of US history, priests were imagined as the bogeymen of America's democratic state, a reputation born of a constant demand for conformity and their management of an array of opaque institutions; but in the twentieth century, in confessionals and in response to conscription, in contests over birth control and abortion, priests consistently sided with conscience and subjectivity, making a central contribution to the development of a modern democratic culture.

Yet priesthood is not a class but a particular occupation, a vocation that can be used for good or evil. The same years that priests rallied for freedom of subjectivity in sex and war were also those in which the sexual abuse of thousands of young people by priests came to light. A narrative about liberation of individuals shares no straightforward relationship with the rise of sexual deviance: liberation and domination are both characteristics of the modern priesthood that sometimes share a space in an individual cleric. Father James Rausch, general secretary of the United States Conference of Catholic Bishops from 1972 to 1977 and a consistent defender of the conscience clause before the House of Representatives and the Senate throughout the 1970s, was accused of abusing a seventeen-year-old boy in 1979, which resulted in a legal settlement in 2002. But neither narrative about the modern American Catholic priesthood—whether agents of liberation or figures of sexual domination—should erase the other. Each narrative, properly explored, increases our understanding of the American past considerably. In the long history of the American Catholic priesthood, liberation and domination paradoxically coexist, intricate characteristics of a modern and medieval American religious culture.

ACKNOWLEDGMENTS

This project has been nearly a decade in the making, and now it is my pleasure to thank the many people who made its completion possible. I have accrued too many debts to friends and institutions to name them all. But here I want to start by thanking my parents, Amie and Phil. Thank you for always supporting and encouraging me. The unconditional love you have offered me over the years has manifested in many ways, from helping me pack moving trucks, to driving me to innumerable basketball practices, to listening to my dinner table harangues. I am beyond fortunate to have you as parents. This book would not have happened without your devotion to me. My sister, Lindsay, has said many kind words to me, even if she would deny having done so. Thank you for your support; it means more than I can express. I'm proud of the person you have become—and I am thankful that you brought Jamie and Lucas into our family. My grandpa John read several chapter drafts and let loose via email with characteristic candor to keep me on the right track. He has always been there cheering me on. My grandma Dorothy offered crucial support. I love you both. Thanks also go to Tim, Jake, Annette, Dave, Stacy, Tom, and Sarah.

In August of 2015, I married into a large Irish family, which has been a constant source of inspiration and entertainment. I would like to think that I became the cool American uncle to fourteen Irish nieces and nephews. For welcoming me into their crew, I would like to thank Joseph, Cathal, Orlagh, Donál, Ethan, Dillon, Molly, Bronagh, Clodagh, Ronan, Darragh, Niall, Cormac, and Evelyn. My brother- and sisters-in-law—Pat, Roisin, Niall, Mary, Ashley, Ruairí, Siobhan, Gareth, Naomh, Patrick, Eimear, and Jason—have always checked in on me to ask about my writing and research. They welcomed me into their homes and lives with tremendous warmth. Special thanks to Brendan, Elizabeth, Peter, and Sheila for the food, the wine, and the conversations. The generosity and intellectual curiosity of my mother- and father-in-law, Peter and Marie, seem boundless. Peter gave me his office when I needed space to write the first chapter drafts. Marie welcomed me into her home for months at a time and challenged me to be a better writer, thinker, and person. I love you both, and I am in constant awe of your accomplishments and selflessness.

I am blessed to have studied with excellent teachers. Jason Anderson, T. K. Griffith, and Brother Joseph LeBon stuck with me during my time at Archbishop Hoban High School. The History Department at the University of Dayton was an amazing place to be an undergraduate student; I am so thankful for the many professors who took the time to familiarize me with the discipline. Michael Carter introduced me to American Catholic studies. John Heitmann hired me as his research assistant the semester after I graduated. John taught me so much about the craft of history, and I still feel very privileged to have learned directly from such an accomplished scholar. I took four classes from Bill Trollinger. I am grateful for his teaching, scholarship, and mentorship. Thanks also to Una Cadegan, Tony Smith, John Putka, Larry Flockerzie, and Chris Duncan.

My friends at Dayton—Sutton, Justin, Emily, Evan, Yako, Derek, Eric, Tracy, Drew, Clare, Caroline, Brad, Brett, Kaitlin, Gordon, Katie, Kellie, Anna, Laura, Andy, Katy Jo, Jose, Lofton, Maroon, Helen, Tony, Whaley, and Kim—were among my best teachers. This book would never have been possible without their encouragement and humor. At Marquette University, I learned American Catholic history from one of the best: Steve Avella, an encounter I still see as formative. Thank you for your rigor and your generosity. Dominic Faraone was kind and wise; Charissa Keup taught me much about research and writing.

I was lucky to find my way to the Boston College History Department, which is full of ambitious and passionate scholars. My thanks to Julian Bourg, Charles Gallagher, Kevin Kenny, Alan Rogers, Devin Pendas, Oliver Rafferty, and Sarah Ross for their encouragement. Virginia Reinburg took time to counsel me on life, scholarship, and the profession. James O'Toole is the type of scholarly mentor who, to put it simply, is always there for his students. He was committed to this project at all stages and went well beyond the call of duty in guiding me. His scholarship and teaching set a high standard of excellence. Thank you for your commitment to making me a better researcher and for letting me explore religious history. Close friendships with Jesse Tumblin, Adam Rathge, Craig Gallagher, and James Clifton made my time in Boston memorable. And I was lucky to be surrounded with brilliant and kind friends like Andrea Wenz, Chris Stayzniak,

Allison Vander Broek, Joanna Kelly, Elise Franklin, Amy Limoncelli, Carolyn Twomey, Kasper Volk, Ian Delahanty, Hidetaka Hirota, Seth Meehan, and Philip Stetzel.

Several institutions and programs provided crucial support for this project. It is a privilege to note their magnanimity. A fellowship from the Louisville Institute helped me complete this project and conduct additional archival research. The American Catholic History Research Center at the Catholic University of America granted me a Dorothy Mohler Research Grant that brought me in contact with sources that led to several of my key conclusions. At Boston College, the History Department, the Clough Center for Constitutional Democracy, the Center for Christian-Jewish Learning, the Center for Human Rights and International Justice, and the Woods School of Advancing Studies all provided timely support, as did the American Catholic Historical Association, which awarded this project a Summer Research Grant. Several archivists also provided crucial support. My thanks go to Maria Mazzenga, William John Shephard, Shane MacDonald, Joe Smith, Kevin Cawley, Patrick Hayes, Christine Orozco, Michelle Levy, and Jean McManus.

I owe a profound debt of gratitude to the Cushwa Center for the Study of American Catholicism at the University of Notre Dame. An appointment as a postdoctoral research associate at Cushwa from 2016 to 2018 provided me with ample time for writing this book, and it put me in constant contact with a supportive research community. I would like to thank Bill and Jean Cushwa for their commitment to our field. Maggie Elmore, Ben Wetzel, and Philip Byers were tremendous interlocutors. Shane Ulbrich and Madonna Noak are the best colleagues I could ask for. Above all, I wish to thank Kathleen Sprows Cummings. She placed a tremendous amount of faith in me when she offered me the position. I am so grateful. It is simply impossible to adequately convey my thanks—except to say that Kathy's support made this book a reality, and her advising contributed to my development as a scholar and as a person. As I like to put it, she offers a master class in academic life. I am exceptionally lucky to have taken this class.

I have many people to thank from the wider Notre Dame community. My colleagues in the Department of American Studies have been welcoming and energetic. Thanks to Perin Gurel, Katie Schlodfelt, Mary Jo Young, Tom Tweed, Jennifer Huynh, Jason Ruiz, Korey Garibaldi, Sophie White, Ben Giamo, Bob Walls, Erika Doss, Richard Jones, Victoria St. Martin, and Annie Coleman. John McGreevy has always been one of my favorite historians, and it is now an honor of mine to count him as a friend and a mentor. He always took time out of a busy schedule to meet with me. All the participants of the Colloquium on Religion in American History—including

Darren Dochuk, Susanna De Stradis, Jonathan Riddle, Suzanna Krivulskaya, Linda Pryzbyszweksi, Ian Van Dyke, Tomas Valle, Sarah Shorthall, and Lauren Hamblen—improved this project immensely. Thank you.

Several individuals invested an inordinate amount of time in making this project into a book. Tim Mennel of the University of Chicago Press guided my manuscript with a steady hand from start to finish. From our first communication by email in 2014, he has been generous, thorough, and encouraging. I appreciate so deeply the opportunity he gave me to work with the press. Its staff and its other editors, especially Susannah Engstrom, have been accommodating and deeply committed. Daniel Williams read the manuscript and offered perceptive comments; I am thankful that he brought his immense erudition to bear on it. Thomas Rzeznik read an early draft and pushed my work in new directions. Daniel Silliman has been a good friend from whom I have learned much. The manuscript's two anonymous reviewers for the University of Chicago Press improved it immensely—helping me say what I wanted to say with more clarity, efficiency, and precision. I hope I have heeded their advice. I would also like to thank my crew from the American Catholic Historical Association: Charles Strauss, Monica Mercado, Jack Downey, Mary Beth Connoly, Bill Cossen, Erin Bartram, Sean Blanchard, Kathleen Holscher, Matthew Cressler, Brian Clites, John Seitz, and Catherine Osbourne. You all continue to inspire me to research and write about American Catholics. I offer my thanks as well to the officers and leaders of the Society of United States Intellectual History for providing a much-needed space in the wider discipline.

My greatest debt of all is owed to my wife, Gráinne. Her scholarship and teaching have always energized me, and her own work on religious intellectuals helped develop my interest in the topic. She writes and speaks with a precision and depth that continuously expand my thinking. Moreover, I never would have seen the ink dry on these pages without her encouragement and support over the past decade. She has listened to me prattle on about theological technicalities, and she has endured my lectures about the importance of ideas in American history. Together we have explored politics, immigration, feminism, and religion as intellectual partners. Sometimes I would immerse myself completely in this project and wander off into the mists of historical scholarship. It was then that Gráinne would always ground me and remind me about what mattered most: family, relaxation, good films, and tea. She has done so much for me. She left her Irish family and crossed an ocean to support my writing. I will never forget that. Thank you for all you have done. It means more to me than I can express here, except to say that this book is for you.

Killian arrived when I had drafted only three chapters of this book. He has not been—if I am to be honest—a great research assistant. But he has done more for this project and its author than he can imagine. His seemingly indefatigable supply of energy and curiosity illuminates my world. Ruaírí made his debut a few months before this project went into final edits. He and his older brother are sources of unimaginable joy for their parents. I love you both and see a good future for the world when I look into your eyes.

NOTES

Abbreviations

Archives frequently cited have been identified by the following abbreviations:

BPRA   Baltimore Province of the Redemptorists Archives, Philadelphia

CUAA   Catholic University of America Archives, Washington, DC

CULAC Columbia University Library Archival Collection, New York

NEPSJA New England Province of the Society of Jesus Archives, Worcester, MA

UNDA   University of Notre Dame Archives, Notre Dame, IN

INTRODUCTION

1. James McHugh to Augustus F. Hawkins, April 19, 1977. Ad Hoc Committee on Pro-Life Activities, box 63, folder "Pro-Life Activities, 1977, April–June," CUAA.

2. James McHugh to Harrison A. Williams, July 20, 1977. Ad Hoc Committee on Pro-Life Activities, box 63, folder "Pro-Life Activities, 1977, July–December," CUAA.

3. James A. Straukamp to the Adjutant General, May 2, 1968. In *On Writ of Certiorari to the United States Court of Appeals for the Ninth Circuit*, Louis A. Negre v. Stanley R. Larsen, et al., no. 325, October Term 1970, 27.

4. Shane MacCarthy, Homily Notes, August 1968, 5. Shane MacCarthy Humanae Vitae Collection, box 2, folder 8, CUAA.

5. Chris Beneke, *Beyond Toleration: The Religious Origins of American Pluralism* (Oxford: Oxford University Press, 2006); Daniel Walker Howe, *Making the American Self: Jonathan Edwards to Abraham Lincoln* (Oxford: Oxford University Press, 2009); Allen C. Guelzo, *Edwards on the Will: A Century of American Theological Debate* (Middletown, CT: Wesleyan University Press, 1989); Amy Kittlestrom, *The Religion of Democracy: Seven Liberals and the American Moral Tradition* (New York: Penguin, 2015); Louis Menand, *The Metaphysical Club: A Story of Ideas in America* (New York: Farrar, Straus and Giroux, 2001); Terry Anderson, *The Movement and the Sixties: Protest in America from Greensboro to Wounded Knee* (Oxford: Oxford University Press, 1995); Wilfred M. McClay, *The Masterless: Self and Society in Modern America* (Chapel Hill: University of North Carolina Press, 1994).

6. On the rise of Thomism, see Gerard A. McCool, *From Unity to Pluralism: The Internal Evolution of Thomism* (New York: Fordham University Press, 1988) and *The*

Neo-Thomists (Milwaukee: Marquette University Press, 1994). For the impact of Thomism on Catholic epistemology, see William M. Halsey, *The Survival of American Innocence: Catholicism in an Era of Disillusionment, 1920–1940* (South Bend, IN: Notre Dame University Press, 1980).

7. On war as its own track, see for example Joseph Kip Kosek, *Acts of Conscience: Christian Non-Violence and Modern American Democracy* (New York: Columbia University Press, 2009); Michael S. Foley, *Confronting the War Machine: Draft Resistance during the Vietnam War* (Chapel Hill: University of North Carolina Press, 2003). On sexuality as its own arena, see for example Daniel Williams, *Defenders of the Unborn: The Pro-Life Movement before "Roe v. Wade"* (Oxford: Oxford University Press, 2016); Leslie Tentler, *Catholics and Contraception: An American History* (Ithaca, NY: Cornell University Press, 2004); R. Marie Griffith, *Moral Combat: How Sex Divided American Christians and Fractured American Politics* (New York: Basic Books, 2017). For a study that charts the growth of state power and the regulation of sexuality, see Margot Canaday, *The Straight State: Sexuality and Citizenship in Twentieth Century America* (Princeton, NJ: Princeton University Press, 2009).

8. John T. McGreevy, *Catholicism and American Freedom: A History* (New York: W. W. Norton, 2003).

9. On priests as papal agents and anti-individualists, see Jenny Franchot, *Roads to Rome: The Antebellum Encounter with Catholicism* (Berkeley: University of California Press, 1994); Elizabeth Fenton, *Religious Liberties: Anti-Catholicism and Liberal Democracy in Nineteenth-Century U.S. Literature and Culture* (New York: Oxford University Press, 2011).

10. James Kloppenberg, *Toward Democracy: The Struggle for Self-Rule in European and American Thought* (Oxford: Oxford University Press, 2016), 8.

11. On rights language and authority, see Samuel Moyn, *The Last Utopia: Human Rights in History* (Cambridge, MA: Harvard University Press, 2012); Daniel Rogers, *Age of Fracture* (Cambridge, MA: Belknap Press of Harvard University Press, 2012); Andrew Hartman, *A War for the Soul of America: A History of the Culture Wars* (Chicago: University of Chicago Press, 2015).

12. Sarah Igo, "Toward a Free Range Intellectual History," in *The Worlds of American Intellectual History*, ed. Joel Isaac, James T. Kloppenberg, Michael O'Brien, and Jennifer Ratner-Rosenhagen (Oxford: Oxford University Press, 2017), 327.

13. David A. Hollinger, *In the American Province: Studies in the History and Historiography of Ideas* (Bloomington: Indiana University Press, 1985), 130–51.

14. The population attending Catholic primary and secondary schools swelled in the first third of the twentieth century, growing from 755,038 in 1895 to 2,469,032 by 1930. Nationwide, these schools added another 3.1 million names to the rolls between 1945 and 1960. The number of students attending Catholic colleges, growing apace with primary and secondary institutions, increased by an astonishing 300 percent, rising from 92,426 students in 1945 to 384,526 in 1960. For data, see Patrick Carey, *Catholics in America: A History* (Westport, CT: Praeger, 2004), 93; Ann Marie Ryan, "Negotiating Assimilation: Chicago Catholic High Schools' Pursuit of Accreditation in the Early Twentieth Century," *History of Education Quarterly* 46 (Fall 2006): 352; McGreevy, *Catholicism and American Freedom*, 114.

CHAPTER ONE

1. Edward G. Rosenberger and Francis J. Sugrue, *Outlines of Religion for Catholic Youth* (New York: George Grady, 1953), 398.

2. John Courtney Murray, "Freedom of Conscience: The Ethical Problem," *Theological Studies* 6 (June 1945): 257.

3. As Robert Orsi has shown, twentieth-century Catholic educators felt a strong tension between asking pupils to memorize doctrines on the one hand and stoke a supernatural imagination about the saints and the real presence of the Eucharist on the other. Students were asked to memorize "technical terminology of scholastic opacity" but also to experience Catholicism with a "full sensorium." Robert A. Orsi, *History and Presence* (Cambridge, MA: Belknap Press of Harvard University Press, 2016), 123–30.

4. Quoted in Edward G. Andrew, *Conscience and Its Critics: Protestant Conscience, Enlightenment Reason, and Modern Subjectivity* (Toronto: University of Toronto Press, 2012), 16.

5. John Winthrop as quoted in David D. Hall, ed., *The Antinomian Controversy, 1636–1638: A Documentary History* (Middletown, CT: Wesleyan University Press, 1968), 312.

6. Anne Hutchinson as quoted in Hall, 337.

7. Beneke, *Beyond Toleration*, 33.

8. Roger Williams, *The Bloudy Tenet of Persecution for Cause of Conscience*, in *The American Intellectual Tradition*, vol. 1, *1630–1865*, ed. David A. Hollinger and Charles Capper (Oxford: Oxford University Press, 2016), 41.

9. For excellent commentary on *The Bloudy Tenet*, see Edwin S. Gaustad, *Liberty of Conscience: Roger Williams in America* (Valley Forge, PA: Judson, 1999), 71–80.

10. Quoted in Andrew R. Murphy, *Liberty, Conscience, and Toleration: The Political Thought of William Penn* (Oxford: Oxford University Press, 2016), 42.

11. Quoted in Murphy, 42.

12. Quoted in *The Political Writings of William Penn*, ed. Andrew Murphy (Indianapolis: Liberty Fund, 2002), xix.

13. Murphy, *Liberty, Conscience, and Toleration*, 118.

14. Tisa Wenger, *Religious Freedom: The Contested History of An American Ideal* (Chapel Hill: University of North Carolina Press, 2017).

15. McGreevy, *Catholicism and American Freedom*, 177–78.

16. David Wootton, ed., *John Locke: Political Writings* (London: Penguin, 1993), 202.

17. Milton, *Paradise Lost*, bk. 12, lines 521–23.

18. Paul Tillich, "Conscience in Western Thought and the Idea of a Transmoral Conscience," *Crozer Quarterly* 22 (October 1945): 293–94.

19. Quoted in McGreevy, *Catholicism and American Freedom*, 180.

20. Amy Kittlestrom, *The Religion of Democracy: Seven Liberals and the American Moral Tradition* (New York: Penguin, 2015), 29.

21. Thomas Aquinas, *The Disputed Questions on Truth*, vol. 2, trans. James V. McGlynn (Chicago: Henry Regnery, 1953), 328.

22. Thomas Aquinas, 331.

23. Bertrand L. Conway, *Question Box Answers: Replies to Questions Received on Missions to Non-Catholics* (New York: Catholic Book Exchange, 1903), 130.

24. Thomas Aquinas, *The Disputed Questions on Truth*, 336.

25. Thomas Aquinas, *Summa Theologica* (Claremont, CA: Coyote Canyon, 2018), 315.

26. Alphonsus Liguori, *Conscience: Writings from "Moral Theology" by Saint Alphonsus*, trans. Raphael Gallagher (Liguori, MO: Liguori Press, 2019), 69.

27. On the implementation of *Pascendi*, see Thomas V. Gannon, "Before and after Modernism: The Intellectual Isolation of the American Priest," in *The Catholic Priest in the United States: Historical Investigations*, ed. John Tracy Ellis (Collegeville, MN: Saint John's University Press, 1971), 293–383.

28. William M. Halsey, *The Survival of American Innocence: Catholicism in the Era of Disillusionment* (South Bend, IN: Notre Dame University Press, 1980).

29. Paul Blanshard, *Communism, Democracy, and Catholic Power* (London: Jonathan Cape, 1952), 217.

30. Antonio Lanza and Pietro Palazzini, *General Moral Theology*, trans. W. J. Collins (Boston: Daughters of St. Paul, 1961), 184.

31. Lanza and Palazzini, 182.

32. Anthony J. Flynn, Sister Vincent Loretto, and Mother Mary Simeon, *Living Our Faith*, bk. 3 (New York: W. H. Sadlier, 1945), 41.

33. Anthony F. Alexander, *College Moral Theology* (Chicago: Henry Regnery, 1958), 47.

34. James Martin Gillis, "Conscience," November 30, 1931, in *The Moral Law: Eight Addresses Delivered in "The Catholic Hour,"* ed. National Council of Catholic Men, 15. James Martin Gillis Papers, box 34, folder "Catholic Hour Radio Talks," Office of Paulist Archives, New York.

35. Peter D'Agostino, *Rome in America: Transnational Catholic Ideology from the Risorgimento to Fascism* (Chapel Hill: University of North Carolina Press, 2004), 258. For a biography of Gillis, see Richard Gribble, *Guardian of America: The Life of James Martin Gillis CSP* (New York: Paulist Press, 1998).

36. Francis J. Connell, *Outlines of Moral Theology* (Milwaukee: Bruce, 1953), 38.

37. See also John A. O'Brien, "Does Conscience Bear Witness to God?," *Ecclesiastical Review* 107 (December 1942): 451–52; Damian J. Blaher, "Any More about Conscience?," *Friar* 11 (February 1959): 63.

38. Francis J. Connell, *Freedom of Worship: The Catholic Position* (New York: Paulist Press, 1944).

39. On Connell, see R. Scott Appleby and John H. Haas, "The Last Supernaturalists: Fenton, Connell, and the Threat of Catholic Indifferentism," *U.S. Catholic Historian* 13 (Spring 1995): 23–48.

40. Catechisms allowed Catholics to apprehend the realities of the world with the powers of reason. Historian William Halsey makes the important point that catechisms were "popular condensations of more complex Scholastic arguments." Halsey, *The Survival of American Innocence*, 155.

41. Hilary J. Carpenter, "The Meaning of Conscience," *Blackfriars* 12 (May 1931): 287.

42. James O'Toole, "In the Court of Conscience: American Catholics and Confession, 1900–1975," in *Habits of Devotion: Catholic Religious Practice in Twentieth-Century America*, ed. James O'Toole (Ithaca, NY: Cornell University Press, 2004), 134–35.

43. Aloysius J. Heeg, *A Little Child's Confession Book: Prayers, Directions, and Examination of Conscience Suitable for Children in the Lower Grades* (St. Louis: Queen's Work Press, 1941), 6.

44. Heeg, 5.

45. John Joseph McVey, *Catechism of Christian Doctrine No. 4, Revised according to the Code of 1918* (Philadelphia: Institute of the Brothers of the Christian Schools, 1926), 112–113.

46. *A Catholic Catechism* (New York: Herder and Herder, 1957), 304.

47. Eric Marcelo O. Genilo, *John Cuthbert Ford, SJ: Moral Theologian at the End of the Manualist Era* (Washington, DC: Georgetown University Press, 2007); McGreevy, *Catholicism and American Freedom*, 216–22, 238–48. See also Germain Grisez, "About John C. Ford," March 23, 2015, The Way of the Lord Jesus, http://www.twotlj.org /Ford.html; Peter Cajka, "'Each Individual Catholic Can and Does Form His Own

Conscience on This and Every Other Subject': John Ford, S.J., and the Theology of Conscience, 1941–1969," in *Crossings and Dwellings: Restored Jesuits, Women Religious, American Experience, 1814–2014*, ed. Kyle B. Roberts and Stephen R. Schloesser (Leiden: Brill, 2017): 567–602.

48. John C. Ford, "Pastoral Remarks on the Erroneous Conscience." John Ford Papers, box 14, folder 1, NEPSJA.

49. Ford, "Pastoral Remarks."

50. O'Brien, "Does Conscience Bear Witness to God?"

51. John C. Ford and Gerald Kelly, *Contemporary Moral Theology*, vol. 1 (Westminster, MD: Newman, 1958), 109–11.

52. "Perverting Conscience," editorial, *Commonweal*, June 21, 1940, 178.

53. Daniel Lord, *When We Go to Confession* (St. Louis: Queen's Work Press, 1941), 5.

54. Pius XII, "Christian Conscience as an Object of Education," *Catholic Action* 34 (May 1952): 17.

55. Henry Davis, *Moral and Pastoral Theology* (New York: Sheed and Ward, 1952), 7.

56. Clarence E. Elwell, Anthony J. Fuerst, Sister Mary Rosalia Paulus, James T. O'Dowd, and John J. Voight, *Through Christ Our Lord: Our Quest for Happiness*, bk. 2, *Sophomore Year* (Chicago: Mentzer, Bush, 1948), 133.

57. Edwin F. Healy, *Moral Guidance: A Textbook in Principles of Conduct for Colleges and Universities* (Chicago: Loyola University Press, 1942), 28.

58. Heribert Jone and Urban Adelman, *Moral Theology*, 18th ed. (Westminster, MD: Newman, 1963), 41; Dominicus Prümmer, *Handbook of Moral Theology*, trans. Reverend Gerald Shelton and ed. John Galvin Noland (New York: P. J. Kenedy and Sons, 1957), 64; Alexander, *College Moral Theology*, 49.

59. Francis B. Cassilly, *Religion: Doctrine and Practice for Use in Catholic High Schools* (Chicago: Loyola University Press, 1931), 36.

60. Elwell et al., *Through Christ Our Lord*, 528.

61. Bede Jarrett, "Infallibility of Conscience," *Catholic Worker*, November 1941, 4. Original quotation appears in Bede Jarrett, *Meditations for Layfolk* (London: Catholic Truth Society, 1915), 211.

62. Connell, *Outlines of Moral Theology*, 41–43.

63. D. F. Miller, *What Is Your Conscience?* (Liguori, MO: Liguorian Pamphlets, 1956), 16.

64. Thomas Deman, "The Dignity of Conscience," *Blackfriars* 34 (March 1953): 115.

65. Ulrich Lehner, *The Catholic Enlightenment: The Forgotten History of a Global Catholic Movement* (New York: Oxford University Press, 2016), 48.

66. Cassilly, *Religion: Doctrine and Practice*, 35.

67. Dominicus Prümmer, *Handbook of Moral Theology*, trans. Reverend Gerald Shelton and ed. John Galvin Noland (New York: P. J. Kenedy and Sons, 1957), 60.

68. John C. Ford, "The Conscience in General." John Ford Papers, box 14, folder 1, NEPSJA.

69. Francis J. Connell, "The Virtue of Prudence," 3. Francis Connell C.Ss.R. Papers, folder "Moral Virtues," BPRA.

70. Francis J. Connell, "The Formation of a Christian Conscience," 1. Francis Connell C.Ss.R. Papers, folder "Conscience," BPRA.

71. Prümmer, *Handbook of Moral Theology*, 60.

72. Brendan Larnen, *The Four Freedoms* (Washington, DC: National Council of Catholic Men, 1944), 8; Healy, *Moral Guidance*, 28; Lanza and Palazzini, *General Moral Theology*, 162.

73. Ford, "The Conscience in General."

74. McVey, *Catechism of Christian Doctrine No. 4*, 112–13.
75. Rev. Ferreol Girardey, C.Ss.R., ed., *Commentary on the Catechism of Rev. W. Faeber for the Parochial Schools of the United States* (St. Louis: B. Herder, 1930), 257.
76. Felix M. Kirsch and Sister M. Brendan, *Catholic Faith Explained: A Teacher Manual for Catholic Faith* (Washington, DC: Catholic University of America Press, 1939), 340.
77. *A Catholic Catechism*, 303.
78. Girardey, *Commentary on the Catechism of Rev. W. Faeber*, 257.
79. *A Catholic Catechism*, 304.
80. Gillis, "Conscience," 17.
81. Robert Lord, "The Church and Conscience," *Catholic World* 36 (June 1938): 248.
82. Davis, *Moral and Pastoral Theology*, 7.
83. Deman, "The Dignity of Conscience," 116.
84. Gillis, "Conscience and Casuistry," 6. James Martin Gillis Papers, box 19, folder "Conscience," Office of Paulist Archives, New York.
85. Gillis, 6.
86. Gribble, *Guardian of America*.
87. Gillis, "Conscience," 17.
88. Gillis, "Conscience and Casuistry," 6.
89. Francis J. Connell, "Confusion in Modern Morals," December 18, 1949, 3. Francis Connell C.Ss.R. Papers, folder "Morality," BPRA.
90. Francis J. Connell, "Catholic Hour on Television: Moral Decisions, Part One; The Individual and His Freedom," National Broadcasting Company, January 2, 1955, 17. Francis Connell C.Ss.R. Papers, folder "Moral Decisions III," BPRA.
91. Connell, 28.
92. Francis J. Connell, "Notes in Moral Theology," 4. Francis Connell C.Ss.R. Papers, folder "Miscellaneous," BPRA.
93. Francis J. Connell, "Restitution because of Damnification." Francis Connell C.Ss.R. Papers, folder "Summer School, Moral," BPRA.
94. Raymond A. Tartre, "The Law and Love," *Emmanuel* 70 (October 1964): 391.
95. Tartre, 389.
96. Tartre, 390.
97. Second Vatican Council, *Pastoral Constitution on the Church in the Modern World*, December 7, 1965, the Vatican website, http://www.vatican.va/archive/hist_councils /ii_vatican_council/documents/vat-ii_cons_19651207_gaudium-et-spes_en.html.
98. Second Vatican Council, *Pastoral Constitution on the Church in the Modern World*.
99. Second Vatican Council, *The Declaration on Religious Freedom*, December 7, 1965, the Vatican website, http://www.vatican.va/archive/hist_councils/ii_vatican_council /documents/vat-ii_decl_19651207_dignitatis-humanae_en.html.

CHAPTER TWO

1. John Ryan, "Conscientious Objection: A Point of View," *Catholic Educational Review* 39 (June 1941): 324.
2. Ryan, 325.
3. Henry David Thoreau, *Civil Disobedience: Resistance to Civil Government* (Boonton, NJ: Liberty Library, 1946), 9.
4. Thomas Hobbes, *Leviathan*, ed. Michael Oakeshott (New York: Collier Books, 1962), 238. Hobbes ranked the proposition that one sins by acting against conscience—a tenet of Catholic doctrine since the thirteenth century—high on his list of "those things that weaken, or tend to the Dissolution of a Commonwealth" (237).

5. Bede Jarrett, "Infallibility of Conscience," *Catholic Worker*, November 1941, 4. Original quotation appears in Bede Jarrett, *Meditations for Layfolk* (London: Catholic Truth Society, 1915), 210.

6. Paul Blakeley, "An Answer to the Objectors Who Deny Any War Is Just," *America*, March 3, 1942, 594.

7. The just-war theory boiled down to a short list of propositions. For a war to be just, it must be declared by a legitimately constituted state (whether the state was democratic, monarchist, or totalitarian). The war must be defensive in nature, and the tactics utilized to win the war must recognize the dignity of civilian innocents. The just-war theory also distinguished between formation of conscience before a war (*jus ad bellum*) and the formation of conscience in response to specific commands during war (*jus in bello*). Catholics might enter a just war but opt to follow conscience in the face of a specific order during the war to commit an unjust action. Finally, war must be a last resort and deemed absolutely necessary. Catholics remained committed in the 1940s and 1950s to the possibility that war could be just, even as the Soviet Union and the United States expanded their nuclear stockpiles. Indeed, Pope Pius XII used his 1956 Christmas Address to argue that the just-war theory holds in the atomic age. See Pius XII, "The Contradiction of Our Age," *The Pope Speaks*, Winter 1956–57, 343.

8. John Joseph McVey, *Catechism of Christian Doctrine No. 4, Revised according to the Code of 1918* (Philadelphia: Institute of the Brothers of the Christian Schools, 1926), 115.

9. Raymond J. Campion and Ellamay Horan, *Religion: A Secondary School Course*, bk. 3, *Emerging Catholic Action* (New York: William H. Sadlier, 1932), 252.

10. Campion and Horan, 253.

11. Patricia McNeal, "Catholic Conscientious Objection during World War II," *Catholic Historical Review* 61 (April 1975): 222. On conscientious objection during World War II, see Jeremy K. Kessler, "A War for Liberty: On the Law of Conscientious Objection," in *The Cambridge History of World War II*, ed. Michael Geyer and Adam Tooze (Cambridge: Cambridge University Press, 2015), 447–74. The US lawmakers did leave room for conscientious objection, Kessler notes, even as they constructed an administrative state that ignored individual rights in the name of waging wars abroad. These nearly twelve thousand official COs were assigned to perform works of "national importance" in the Civilian Public Service camps administered during the war by members of peace churches, like the Jehovah's Witnesses and the Quakers. Catholics were also found among the twenty-five thousand COs assigned to noncombatant service in the military. The draft laws of World War II did recognize COs who by "religious training and belief" were legitimately opposed to war, making space for members of peace churches.

12. Peter D'Agostino, *Rome in America: Transnational Catholic Ideology from the Risorgimento to Fascism* (Chapel Hill: University of North Carolina Press, 2004), 259.

13. James Martin Gillis, "The Rights of Conscience vs the Constitution?," *Sursum Corda*, July 15, 1929, 1. James Martin Gillis Papers, box 36, folder "Sursum Corda, 1–299," Office of Paulist Archives, New York.

14. James Martin Gillis, "The State above God?," *Sursum Corda*, January 27, 1930, 1. James Martin Gillis Papers, box 36, folder "Sursum Corda, 1–299," Office of Paulist Archives, New York.

15. "Conscience and Law," *America*, December 15, 1934, 217.

16. "Conscience and Law," 217.

17. Samuel Moyn, *Christian Human Rights* (Philadelphia: University of Pennsylvania Press, 2015), 1–3. On saint-making and ecclesiastical politics, see Kathleen Sprows

Cummings, *A Saint of Our Own: How the Quest for a Holy Hero Helped Catholics Become American* (Chapel Hill: University of North Carolina Press, 2019).

18. Pius XI, "The English Martyrs," *Catholic Mind* 33 (May 1935): 165.

19. Historians Sam Moyn and James Chappell have identified the 1930s as the period when the Catholic Church embraced human rights and much of what we consider modern. In response to totalitarianism, Catholics began to lobby for liberties from the state, ceasing their calls that the *modern state be made Catholic*. Moyn shows how French Catholic philosopher Jacques Maritain abandoned his critique of modern individualism after Hitler and Mussolini took power, turning instead to a new argument about how natural law supports human rights and the inherent dignity of the person. The persecution of churches, deportations, labor camps, and unmitigated violence spurred the shift in his thinking. James Chappell demonstrates that encounters with the twin horrors of fascism and communism convinced Catholics that the state must be constrained and individual freedoms preserved. "Faced with totalitarianism of the right (fascism) and the left (Stalinism)," Chappell writes, "Catholics across Europe engaged in a robust rethinking of what it meant to be Catholic and what role the Church should play in the world." Suddenly, they embraced dignity, personalism, religious liberty, pluralism, and human rights. Moyn, *Christian Human Rights*, 11; James Chappell, *Catholic Modern: The Challenge of Totalitarianism and the Remaking of the Church* (Cambridge, MA: Harvard University Press, 2018), 11.

20. Francis Talbot, "Fisher and More: Saints," *America*, April 6, 1935, 611.

21. Edward Quinn, "The Consistency of Martyrs," *Downside Review* 53 (January 1935): 14–15.

22. James A. Magner, "Two English Martyrs," *Extension Magazine* 30 (July 1935), 55.

23. Mel Piehl, *Breaking Bread: The Catholic Worker Movement and the Origin of Catholic Radicalism in America* (Philadelphia: Temple University Press, 1982), 196–97. The existence of two responses to war evinced contention in the Worker movement rather than healthy plurality: Day took a stand for total pacifism, with which many Worker communities disagreed.

24. "Study of Medieval Theologians and Conscientious Objection," *Catholic Worker*, September 1938, 6.

25. "Study of Medieval Theologians and Conscientious Objection," 6.

26. Patrick C. Coy, "Conscription and the Catholic Conscience in World War II," in *American Catholic Pacifism: The Influence of Dorothy Day and the Catholic Worker Movement*, ed. Anne Klejment and Nancy L. Roberts (Westport, CT: Praeger, 1996), 51.

27. George Barry O'Toole, *War and Conscription at the Bar of Christian Morals* (New York: Catholic Worker Press, 1941), 37.

28. O'Toole, 36.

29. Daniel Lord, *So You Won't Fight, Eh?* (St. Louis: Queen's Work Press, 1939,) 3.

30. Lord, 7.

31. Lord, 16.

32. Cyprian Emmanuel, "Conscientious Objection to War," *Catholic Mind*, October 22, 1940, 395.

33. "Conscientious Objectors," *America*, December 13, 1941, 266.

34. "War and Conscience," *America*, December 27, 1941, 322.

35. "War and Conscience," 322.

36. Paul L. Blakeley, "An Answer to the Objectors Who Deny Any War Is Just," *America*, March 7, 1942, 593.

37. Stephen Brown, "A Discourse on Conscience," *Homiletic and Pastoral Review* 42 (September 1942): 1095–96.

38. John C. Ford, "Current Theology: Notes on Moral Theology, 1942," *Theological Studies* 3 (1942): 581.

39. Father Cyprian Emmanuel, *The Morality of Conscientious Objection to War: A Report to the Ethics Committee* (Washington, DC: Catholic Association for International Peace, 1941), 20.

40. Emmanuel, 22.

41. John F. O'Brien, "Who in Conscience May Object to Military Service?" (S.T.L. diss., Catholic University of America, 1942), 29.

42. Leslie Tentler, *Catholics and Contraception: An American History* (Ithaca, NY: Cornell University Press, 2004), 164–66.

43. Aine Collier, *The Humble Little Condom: A History* (New York: Prometheus Books, 2007), 238.

44. Joseph LaRue to John F. O'Hara, August 6, 1942. Francis Connell C.Ss.R. Papers, folder "Contraception," BPRA.

45. John F. O'Hara to Joseph LaRue, August 12, 1942. Francis Connell C.Ss.R. Papers, folder "Contraception," BPRA.

46. O'Hara to LaRue, August 12, 1942.

47. John C. Ford, "Notes on Moral Theology, 1944," *Theological Studies* 5 (1944): 521.

48. Eric Marcelo O. Genilo, *John Cuthbert Ford, SJ: Moral Theologian at the End of the Manualist Era* (Washington, DC: Georgetown University Press, 2007), 35–76.

49. John C. Ford, "The Morality of Obliteration Bombing," *Theological Studies* 5 (1944): 264–68.

50. Jörg Friedrich, *The Fire: The Bombing of Germany, 1940–1945*, trans. Allison Brown (New York: Columbia University Press, 2006): 96–97.

51. Joseph Connor, "The Catholic Conscientious Objector," *Ecclesiastical Review* 108 (January–June 1943): 137.

52. Connor, 138.

53. On the national security state, see Michael Hogan, *A Cross of Iron: Harry S. Truman and the Origins of the National Security State, 1945–1954* (New York: Cambridge University Press, 1998); Melvyn Leffler, *A Preponderance of Power: National Security, the Truman Administration, and the Cold War* (Palo Alto, CA: Stanford University Press, 1993).

54. James Martin Gillis, "Conscience and the Draft for War," *Boston Pilot*, September 10, 1949.

55. James Martin Gillis, "Conscience Again," *Boston Pilot*, September 17, 1949.

56. Robert Drinan, "Is Pacifist Larry Gara a Criminal?," *Catholic World* 172 (March 1951), 410.

57. Drinan, 415.

58. Patrick O'Boyle to T. Oscar Smith, May 10, 1957. Francis Connell C.Ss.R. Papers, folder "Conscientious Objection," BPRA.

59. O'Boyle to Smith, May 10, 1957.

60. Pius XII, "The Contradiction of Our Age," 343.

61. John C. Ford, "Opinion of John C. Ford SJ on the Letter of T. Oscar Smith of the US Department of Justice, to Archbishop Patrick O'Boyle, concerning the Pope's Annual Christmas Message (1956) and Catholic Conscientious Objection," February/March 1957. John Ford Papers, box 6, folder 46, NEPSJA.

62. Francis J. Connell, "The Catholic Conscientious Objector," February/March 1957. John Ford Papers, box 6, folder 46, NEPSJA.

CHAPTER THREE

1. Patrick Carey, *Catholics in America: A History* (Westport, CT: Praeger, 2004), 93.
2. Andrew Vincenzo, "Panel A Questions Continued," October 4, 1965. Catholic Peace Fellowship Records, box 24, folder "Correspondence, A, 1965–1967," UNDA. Andrew Vincenzo is a pseudonym. Nearly all the draft dossiers—except for Stephen Spiro's papers—reside in the University of Notre Dame Archives. The Notre Dame archivist asked me to sign a contract withholding the names of the Catholic conscientious objectors found in the Form 150 and related correspondence, and I consented. I have changed the names of the COs who filed paperwork with the Catholic Peace Fellowship and the draft boards. This applies only to the Catholic COs and not the officers of the Catholic Peace Fellowship or the priests who wrote character letters for the COs.
3. Historians have identified the burning of draft cards, the protest vigil, and the famous draft board raids as significant modes of Catholic draft resistance, but the lay Catholic draft essay, with its elucidation of the church's teaching on conscience, marked an important and perhaps more frequent exercise of remonstrance. Jason C. Bivins, *The Fracture of Good Order: Christian Antiliberalism and the Challenge of American Politics* (Chapel Hill: University of North Carolina Press, 2003): 115–52; Shawn Francis Peters, *The Cantonsville Nine: A Story of Faith and Resistance in the Vietnam Era* (Oxford: Oxford University Press, 2013); Michael S. Foley, *Confronting the War Machine: Draft Resistance during the Vietnam War* (Chapel Hill: University of North Carolina Press, 2003); Thomas J. Sugrue, "The Catholic Encounter with the 1960s," in *Catholics in the American Century: Recasting Narratives of US History*, ed. R. Scott Appleby and Kathleen Sprows Cummings (Ithaca, NY: Cornell University Press, 2012), 78.
4. Helen M. Ciernick, "A Matter of Conscience: The Selective Conscientious Objector, Catholic College Students, and the Vietnam War," *U.S. Catholic Historian* 26 (Summer 2008): 42.
5. Ronit Y. Stahl, *Enlisting Faith: How the Military Chaplaincy Shaped Religion and State in Modern America* (Cambridge, MA: Harvard University Press, 2017), 216.
6. Stahl, 219.
7. On the origins of the CPF, see Patricia McNeal, *Harder Than War: Catholic Peacemaking in Twentieth-Century America* (New Brunswick, NJ: Rutgers University Press, 1992), 144; Kip Kosek, *Acts of Conscience: Christian Nonviolence and Modern American Democracy* (New York: Columbia University Press, 2009): 234–36.
8. John Deedy, "Behind the Catholic Peace Fellowship," *U.S. Catholic* 34 (August 1968), 14.
9. Deedy, 18.
10. James Forest to Gerald Worski, August 29, 1968, 2. Catholic Peace Fellowship Records, box 34, folder "W," UNDA.
11. Thomas Cornell to Ignacz McDermott, July 18, 1969. United States Catholic Conference, box 104, folder "Military Affairs: Selective Service, Conscious Objection, 1968–1969," CUAA. Cornell explained to a staffer at the United States Conference of Catholic Bishops that this office received twenty letters a week from Catholic men seeking basic information on the draft and Catholic peace teachings.
12. Penelope Adams Moon, "'Peace on Earth: Peace in Vietnam': The Catholic Peace Fellowship and Antiwar Witness, 1964–1976," *Journal of Social History* 36 (Summer 2003): 1048. Moon contends that the number of men seeking advice from the CPF

each week—by letter or drop-in visit—ranged from forty to fifty between 1966 and 1968, the years when the Selective Service System brought thirty thousand male citizens a month into the military. In his letter to McDermott, Cornell estimated that twenty-five men visited the office in person each week.

13. Thomas Cornell to Donald Blight, May 23, 1967. Catholic Peace Fellowship Records, box 24, folder "Correspondence, B, 1965–1970," UNDA.

14. Cornell to Blight, May 23, 1967.

15. Deedy, "Behind the Catholic Peace Fellowship," 14.

16. James Forest, *Catholics and Conscientious Objection* (New York: Catholic Peace Fellowship, 1966), 5.

17. Lyle Young to Robert Jimenez, December 13, 1968. Catholic Peace Fellowship Records, box 33, folder R, UNDA.

18. Lyle Young to Kip Stepheson, June 6, 1969. Catholic Peace Fellowship Records, box 32, folder K, UNDA.

19. Forest, *Catholics and Conscientious Objection*, 10, 4.

20. Jim Forest to Allen Westmore, November 2, 1965. Catholic Peace Fellowship Records, box 25, folder "Correspondence, E, 1965–1967," UNDA.

21. Forest to Westmore, November 2, 1965.

22. Stephen Spiro, "Appeal Board, Panel No. 1, State of New Jersey, Selective Service System," October 12, 1964. John Ford Papers, box 46, folder 5, NEPSJA.

23. John Ford to James Forest, January 16, 1965. John Ford Papers, box 46, folder 5, NEPSJA.

24. Daniel Berrigan to General Lewis B. Hershey, January 15, 1965. Catholic Peace Fellowship Records, box 29, folder "Correspondence, S, 1965–1970," UNDA.

25. Jim Forest to John Wright, February 1, 1965. Catholic Peace Fellowship Records, box 29, folder "Correspondence, S, 1965–1970," UNDA. Wright gave the McGreary Foundation Lecture to members of the Thomas More Association in early 1964. See John J. Wright, "Reflections on Conscience and Authority," *Critic: A Catholic Review of Books and the Arts*, April–May 1964, 11–28.

26. Marilyn B. Young, *The Vietnam Wars, 1945–1990* (New York: HarperCollins, 1991), 217.

27. Vincenzo, "Panel A Questions Continued," 2.

28. Norris Davidson, "Selective Service System Special Form for Conscientious Objector," April 1966, 2. Catholic Peace Fellowship Records, box 33, folder N, UNDA.

29. Anthony Francis, "Selective Service System: Special Form for Conscientious Objector," January 8, 1971, 3-p2. Catholic Peace Fellowship Records, box 33, folder M, UNDA.

30. Second Vatican Council, *Pastoral Constitution on the Church in the Modern World*, December 7, 1965, the Vatican website, http://www.vatican.va/archive/hist_councils /ii_vatican_council/documents/vat-ii_cons_19651207_gaudium-et-spes_en.html.

31. As historian John O'Malley noted in his history of the Second Vatican Council, the bishops and their expert theologians wrote documents in a pastoral language intending to heal the brokenness of the modern world. They also paid special attention to interiority. John O'Malley, *What Happened at Vatican II* (Cambridge, MA: Belknap Press of Harvard University Press, 2010).

32. Charles Bronson, "Series II. No. 2.," December 29, 1967, attached page No. 2. Catholic Peace Fellowship Records, box 24, folder "Correspondence, B, 1965–1970," UNDA.

33. Edmund Thompson, "Series II. Religious Training and Belief," June 12, 1969. Catholic Peace Fellowship Records, box 33, folder Q+R" UNDA. The *Pastoral Constitution on*

the Church in the Modern World was not as unequivocal as these COs wanted American draft boards to believe, but neither was the text without sentences and clauses that supported a Catholic conscience follower's cause. The documents acknowledged Catholics' right to follow conscience but also pointed out the limits of that right. Lay Catholics were creatively reinterpreting the documents in the context of an increasingly vocal antiwar movement: in 1967, 100,000 Americans arrived in Washington, DC, to protest the war; just two years later in 1969, a throng of 250,000 antiwar protesters took over its streets.

34. The Catholic press in the United States imported the phrase for readers after "primacy of conscience" aired conspicuously in 1964 on Dutch television, in an address by Bishop Willem Bekkers. That July, a Catholic newspaper in Davenport, Indiana, reported that Bekkers gave an address "stressing the 'primacy of personal conscience,'" and quoted the bishop as saying, "In our life we are confronted daily with situations that compel us . . . to a personal decision of conscience." See "Dutch Prelate Stresses That Conscience Is Chief Guide," *Catholic Messenger* (Davenport, IN), July 2, 1964. Also in that year, a priest wrote a letter to the theological experts at the *American Ecclesiastical Review* to report that "much is being said nowadays about the 'primacy of conscience,'" and warned his fellow confessors about imminent confrontations with laypeople. See "Answers to Questions: The Primacy of Conscience," *American Ecclesiastical Review* 151 (1964): 343.

35. Lyle Young to Devin O'Rourke, August 13, 1969. Catholic Peace Fellowship Records, box 33, folder O, UNDA.

36. James Upton, "Question I," November 11, 1969. Catholic Peace Fellowship Records, box 34, folder T, UNDA.

37. Patrick O'Sullivan, "Series II—Religious Training and Belief: Answer to Question Two." Catholic Peace Fellowship Records, box 25, folder "Correspondence, D, 1962–1967," UNDA.

38. Jacob Reisman, "Selective Service System: Special Form for Conscientious Objector," October 3, 1966. Catholic Peace Fellowship Records, box 34, folder S, UNDA.

39. Robert A. Orsi, *History and Presence* (Cambridge, MA: Belknap Press of Harvard University Press, 2016), 6; Ruth Harris, *Lourdes: Body and Spirit in a Secular Age* (New York: Penguin Books, 2000); John T. McGreevy, *American Jesuits and the World: How an Embattled Religious Order Made Catholicism Global* (Princeton, NJ: Princeton University Press, 2016), 104–43.

40. Matteo Ammiani, "Religious Training and Beliefs," December 23, 1970, Catholic Peace Fellowship Records, box 31, folder A, UNDA.

41. Drake Wiesman, "Outline of What I Want to Say at Personal Interview before Local Selective Service Board #101," August 19, 1968, 4. Catholic Peace Fellowship Records, box 34, folder W, UNDA.

42. Brody Jacobson to Chief of Naval Personnel, April 24, 1965. Catholic Peace Fellowship Records, box 24, folder "Correspondence, B, 1965–1970," UNDA.

43. Quentin Clarkson, "Series II—Religious Training and Belief," December 15, 1967. Catholic Peace Fellowship Records, box 31, folder C, UNDA.

44. Yani Turkic, "Answers for Questions in Series II," 2. Catholic Peace Fellowship Records, box 34, folder T, UNDA.

45. George Schultz, "Required Information Sheet," December 1968, 6. Catholic Peace Fellowship Records, box 34, folder S, UNDA.

46. Stanley O'Leary, "IV: 2e." 6; Larson Peters, "Summary of Hearing with Local Board 83." Catholic Peace Fellowship Records, box 28, folder "Correspondence, O, 1965–1967," UNDA.

47. Stanley O'Leary, "Hearing Before the Local Board," April 26, 1966, 5. Catholic Peace Fellowship Records, box 28, folder "Correspondence, O, 1965–1967," UNDA.

48. Dennis Ackerman, "Question 2," December 1966. Catholic Peace Fellowship Records, box 24, folder "Correspondence, A, 1965–1967," UNDA.

49. Jimmy Saddles, "Series II: Religious Training and Belief," October 2, 1967, 4. Catholic Peace Fellowship Records, box 28, folder "Correspondence, S, 1965–1970," UNDA.

50. Darren Scaft, "Copy of SSS Form #150," March 1967, 3. Catholic Peace Fellowship Records, box 29, folder "Correspondence, S, 1965–1970," UNDA.

51. Schultz, "Required Information Sheet," December 1968, 6.

52. Martin Luther King, *Why We Can't Wait* (New York: Berkley, 1963), 94.

53. King, 88.

54. Terence O'Shaughnessy to Michigan Draft Board, November 27, 1967. Catholic Peace Fellowship Records, box 24, folder "Correspondence, B, 1965–1970," UNDA.

55. Francis Connolly to Local Board 77, February 4, 1972. Catholic Peace Fellowship Records, box 25, folder "Correspondence, D, 1962–1967," UNDA.

56. Thomas Cornell, "Memorial: Stephen J. Spiro," December 1, 2007. *Homilies, Sermons, and Harangues* (blog), http://homiliessermonsharangues.blogspot.com/2007/12/memorial-stephen-j-spiro.html.

57. Foley, *Confronting the War Machine*, 156.

58. William Bier, introduction to *Conscience: Its Freedoms and Limitations*, ed. William Bier (New York: Fordham University Press, 1971), x.

59. Bier, xi.

60. Bier, xi.

CHAPTER FOUR

1. Morris J. MacGregor, *Steadfast in the Faith: The Life of Cardinal O'Boyle* (Washington, DC: Catholic University of America, 2005), 348.

2. "Roman Catholics," *Time*, September 13, 1968, 38.

3. Kenneth Dole, "Priest Tells His View of Conscience," *Washington Post*, December 23, 1968.

4. On global 1968, see Jeremy Varon, *Bringing the War Home: The Weather Underground, the Red Army Faction, and Revolutionary Violence in the Sixties and the Seventies* (Berkeley: University of California Press, 2004); Gerd-Rainer Horn, *The Spirit of '68: Rebellion in Western Europe and Northern America* (Oxford: Oxford University Press, 2007); Mark Kurlansky, *1968: The Year That Rocked the World* (New York: Ballantine, 2004); Jeremy Suri, *Protest and Power: Global Revolution the Rise of Détente* (Cambridge, MA: Harvard University Press, 2005).

5. On existentialism, alienation, and the student New Left, see Douglas Rossinow, *The Politics of Authenticity: Liberalism, Christianity, and the New Left in America* (New York: Columbia University Press, 1998).

6. Pius XI, *Casti connubii*, December 31, 1930, https://w2.vatican.va/content/pius-xi/en/encyclicals/documents/hf_p-xi_enc_19301231_casti-connubii.html, accessed January 25, 2019.

7. MacGregor, *Steadfast in the Faith*, 338.

8. See "O'Donoghue Appeals to Pope to 'Give Help' to Cardinal," *Evening Star* (Washington, DC), Friday, October 11, 1968. Shane MacCarthy Humanae Vitae Collection, box 3, folder 5, CUAA. The article notes that O'Boyle ceased paying the tuition fees ($250 a year) in October for AWP members' classes at Catholic University of America.

9. For an interpretation of the Second Vatican Council as a response to the crises of decolonization and Cold War arms races, see Stephen Schloesser, "Against Forgetting: Memory, History, Vatican II," *Theological Studies* 67 (June 2006): 275–319. On content and form of council documents, see John O'Malley, *What Happened at Vatican II* (Cambridge, MA: Belknap Press of Harvard University Press, 2010).

10. Executive Council of the Association of Washington Priests to Patrick O'Boyle, July 19, 1968. Shane MacCarthy Humanae Vitae Collection, box 1, folder 2, CUAA.

11. "Chronology of Events," n.d. Shane MacCarthy Humanae Vitae Collection, box 1, folder 11, CUAA.

12. Association of Washington Priests, "The Statement of Conscience," July 28, 1968. Shane MacCarthy Humanae Vitae Collection, box 1, folder 2, CUAA.

13. Association of Washington Priests, "The Statement of Conscience."

14. Association of Washington Priests, press release, September 14, 1968. Shane Mac-Carthy Humanae Vitae Collection, box 1, folder 11, CUAA.

15. Association of Washington Priests, press release, September 14, 1968.

16. Father, Bronx, NY, to *Jubilee* magazine, n.d. Edward Rice Papers, box 4, folder 53, Georgetown University Archives. *Jubilee: A Magazine for the Church and Her People* conducted an open-forum discussion of the birth control ban after publishing articles by Rosemary Radford Reuther, a graduate student and mother of three, and Bruce Cooper, an English Catholic father of five—both generally critical of the church's stance. Reuther would go on to a successful career as a theologian. Leslie Tentler, *Catholics and Contraception: An American History* (Ithaca, NY: Cornell University Press, 2004): 212–20. According to Tentler, *Jubilee* received hundreds of letters from laypeople who were "in the main both devout and well-educated" (213).

17. William J. Jacobs, "Conscience and Authority: An Ancient and Modern Dilemma," *Ave Maria*, May 16, 1964, 18.

18. Anonymous, "The Primacy of Conscience," *American Ecclesiastical Review* 151 (August 1964): 343.

19. Elaine Tyler May, *America and the Pill: A History of Promise, Peril and Liberation* (New York: Basic Books, 2010), 1–2. By 1962, as May, a historian, notes, 1.2 million women—Catholics among them—were taking the Pill each day. By 1964, just two years later, 6.5 million married women had been using oral contraceptives along with an "untold number of unmarried women" (2).

20. Bernard Häring, "Theology of Married Love," August 1965, 17. John Ford Papers, box 55, folder 2, NEPSJA.

21. Bernard Häring, "Conscience and Freedom," March 1966.John Ford Papers, box 2, folder 8, NEPSJA.

22. "Catechism in Dutch," *Time*, December 1, 1967, 100.

23. Higher Catechetical Institute at Nijmegen, *A New Catechism: Catholic Faith for Adults*, trans. Kevin Smith (New York: Herder and Herder, 1969), 375.

24. Higher Catechetical Institute, 375.

25. Higher Catechetical Institute, 403. The AWP wondered aloud in a memo to O'Boyle how he could claim to teach the authentic magisterium when an official source—the American translations bore the imprimatur of a bishop from Vermont—endorsed conscience with such enthusiasm. Executive Committee to Patrick O'Boyle, July 19, 1968. Shane MacCarthy Humanae Vitae Collection, box 1, folder 2, CUAA.

26. Patty Crowley lived out the calling of the organization she designed to help Catholic couples place Christ at the center of marriage. She and her husband, Pat, married in 1937; they had five kids of their own and raised more than fifty foster children in their

suburban Chicago home. Patty and Pat were at the forefront of a postwar effort led by the laity to sanctify family life. In the aftermath of Vatican II, the Crowleys were appointed to the birth control commission, as historian James O'Toole notes, "so as to include the perspective of a married couple." James O'Toole, *The Faithful: A History of Catholics in America* (Cambridge, MA: Belknap Press of Harvard University Press, 2008), 200.

27. Lansing, MI, "Complete Rhythm Questionnaire, 1965. RWL, CWRL/13, "Completed Rhythm Questionnaire," Patrick and Patricia Crowley: Manuscripts, Patrick and Patricia Crowley Papers, UNDA.

28. Los Angeles, CA, "Complete Rhythm Questionnaire," 1965. RWL, CWRL/13, "Completed Rhythm Questionnaire," Patrick and Patricia Crowley: Manuscripts, Patrick and Patricia Crowley Papers, UNDA.

29. San Diego, CA, "Complete Rhythm Questionnaire," 1965. RWL, CWRL/13, "Completed Rhythm Questionnaire," Patrick and Patricia Crowley: Manuscripts, Patrick and Patricia Crowley Papers, UNDA.

30. Shane MacCarthy, Homily, August 4, 1968, 2. Shane MacCarthy Humanae Vitae Collection, box 2, folder 8, CUAA.

31. MacCarthy, Homily, August 4, 1968, 2.

32. Shane MacCarthy, Homily Notes, 1968, 5. Shane MacCarthy Humanae Vitae Collection, box 2, folder 8, CUAA.

33. MacCarthy, Homily Notes, 1968, 6.

34. MacCarthy, Homily Notes, 1968, 8.

35. Shane MacCarthy to Patrick O'Boyle, September 14, 1968. Shane MacCarthy Humanae Vitae Collection, box 1, folder 4, CUAA.

36. Mark Massa, *The Structures of Theological Revolutions: How the Fight over Birth Control Transformed American Catholicism* (Oxford: Oxford University Press, 2018), 106–27.

37. Germain Grisez, "About John C. Ford," March 23, 2015, The Way of the Lord Jesus, http://www.twotlj.org/Ford.html.

38. Patrick A. O'Boyle, "Dear Friends in Christ," August 2, 1968. Shane MacCarthy Humanae Vitae Collection, box 1, folder 2, CUAA.

39. Patrick A. O'Boyle to Shane MacCarthy, August 10, 1968, 7. Shane MacCarthy Humanae Vitae Collection, box 1, folder 2, CUAA.

40. O'Boyle to MacCarthy, August 10, 1968, 7.

41. Patrick A. O'Boyle to Shane MacCarthy, September 7, 1968. Shane MacCarthy Humanae Vitae Collection, box 1, folder 4, CUAA.

42. O'Boyle to MacCarthy, September 7, 1968.

43. Association of Washington Priests, "Clarification of the Statement of Conscience," press release, September 11, 1968. Shane MacCarthy Humanae Vitae Collection, box 3, folder 4, CUAA. The press release is not dated, but the release date appears on "Chronology of Events." Shane MacCarthy Humanae Vitae Collection, box 1, folder 11, CUAA.

44. Association of Washington Priests, press release, September 14, 1968. Shane MacCarthy Humanae Vitae Collection, box 1, folder 11, CUAA.

45. Patrick A. O'Boyle, "Dear Friends in Christ," September 22, 1968. Shane MacCarthy Humanae Vitae Collection, box 1, folder 11, CUAA.

46. O'Boyle, "Dear Friends in Christ."

47. "200 Leave Mass as O'Boyle Speaks," *Boston Globe*, September 23, 1968; "An Act of Faith," *Washington Post*, September 25, 1968.

48. Patrick A. O'Boyle, "Birth Control and Public Policy," sermon, St. Matthew's Cathedral, Sunday, August 29, 1965. John Ford Papers, box 21, folder 14, NEPSJA.

49. The 47 (Association of Washington Priests) to Patrick A. O'Boyle, September 27, 1968. Shane MacCarthy Humanae Vitae Collection, box 1, folder 4, CUAA.

50. David J. Endres, *Many Tongues, One Faith: A History of Franciscan Parish Life in the United States* (Oceanside, CA: Academy of American Franciscan History, 2018), 120.

51. Patrick A. O'Boyle, press release, October 1, 1968. Shane MacCarthy Humanae Vitae Collection, box 1, folder 5, CUAA.

52. MacGregor, *Steadfast in the Faith*, 1–42, 166–97, 304–34.

53. John F. Corrigan, press release, October 2, 1968. Shane MacCarthy Humanae Vitae Collection, box 2, folder 8, CUAA.

54. Corrigan, press release, October 2, 1968.

55. Martin Well, "Rally of 800 Hears Ousted Priest," *Washington Post*, n.d. but early September. Shane MacCarthy Humanae Vitae Collection, box 3, folder 3, CUAA.

56. Well, "Rally of 800 Hears Ousted Priest."

57. MacGregor, *Steadfast in the Faith*, 355–56.

58. Center for Christian Renewal, "Unity Day Rally," n.d. but September or October 1968. Shane MacCarthy Humanae Vitae Collection, box 3, folder 6, CUAA. The rally was held on November 10, 1968, at 2 p.m. Center for Christian Renewal flyer, n.d. Shane MacCarthy Humanae Vitae Collection, box 2, folder 8, CUAA. AWP members organized the group's letter-writing campaign, asking laypeople and priests across the United States to send letters to their own local authorities, important cardinals and archbishops, along with Archbishop Dearden (president of the US Conference of Catholic Bishops), Cardinal Shehan (chairman of the Bishops' Committee on Arbitration and Mediation), and Cardinal Archbishop O'Boyle.

59. Mary McGrory, "Happy Throng Strikes a Blow for Dissent," *Evening Star* (Washington, DC), November 11, 1968. Shane MacCarthy Humanae Vitae Collection, box 3, folder 6, CUAA.

60. "Priests Stage Sit-in at Bishops Hotel," *Evening Star* (Washington, DC), November 11, 1968. Shane MacCarthy Humanae Vitae Collection, box 3, folder 6, CUAA.

61. Group of Laypeople to Lawrence Cardinal Shehan, November 1, 1968. Lawrence Cardinal Shehan Papers, box 7, folder "Correspondence with Laity, Re: Situation in Washington D.C.," Archives of the Archdiocese of Baltimore. Approximately a dozen laypeople from Kentucky sent this letter to Dearden, O'Boyle, Shehan, and the bishop of Covington, Kentucky.

62. D. C. Duivestiejn, "Personal Conscience and Church Authority," *Clergy Review* 53 (November 1968): 868.

63. John Dedek, "Freedom of the Catholic Conscience," *Chicago Studies* 7 (Summer 1968): 124.

64. Gregory Kenny, *How Conscience Can Be Your Guide* (Chicago: Claretian Publications, 1972), 18.

65. Patrick O'Boyle, "The Catholic Conscience," October 9, 1968, 2. Shane MacCarthy Humanae Vitae Collection, box 3, folder 4, CUAA.

66. Knights of Columbus, *Sex in Marriage: Questions Asked since the Encyclical* Humanae Vitae (New Haven, CT: Knights of Columbus, 1968), 1.

67. In a book published in 1969, German émigré and Fordham philosopher Dietrich von Hildebrand wrote, "The thesis that the decision to practice contraception ought to be left to the consciences of individual Catholics has become quite fashionable. . . . [It is], however, a confusion—an utterly false understanding of conscience." Dietrich von Hildebrand, *Love, Marriage, and the Catholic Conscience* (Manchester, NH: Sophia Press, 1969), 77.

68. William Buckley, "Freedom of Conscience vis a vis Church Authority," in *Spectrum of Catholic Attitudes*, ed. Robert Campbell (Milwaukee: Bruce, 1969), 83.

69. Paul VI, "Conscience: Its Dignity and Limitation," *The Pope Speaks*, February 1969, 10.

70. Knights of Columbus, *Sex in Marriage*, 1.

71. O'Boyle, "The Catholic Conscience," 3.

72. O'Boyle, 3.

73. O'Boyle, 3.

74. Robert W. Lawson, "Conscience or Canon Law," *Boston Globe*, December 3, 1968.

75. William J. Kenneally to Lawrence Cardinal Shehan, October 28, 1968. LCSP, box 7, folder "Correspondence with Laity, Re: Situation in Washington DC," AAB.

76. Kenneally to Shehan, October 28, 1968.

77. "Day with a Priest Who Can't Teach or Preach," *Washington Daily News*, October 7, 1968. Shane MacCarthy Humanae Vitae Collection, box 3, folder 5, CUAA.

78. "Day with a Priest Who Can't Teach or Preach."

79. John Deedy, editorial in "News and Views," *Commonweal*, November 1, 1968, 138.

80. Deedy, 138.

81. Deedy, 138.

82. National Conference of Catholic Bishops, *Human Life in Our Day*, November 15, 1968. Priests for Life, June 2015, http://www.priestsforlife.org/magisterium/bishops/68-11-15humanlifeinourdaynccb.htm.

83. Quoted in "Dearden Emphasizes Conscience," *National Catholic Reporter*, December 11, 1968, 7.

84. MacGregor, *Steadfast in the Faith*, 366.

85. Tentler, *Catholics and Contraception*, 274–75.

86. Sacra Congregatio pro Clericis, April 26, 1971. Shane MacCarthy Humanae Vitae Collection, box 1, folder 10, CUAA.

CHAPTER FIVE

1. W. Norris Clarke, "The Mature Conscience in Philosophical Perspective," in *Conscience: Its Freedom and Limitations*, ed. William Bier (New York: Fordham University Press, 1971), 358.

2. Clarke, 359.

3. Bernard Lonergan, "The Transition from a Classicist World-View to Historical-Mindedness," in *A Second Collection*, ed. William F. J. Ryan and Bernard J. Tyrell (Philadelphia: Westminster, 1966): 1–9.

4. William M. Halsey, *The Survival of American Innocence: Catholicism in an Era of Disillusionment, 1920–1940* (South Bend, IN: Notre Dame University Press, 1980); Paula M. Kane, "Confessional and Couch: E. Boyd Barrett, Priest-Psychoanalyst," in *Crossings and Dwellings: Restored Jesuits, Women Religious, and American Experience, 1814–2014*, ed. Kyle B. Roberts and Stephen R. Schloesser (Leiden: Brill, 2017): 409–53; C. Kevin Gillespie, *Psychology and American Catholicism: From Confession to Therapy?* (New York: Cross Roads, 2001).

5. Robert Kugelmann, "An Encounter between Psychology and Religion: Humanistic Psychology and the Immaculate Heart of Mary Nuns," *Journal of the History of the Behavioral Sciences* 41 (Fall 2005): 347–65.

6. Robert Kugelmann, the historian who has explored the relationship between psychology and Catholicism in the greatest depth, credits psychology with the breakdown of a classicist worldview in American Catholic life. Robert Kugelmann, *Psychology and Catholicism: Contested Boundaries* (Cambridge: Cambridge University Press, 2011), 331.

7. John C. Ford, *Religious Superiors, Subjects and Psychiatrists* (Westminster, MD: Newman Press, 1963); Francis J. Connell, *Outlines of Moral Theology* (Milwaukee: Bruce, 1953), 38.
8. Fulton Sheen, *Peace of Soul* (New York: McGraw-Hill, 1949), 111.
9. Bernard Häring, "Invincible Ignorance," September 1963, 27. Unprocessed Häring Lectures, Mount St. Alphonsus Collection, BPRA.
10. Michael Stock, "Conscience and Superego," *Thomist: A Speculative Quarterly Review* 24 (April 1, 1961), 544.
11. Stock, "Conscience and Superego," 561.
12. Louis Janssens, *Freedom of Conscience and Religious Freedom*, trans. Brother Lorenzo, CFX (Staten Island, NY: Alba House, 1965), 55.
13. Raymond Gardella, "Morality and the Law," *Perspectives* 10 (June–July 1965): 77.
14. Charles Davis, "Announcing Mortal Sins," *America*, February 6, 1965, 193. A psychiatrist thought he found empirical evidence that a preponderance of superegos could be found in the American Catholic community, and he published the findings in the *Journal of Religion and Health* in 1966. "The psychiatric disorders seen among Catholics tend to be characterized by one of two clinical syndromes," he wrote. These were either outsized superegos (attachment to the law) or a struggle against the superego (anger at the pain received from disobeying the law). John E. Kysar, "Mental-Health Implications of Aggiornamento," *Journal of Religion and Health* 5 (1966), 38.
15. Erich Fromm, *Man for Himself* (New York: Routledge, 2003), 118–29. First published 1947.
16. Fromm, 118.
17. John P. Lavin, "Conscience or Mob Consciousness," *Liguorian*, August 1966, 47.
18. "The Split-Level Conscience," *Sign*, February 1966, 34; Fank Marbach, "To Catch the Conscience of the Child," *St. Anthony Messenger*, March 1967, 30; Xavier G. Colavechio, "Conscience: A Personalist Perspective," *Continuum*, Summer 1967, 203–10.
19. Louis Monden, *Sin, Liberty and Law*, trans. Joseph Donceel (London: Geoffery Chapman, 1966), 4.
20. Monden, 7.
21. Monden, 102–3.
22. Marbach, "To Catch the Conscience of the Child," 30.
23. Felicitas Betz, "How the Child's Conscience Develops," in *Making Sense of Confession: A New Approach for Parents, Teachers and Clergy*, ed. Otto Betz and trans. Hilda Graf (Chicago: Franciscan Herald,1968), 37.
24. Betz, 40.
25. John W. Glaser, "Conscience and the Superego: A Key Distinction," *Theological Studies* 32 (March 1971): 46.
26. Glaser, 46.
27. John J. Ferrante, "Forming the Conscience," *Priest* 28 (February 1972): 69.
28. Gabriel Moran, "Creating Mature Consciences," *National Catholic Register*, March 30, 1969, 10.
29. William Reedy, "Consult, Think, Pray," *National Catholic Register*, March 30, 1969, 10.
30. Gerard S. Sloyan, "Love Is the Measure," *National Catholic Register*, March 30, 1969, 10.
31. Ferrante, "Forming the Conscience," 69.
32. Kevin O'Rourke, "Conscience, the Church, and You," *St. Cloud Visitor*, November 5, 1970.
33. John R. Cavanagh, "The Mature Conscience as Seen by a Psychiatrist," in *Conscience: Its Freedoms and Limitations*, ed. William Bier (New York: Fordham University, 1971), 384.

34. Leonard Foley, "You (and) Your Conscience," *St. Anthony Messenger*, June 1964, 15.
35. Bernard Häring, "Lecture Twelve: The Formation of a Christian Conscience," September 1963, 82. Unprocessed Häring Lectures, Mount St. Alphonsus Collection, BPRA.
36. Marbach, "To Catch the Conscience of the Child," 30.
37. Nicholas Lohkamp, "Conscience = Response-Ability," *St. Anthony Messenger*, October 1970, 40.
38. Häring, "Lecture 12: The Formation of Conscience," September 1963, 80.
39. Colavechio, "Conscience: A Personalist Perspective," 204.
40. Marbach, "To Catch the Conscience of the Child," 30.
41. Häring, "Lecture 12: The Formation of Conscience," September 1963, 80; Janssens, *Freedom of Conscience and Religious Freedom*, 57.
42. Foley, "You (and) Your Conscience," 15.
43. Arnold Tkacik, "Conscience: Conscious and Unconscious," *Journal of Religion and Health* 4 (1964): 80.
44. Gerald R. Garguilo, "Witness to Love," *Perspectives* 10 (May/June 1965): 76.
45. Monden, *Sin, Liberty and Law*, 7.
46. "Moral Order and Freedom of Conscience," *New Blackfriars* 46 (June 1965): 495.
47. Robert J. Rigali, "Notes on Conscience Formation," *Priest* 31 (October 1975): 38.
48. Robert H. Springer, *Conscience and the Behavioral Sciences* (Washington, DC: Corpus Books, 1968), 2.
49. Springer, 19.
50. Springer, 27.
51. Springer, 28.
52. Springer, 24.
53. Harvard psychologist Robert White's 1948 textbook, *The Abnormal Personality*, assigned to university students throughout the 1950s and 1960s (a second edition arrived in 1956 and a third in 1964), offered readers a two-page summary on the deficiencies of the superego. White observed that "many writers do not distinguish between super-ego and mature conscience," and then he drew a sharp distinction between the concepts. Developmental psychologist Lawrence Kohlberg followed up on White's suggestion in a breakthrough article published in 1963. In it, he presented evidence that conscience matured as individuals progressed through a series of age-based stages. As the individual moves through these moral stages, Kohlberg argued, he or she stops obeying law for the sake of obeying law, and instead follows the rules after voluntarily consenting to an intragroup agreement. Robert White, *The Abnormal Personality* (New York: Ronald Press, 1948), 371. Lawrence Kohlberg, "Moral Development and Identification," in *Child Psychology: The Sixty-Second Yearbook of the National Society for the Study of Education* (Chicago: University of Chicago Press, 1963), 295.
54. Lawrence Kohlberg, "Stages and Aging in Moral Development: Some Speculations," *Gerontologist* 4 (January–March 1973): 499. Kohlberg sketched the principles and stages as early as 1968, but he published the refined schema in 1973. For the earlier typology, see Lawrence Kohlberg, "Stages in Moral Growth," *International Journal of Religious Education* 44 (September–October 1968): 8–9, 40–41.
55. Paul J. Philibert, "Conscience: Developmental Perspectives from Rogers and Kohlberg," *Horizons* 6, no. 1 (1979): 1.
56. Jeffrey Keefe, "Conscience—More Than Judgement," *Catechist* 11 (January 1978): 6.
57. Keefe, 6.
58. Keefe, 6.

59. Robert T. Reilly, "Catholic Morality: Bless Me, Father, For Maybe I Sinned," *U.S. Catholic* 48 (September 1983): 53–54.

60. James J. DiGiacomo, "Follow Your Conscience," *Living Light* 15 (Fall 1978): 398.

61. Lawrence Kohlberg, "The Claim to Moral Adequacy of a Highest Stage of Moral Judgement," *Journal of Philosophy* 70 (1973): 632.

62. Lawrence Kohlberg with Rochelle Mayer, "Education for Justice," in *Essays on Moral Development* (San Francisco: Harper and Row, 1981), 1:45.

63. Lawrence Kohlberg, "Moral Stages and Moralization: The Cognitive-Developmental Approach," in *The Psychology of Moral Development* (San Francisco: Harper and Row, 1984), 2:179.

64. Kohlberg, 2:179.

65. Kohlberg, 2:179.

66. John T. McGreevy, *Catholicism and American Freedom: A History* (New York: W. W. Norton, 2003): 138–41.

67. Lawrence Kohlberg, "Development as the Aim of Education," in *Essays on Moral Development* (San Francisco: Harper and Row, 1981), 1:54.

68. Kohlberg, 1:55.

69. John Rawls, *A Theory of Justice* (Cambridge, MA: Belknap Press of Harvard University Press, 1971). Kohlberg discusses justice in "Moral Stages and Moralization: The Cognitive Development Approach," in *Moral Development and Behavior: Theory, Research, and Social Issues* (New York: Holt, Rinehart and Winston, 1976), 50.

70. For Kohlberg's take on Rawls, see "Justice as Reversability: The Claim to Moral Adequacy of a Highest Stage of Moral Judgment," in *Essays on Moral Development* (San Francisco: Harper and Row, 1981), 1:190–230.

71. Philibert, "Conscience: Developmental Perspectives from Rogers and Kohlberg," 12.

72. Keefe, "Conscience—More Than Judgement," 6.

73. Keefe, 6.

74. Kohlberg, "Stages in Moral Growth," 9.

75. William E. May, "The Natural Law, Conscience, and Developmental Psychology," *Communio* 2 (Spring 1975): 18.

76. Lawrence Kohlberg with Clark Power, "Moral Development, Religious Thinking, and the Question of a Seventh Stage," in *Essays on Moral Development* (San Francisco: Harper and Row, 1981), 1:319.

CHAPTER SIX

1. The bishops passed the statement in October 1971 and it was published in 1972. Quoted in "American Bishops' Declaration on Conscientious Objection," *Catholic World*, February 1972, 53.

2. Howard Everngam, *Pax: News* (Spring 1968). CZHN 6/08617, Gordon Zahn Papers, UNDA.

3. Zahn caused a transatlantic conflict after delivering an academic paper on German Catholic complicity with National Socialism at a 1963 conference. Mark Edward Ruff, *The Battle for the Catholic Past in Germay, 1945–1980* (Cambridge: Cambridge University Press, 2017).

4. American Pax Association, "Purpose of the PAX Campaign," n.d., published after July 1, 1967. United States Conference of Catholic Bishops Social Action Department, box 51, folder 8, CUAA.

5. Reverend Joseph M. Nelligan to Gordon Zahn, July 7, 1945. CZHN 1/01367, Gordon Zahn Papers, UNDA.

6. Gordon Zahn to Reverend Joseph M. Nelligan, July 10, 1945. CZHN 1/10368, Gordon Zahn Papers, UNDA.

7. Gordon Zahn to Reverend Carthy, September 29, 1945. CZHN 1/01369, Gordon Zahn Papers, UNDA.

8. Benjamin Peters, "'A Completely Fresh Reappraisal of War': Americanism, Radicalism, and the Catholic Pacifism of Gordon Zahn," *American Catholic Studies* 128 (Winter 2017): 6.

9. Gordon Zahn, "The Private Conscience and Legitimate Authority," *Commonweal*, March 30, 1962, 12. For a brief biography of Zahn, see David O'Brien, "Gordon C. Zahn," *American Catholic Studies* 126 (Fall 2015): 107–11.

10. Zahn, "The Private Conscience and Legitimate Authority," 12.

11. Zahn, 12.

12. Marilyn B. Young, *The Vietnam Wars, 1945–1990* (New York: HarperCollins, 1991), 103.

13. Gordon Zahn, "He Would Not Serve," *America*, July 5, 1958, 388–90.

14. Thomas Merton to Gordon Zahn, January 11, 1962. CZHN 9/12802, Gordon Zahn Papers, UNDA.

15. Gordon Zahn, *In Solitary Witness: The Life and Death of Franz Jägerstätter* (New York: Holt, Rinehart and Winston, 1964), 76.

16. Zahn, 87.

17. Gordon Zahn to François Houtart, May 17, 1965. CZHN 1/01614, Gordon Zahn Papers, UNDA.

18. Gordon Zahn to George A. Beck, July 23, 1965. CZHN 1/01624, Gordon Zahn Papers, UNDA.

19. Gordon Zahn, "Conscience and the Council," *Chronicle* 4 (Winter 1965): 696.

20. Gordon Zahn to Leo Suenens, July 17, 1965. CZHN 1/01623, Gordon Zahn Papers, UNDA.

21. Zahn to Houtart, May 17, 1965.

22. Thomas D. Roberts, "The Church in the Modern World, Chapter V, Section 101, Conscientious Objection," November 12, 1965, 1. CZHN 9/12322, Gordon Zahn Papers, UNDA. Roberts learned of Jägerstätter firsthand from Zahn when he invited the sociologist to Rome to lecture the British hierarchy on war and conscientious objection. Zahn, a rising academic star after the release of *In Solitary Witness*, had secured an appointment as the Senior Simon Fellow at the University of Manchester in 1964, so he was already in Europe when he received the invitation to serve as an unofficial council expert to the British bishops.

23. Roberts, 1.

24. Roberts, 2.

25. Benita de' Grassi di Pianura to Gordon Zahn, December 30, 1966. CZN 1/02492, Gordon Zahn Papers, UNDA.

26. E. K. Barnard to Gordon Zahn, December 25, 1965. CZN 2/02550, Gordon Zahn Papers, UNDA.

27. Christopher Dennick to Gordon Zahn, April 15, 1965. CZN 2/02512, Gordon Zahn Papers, UNDA.

28. John Wright to Gordon Zahn, February 9, 1966. CZN 9/12317, Gordon Zahn Papers, UNDA.

29. Quoted in "The Church in the World," *Tablet*, January 26, 1963, 43; quoted in "Conscience and Religious Liberty," *St. Anthony Messenger*, February 1964, 10.

30. "Conscience and Judgment," editorial, *Catholic Mind*, March 1966, 3.

31. "Conscience and Judgment," 3.
32. John B. Sheerin, "Thomas More: Conscientious Objector," *Catholic World* 205 (July 1967): 196–98; John B. Sheerin, "Must Conscientious Objectors Be Pacifists?," *Catholic World* 206 (January 1968): 146–47; John B. Sheerin, "Who Speaks for the Church on Vietnam," *Catholic World* 204 (November 1966): 75; John B. Sheerin, "When Is Bad Conscience Good Conscience," *Sum and Substance*, March 18, 1968, 1. George Gilmary Higgins Papers, box 108, folder 1, CUAA.
33. *Vietnam and Your Conscience: A Method of Examining the Moral Issues of the American Involvement in Southeast Asia, Ave Maria* special report (South Bend, IN: Ave Maria Press, 1967), 9, 11.
34. *Vietnam and Your Conscience*, 15.
35. Second Vatican Council, *Pastoral Constitution on the Church in the Modern World*, December 7, 1965, the Vatican website, http://www.vatican.va/archive/hist_coun cils/ii_vatican_council/documents/vat-ii_cons_19651207_gaudium-et-spes_en .html.
36. For a brief biography of Mueller, see William Waters, "Franz Mueller, Eminent Social Economist," *Forum for Social Economics* 17 (2): 51–52.
37. Franz Mueller to Leo Binz, July 5, 1967, 1. United States Conference of Catholic Bishops Social Action Department, box 51, folder 8, CUAA.
38. Mueller to Binz, July 5, 1967, 1.
39. Mueller to Binz, July 5, 1967, 1.
40. The American Pax Association to John J. Wright, September 23, 1968. CZHN 6/08638, Gordon Zahn Papers, UNDA. They sent a cautiously worded memo to bishops in September 1968 to lobby for conscience rights at the annual meeting. In this memo they "strongly recommend" that the bishops "take steps to assure young Catholic men who are called by the consciences to refuse to serve" that the hierarchy will stand in their corner.
41. American Pax Association to the American Bishops, April 3, 1967. United States Conference of Catholic Bishops Social Action Department, Box 51, Folder 8, CUAA.
42. American Pax Association to the American Bishops, April 3, 1967.
43. American Pax Association to the American Bishops, April 3, 1967.
44. Peter J. Henroit to Joseph Bernardin, August 16, 1968. United States Catholic Conference, box 104, folder "Military Affairs: Selective Service; Conscientious Objectors, 1968–1969," CUAA.
45. Henroit to Bernardin, August 16, 1968, 2.
46. National Conference of Catholic Bishops, "Human Life in Our Day," November 15, 1968, Priests for Life, http://www.priestsforlife.org/magisterium/bishops/68-11 -15humanlifeinourdaynccb.htm.
47. Gordon Zahn to Richard Cardinal Cushing, March 1, 1968, 2. CZHN 9/12475, Gordon Zahn Papers, UNDA.
48. Richard Cardinal Cushing to Gordon Zahn, April 15, 1968. CZHN 9/12490, Gordon Zahn Papers, UNDA.
49. Richard Cardinal Cushing to Gordon Zahn, March 8, 1968. CZHN 9/12489, Gordon Zahn Papers, UNDA.
50. John Paul J. Hallinan to Eileen Egan, May 25, 1967. Eileen Egan Papers, box 1, folder 2, UNDA.
51. Albert Fletcher to J. W. Fulbright, June 10, 1970. United States Catholic Conference, box 104, folder "Conscientious Objectors, 1970," CUAA.

52. Peter L. Gerety and Edward C. O'Leary to Edmund S. Muskie, June 1, 1970. United States Catholic Conference, box 104, folder "Conscientious Objectors, 1970," CUAA.

53. Joseph Brunini to G. B. Montgomery, August 10, 1970. United States Catholic Conference, box 104, folder "Conscientious Objectors, 1970," CUAA.

54. John J. Russell, "Catholic Teaching on Conscientious Objection," *Catholic Virginian* (Richmond, VA), June 12, 1970.

55. John J. Russell to Curtis W. Tarr, April 16, 1971. Catholic Peace Fellowship Records, folder L, box 32, UNDA.

56. John T. McGreevy, "The Northern District of California and the Vietnam Draft," *Western Legal History* 2 (Summer/Fall 1989): 268–70.

57. Richard Harrington, "United States District Court for the Northern District of California: Complaint for Declaratory Relief and Injunction," May 10, 1968, 5. United States Catholic Conference, box 104, folder "Conscientious Objectors, 1970," CUAA.

58. Harrington, 5.

59. Quoted in McGreevy, "The Northern District of California and the Vietnam Draft," 270.

60. Helen Ciernik, "A Matter of Conscience: The Selective Conscientious Objector, Catholic College Students, and the Vietnam War," *U.S. Catholic Historian* 26 (Summer 2008): 33–50.

61. John Noonan, "Background Paper: Re Conscientious Objection to War," n.d. but ca. June 31, 1970, 2. United States Catholic Conference, box 104, folder "Conscientious Objection, 1971, Jan–Apr," CUAA.

62. Noonan, 5.

63. Noonan, 3.

64. Timothy Mitchell, "War and Conscientious Objection," *Social Justice Review* 61 (September 1968): 147–54; James Hitchcock, "Conscience and the Draft," *Jubilee: A Magazine for the Church and Her People*, April 1968, 42.

65. Mr. [William] Consedine, "Memorandum to Bishop Bernardin, Subject: Negre v. Larsen," August 25, 1970. United States Conference of Catholic Bishops, box 104, folder "Conscientious Objectors, 1970," CUAA.

66. William Consedine, untitled document, September 15, 1970, 1. United States Catholic Conference, box 104, folder "Conscientious Objectors, 1970," CUAA.

67. Consedine, 1.

68. *On Writ of Certiorari to the United States Court of Appeals for the Ninth Circuit*, Louis A. Negre v. Stanley R. Larsen, et al., no. 325, October Term 1970, 15–26.

69. *On Writ of Certiorari to the United States Court of Appeals for the Ninth Circuit*, 27.

70. Peter J. Donnici and Lawrence S. Lannon, "Brief of the Executive Board of the National Federation of Priests' Councils—Amicus Curiae," October Term, 1970, 2, no. 325, Louis A. Negre v. Stanley R. Larsen.

71. Joseph Bernardin to Philip Hart, May 14, 1971. United States Catholic Conference, box 104, folder "Conscientious Objectors, Jan–Apr 1971," CUAA.

72. Philip Hart to the Senate, June 4, 1971, 2. United States Catholic Conference, box 104, folder "Conscientious Objectors, Jan–Apr 1971," CUAA.

73. Hart to the Senate, June 4, 1971, 2.

74. Joseph Bernardin to John Dearden, October 27, 1971. United States Catholic Conference, box 104, folder "Conscientious Objectors, September–December 1971," CUAA.

75. William Moran to Patrick McDermott, February 19, 1971. United States Catholic Conference, "Conscientious Objectors, Jan–Apr 1971," CUAA.

CHAPTER SEVEN

1. Farrell O'Gorman, *Catholicism and American Borders in the Gothic Literary Imagination* (South Bend, IN: University of Notre Dame Press, 2017): 16–26.

2. Paul Tillich, "Conscience in Western Thought and the Idea of the Transmoral Conscience," *Crozer Quarterly* 22 (October 1945): 293; Paul Blanshard, *Communism, Democracy, and Catholic Power* (London: Jonathan Cape, 1952), 217.

3. David Hollinger, *After Cloven Tongues of Fire: Protestant Liberalism in Modern American History* (Princeton, NJ: Princeton University Press, 2013), 23.

4. Donald L. Berry, "The Rhetoric of Conscience," *Christian Century*, September 4, 1968, 1102.

5. David Little, "A View of Conscience within the Protestant Theological Tradition," in *Conscience: Its Freedom and Limitations*, ed. William C. Bier, SJ, Pastoral Psychology Series, no. 6 (New York: Fordham University Press, 1971), 20.

6. Little, 20.

7. Eric Mount, *Conscience and Responsibility* (Richmond, VA: John Knox, 1969), 10.

8. Paul Lehmann, "Christian Freedom and the Ethical Reality of Conscience," Duodecim Society, May 1963, 2. The Paul Lewis Lehmann Manuscript Collection, box 25, folder 14, Princeton Theological Library Special Collections.

9. Paul Lehmann, "Integrity of Heart: A Comment upon the Preceding Paper," in *Ecumenical Dialogue at Harvard: The Roman Catholic-Protestant Colloquium*, ed. Samuel Howard Miller and G. Ernest Wright (Cambridge, MA: Belknap Press of Harvard University Press, 1964), 275.

10. John Dedek, "Freedom of the Catholic Conscience," *Chicago Studies* 7 (Summer 1968), 116.

11. C. Ellis Nelson to David S. Schuller, September 1, 1972. Carl Ellis Nelson Papers, box H005A, folder "Nelson: Personal: Correspondence, 1970–1981," Austin Presbyterian Theological Seminary. For the broader shift in Nelson's work on conscience, see Peter Cajka, "C. Ellis Nelson, Liberal Protestants, and the Rise of the Catholic Theology of Conscience," *U.S. Catholic Historian* 35 (Summer 2017): 47–74.

12. C. Ellis Nelson, "Notes on Interview with Prof. Vergote," May 23, 1972. Carl Ellis Nelson Papers, box H007a, folder "Nelson: Professional: Educator: Publications—Conscience," Austin Presbyterian Theological Seminary.

13. Hans Schär, "Protestant Problems with Conscience," in *Conscience: Theological and Psychological Perspectives*, ed. C. Ellis Nelson (New York: Newman, 1973), 79.

14. C. Ellis Nelson to Brown Barr, July 23, 1980. Carl Ellis Nelson Papers, box H005B, folder "Nelson: Personal: Correspondence—San Francisco Theological," Austin Presbyterian Theological Seminary.

15. Clergy and Laymen Concerned about Vietnam, "Conscription and Conscience," October 25, 1967. Texas Tech University Vietnam Center and Archive Digital Materials, box 12, folder 50, Social Movements Collection, accessed June 5, 2020, https://www .vietnam.ttu.edu/reports/images.php?img=/images/1451/14511250011.pdf.

16. Roger L. Shinn, "Testimony of Selective Conscientious Objection," April 14, 1967. George Gilmary Higgins Papers, box 108, folder 1, CUAA.

17. Roger L. Shinn, "How Free Can a Society Be?," broadcast on *Frontiers of Faith*, WNBC, New York, April 17, 1966, 14. Roger Shinn Papers, box 1, folder 6, Union Theological Seminary Archives; Piet Fransen, "Grace and Freedom," in *Freedom and Man*, ed. John Courtney Murray (New York: J. P. Kennedy and Sons, 1965), 31–69.

18. Ralph Potter, *Conscientious Objection to Particular Wars*, 1967, 34. George Gilmary Higgins Papers, box 108, folder 1, CUAA; Paul Ramsey, "Selective Conscientious

Objection: Warrants and Reservations," in *The Case for Selective Conscientious Objection: A Conflict of Loyalties*, ed. James Finn (New York: Bobbs-Merrill, 1968); 31–77; Edward LeRoy Long, *War and Conscience in America* (Philadelphia: Westminster, 1968).

19. Mark Philip Bradley, *The World Reimagined: Americans and Human Rights in the Twentieth Century* (New York: Cambridge University Press, 2016), 207.

20. Stephen Hopgood, *Keepers of the Flame: Understanding Amnesty International* (Ithaca, NY: Cornell University Press, 2006), 109.

21. Amnesty International, "Prisoner of Conscience Year: 1977," flyer, 1977. Amnesty International Office of the United States of America, National Office Records, box XI.1.3 430, folder C, CULAC

22. Amnesty International, *Trade Unionists in Prison* (New York: Amnesty International, 1977). Amnesty International Office of the United States of America, National Office Records, box VII.3344, folder 4, CULAC.

23. Amnesty International, *Lawyers in Prison* (New York: Amnesty International, 1977). Amnesty International Office of the United States of America, National Office Records, box VII.3 344, folder 4, CULAC.

24. Charles Taylor, *A Secular Age* (Cambridge, MA: Harvard University Press, 2007); Lincoln Mullen, *The Chance of Salvation: A History of Conversion in America* (Cambridge, MA: Harvard University Press, 2017).

25. Amnesty International, "Today There Is a Way to Help Free Political Prisoners: Amnesty International." Amnesty International Office of the United States of America, National Office Records, box XI.1.3 430, folder C, CULAC.

26. Amnesty International, "And Who Cares about Political Prisoners Today?" 1977. Amnesty International Office of the United States of America, National Office Records, box XI.1.3 430, folder C, CULAC.

27. Amnesty International, *Prisoners of Conscience in the USSR* (London: Amnesty International Publications, 1979). Amnesty International Office of the United States of America, National Office Records, box II.5 10, folder 1, CULAC.

28. Samuel Moyn, *The Last Utopia: Human Rights in History* (Cambridge, MA: Harvard University Press, 2012).

29. Amnesty International, "Inter-Religious Urgent Action Network," ca. 1974. Amnesty International Office of the United States of America, National Office Records, box II.2 6, folder 12, CULAC.

30. Ginetta Sagan to Various Churches, ca. 1974. Amnesty International Office of the United States of America, National Office Records, box II.1 1, folder 14, CULAC.

31. Amnesty International, "Celebrities Publicly Sign the Universal Appeal for Amnesty for All Prisoners of Conscience," December 9, 1983. Amnesty International Office of the United States of America, National Office Records, box XI.3 370, folder 20, CULAC.

32. "Prisoners of Conscience." *America*, December 29, 1984, 434.

33. "Prisoners of Conscience," 434.

34. Sara Dubow, "'A Constitutional Right Rendered Utterly Meaningless': Religious Exemptions and Reproductive Politics, 1973–2014," *Journal of Policy History* 27 (November 2015): 6–9. Church's bill passed in the Senate by a vote of 92–1 and in the House by a vote of 372–1.

35. Ronit Stahl and Ezekiel Emanuel, "Physicians, Not Conscripts—Conscientious Objection in Health Care," *New England Journal of Medicine* 376 (April 2017): 1380–85.

36. United States Catholic Conference, "Statement of the Most Rev. Edward D. Head, Chairman of the Committee of Health Affairs of the United States Catholic

Conferences," January 26, 1973, 4. National Conference of Catholic Bishops, Ad Hoc Committee on Pro-Life Activities, box 63, folder "1973, January to February," CUAA.

37. National Conference of Catholic Bishops, Committee on Pro-Life Activities, memo, February 1973, 2. Ad Hoc Committee on Pro-Life Activities, box 63, folder "1973, January to February," CUAA.

38. James McHugh, "The Supreme Court, Permissive Abortion and the Catholic Hospital," statement, February 20, 1973, 2. Ad Hoc Committee on Pro-Life Activities, box 62, folder "1973, January to February," CUAA. This later appeared in the March 1973 edition of *Hospital Progress*, a publication of the Catholic Hospital Association.

39. James McHugh, "Abortion: The Catholic Hospital and Catholic Health Care Personnel," memo, April 1973, 11. Ad Hoc Committee on Pro-Life Activities, box 62, folder "April–June," CUAA.

40. Steve Bossi to Msgr. Harold Murray, February 20, 1973. Ad Hoc Committee on Pro-Life Activities, box 62, folder "1973, January to February," CUAA.

41. John Dear, *The God of Peace: Towards a Theology of Nonviolence* (New York: Maryknoll, 1994), 158.

42. McHugh, "The Supreme Court, Permissive Abortion and the Catholic Hospital," 2.

43. McHugh, 2.

44. James Rausch to Philip J. Davis, January 28, 1974, 3. Ad Hoc Committee on Pro-Life Activities, box 63, folder "1974, January to June," CUAA.

45. Rausch to Davis, January 28, 1974, 4.

46. Bishops Accountability, "Assignment Record—Bishop James S. Rausch," August 14, 2002. Bishops Accountability.Org, http://www.bishopaccountability.org/assign/Rausch_James_S.htm.

47. United States Conference of Catholic Bishops, "A Critical Analysis of the Report of the U.S. Commission on Civil Rights on Abortion," 1. Ad Hoc Committee on Pro-Life Activities, box 63, folder "Pro-Life Activities, 1975, July–December," CUAA.

48. Terence Cooke to Arthur S. Fleming, March 2, 1976. Ad Hoc Committee on Pro-Life Activities, box 63, folder "Pro-Life Activities, 1976, March," CUAA.

49. Daniel Rogers, "Paths in the Social History of Ideas," in *The Worlds of American Intellectual History*, ed. Joel Isaac, James T. Kloppenberg, Michael O'Brien, and Jennifer Ratner-Rosenhagen (Oxford: Oxford University Press, 2017), 307.

50. Joseph Ratzinger, "Bishops, Theologians, and Morality," in *On Conscience: Two Essays by Joseph Ratzinger*, ed. Edward J. Furton (San Francisco: St. Ignatius, 2007), 51.

51. Joseph Ratzinger, "Conscience and Truth," in *On Conscience: Two Essays by Joseph Ratzinger*, ed. Edward J. Furton (San Francisco: St. Ignatius, 2007): 11–41.

52. John Paul II, *Veritatis Splendor*, August 6, 1993, the Vatican website, http://www.vatican.va/content/john-paul-ii/en/encyclicals/documents/hf_jp-ii_enc_06081993_veritatis-splendor.html.

53. John Paul II, *Veritatis Splendor*.

54. John Paul II, *Veritatis Splendor*.

CODA

1. Francis (pope), *Amoris Laetitia*, March 9, 2016, the Vatican website, https://w2.vatican.va/content/dam/francesco/pdf/apost_exhortations/documents/papa-francesco_esortazione-ap_20160319_amoris-laetitia_en.pdf.

2. Marco Duranti, *The Conservative Human Rights Revolution: European Identity, Transnational Politics, and the Origins of the European Convention* (New York: Oxford University Press, 2017).

3. John Paul II, "Message of His Holiness Pope John Paul II for the XXIV World Day of Peace," January 1, 1991, the Vatican website, http://www.vatican.va/content/john-paul-ii/en/messages/peace/documents/hf_jp-ii_mes_08121990_xxiv-world-day-for-peace.html.

INDEX